Hey AdmissionsMom: Real Talk from Reddit

a no-nonsense, unconventional approach
to college admissions

from the voices of r/ApplyingToCollege
with Carolyn Allison Caplan,
aka u/admissionsmom

Hey AdmissionsMom: Real Talk from Reddit
Copyright © 2019 by AdmissionsMom, LLC

Printed in the United States of America

First Printing, 2019

ISBN - 978-1-7337641-0-0 (Paperback)
ISBN - 978-1-7337641-4-8 (Digital)

AdmissionsMom, LLC
Houston, TX

www.admissionsmom.college

The author has tried to reproduce the questions, advice, and interactions with students as closely as possible to the original engagements on /r/ApplyingToCollege; however, in some cases the language has been edited or paraphrased for consistency, clarity, and/or to accommodate space constraints. Permission was graciously given by each of the contributors whose questions and posts are reproduced in this book. The author has tried her best to credit to those contributors whose engagements with the author allowed her to write this book. At each contributor's preference, the author has used their name or Reddit nickname, when appropriate. In some instances, the author has changed names, content, and/or nicknames to protect the identities of those who requested to remain anonymous. The author does not make any guarantee that following the advice, instruction, or direction provided in this book will result in any specific achievement or goal including, but not limited to, acceptance into a specific college, university, or degree program. Rather, the author hopes that the reader will find support in the shared experiences of others and learn to appreciate the process of applying to college for what it is: a journey.

Book Interior and E-book Design by Amit Dey | amitdey2528@gmail.com *for mom*

Contents

Intro ix

Chapter 1: Just the Basics 1

Chapter 2: Prepping for College Admissions – Juniors
and Seniors. 15

Chapter 3: Course Rigor and Class Selection 27

Chapter 4: It's All About the GPA and Class Rank, or Is It? . 35

Chapter 5: To SAT or ACT? — That Is the Question 41

Chapter 6: Test Scores — Report, Understand,
and Make Peace with Them 49

Chapter 7: Activities, ECs, and Summers, Oh My!. 59

Chapter 8: Letters of Recommendation. 79

Chapter 9: Why Include a Resume? 89

Chapter 10. What to Study? Choosing a Major. 95

Chapter 11: Rankings Schmankings 105

Chapter 12: I Don't Believe in Dream Schools – Finding
Your Fit 113

Chapter 13: Liberal Arts Colleges: The Best Little
Schools You've Never Heard Of 123

Chapter 14: Look for the Vibe and Find Your Tribe:
Campus Visits........................... 129

Chapter 15: EA, ED, RD, SCEA, REA................. 137

Chapter 16: Figuring Out the Finances................. 147

Chapter 17: The Personal Essay Topic? You. 159

Chapter 18: Supplemental Whaaats? More Essays......... 181

Chapter 19: Tell Us More –The Additional Info Essay 189

Chapter 20: The Yucky Parts — Disciplinary Infractions .. 195

Chapter 21: Showing Colleges Some Love — Demonstrated
Interest............................... 199

Chapter 22: Up Close and Personal: The Interview 205

Chapter 23: Taming the Admissions Stress Monster 215

Chapter 24: Grow Your Attitude of Gratitude............ 227

Chapter 25: Mindfulness – An Admissions Journey with
Intention 239

Chapter 26: Dealing with Your Parents 247

Chapter 27: Hello, Parents. This is just for you. 253

Chapter 28: When It Doesn't Go Your Way: The Pain of
Rejection 269

Chapter 29: Hanging in Limbo — The Uncomfortable
World of Being Waitlisted and Deferred...... 285

Chapter 30: Taking a Gap Year...................... 295

Chapter 31: You Did It! Acceptances 299

Chapter 32: International Students – Coming to America .. 309

Chapter 33: Transfers 313

Chapter 34: Veterans — Thank You for Your Service 319

Chapter 35: There's a Place for You: LGBTQ and
First-Gen/Low-Income (including foster
kids and homeless students). 325

Chapter 36: Prepping for College Admissions —
Freshmen and Sophomores 333

Chapter 37: Advice and Updates from Our Community 339

Gen Z Glossary 351

Resources 357

Shout Outs. 371

Acknowledgements. 375

A-Mom's Mom Club. 377

About Carolyn. 379

Intro

who am I?

No, this isn't an esoteric personal statement, but it is an introduction. I did just kind of plop myself onto Reddit one day, and then I started spilling advice without telling anyone who I was. Let's start over.

Hi! I'm AdmissionsMom, and I'm an English teacher, a mom, an independent educational consultant (basically a private college counselor), and a moderator on the subreddit r/ApplyingToCollege. I call myself AdmissionsMom because that's the role I want to play on r/ApplyingToCollege and in this book. When high school kids come to Reddit looking for advice about the college admissions process, I try to offer help and guidance. With this book, I want to smooth those admissions-ruffled feathers and help many of you relax about your college admissions journey while offering advice—both my own and that of many others on our subreddit.

my goals

You might be starting this process. You may be in the middle of your senior year. You may be a year away from applying. You may be a parent wondering how to help your child get into college. Whoever you are, I want to help you navigate this process mindfully and with as little stress as possible.

I want to help students step into their independent selves with confidence. I want to offer you tips about how to get into college and, more importantly, how to go about leading a happy, healthy, and productive life while applying to college (and beyond). All too often, I see a tsunami of anxiety crashing into high schools and overwhelming countless kids. Instead of focusing on who they are, what they want from life, and how college should fit their goals, kids are running themselves ragged trying to turn themselves into someone they think colleges want (spoiler alert: that is the opposite of what they want).

The problem is that, in any given year, around 50,000 students are trying to funnel themselves into the same twenty-five schools. And that's just not going to work. There are literally hundreds of amazing schools that are actively seeking all kinds of students — you simply need to find the one (or more!) out of the many that fit you.

Look, I know there's a lot of pressure to perform. And I'm aware that not everyone has access to the same resources. You might be stuck in a crappy school with less than great teachers. You may be the first person in your family to think about college. You may feel overwhelmed by the whole process. But guess what? You are the determining factor — the captain of your ship. College marks the beginning of your life in a way that you've never experienced before.

This is an awesome opportunity. Don't freak out.

Instead, ask yourself: What do I want out of life when I leave high school? What do I see for myself?

You don't have to know for sure. Sure, the best college applications come from students who have a clear idea of themselves, but sometimes that clear idea of themselves can be that they're unsure about what that idea is. It's ok to be confused and uncertain in high school. That's what being a teenager is all about.

If you already have a fairly strong idea of who you are as a person, congrats! If not, that's ok. We'll get there together. And then we can find the right colleges for you.

how to use this book

If you read this book start to finish, it follows a chronological order from the first things you should be thinking about, like ECs and college FIT (hint, this is not what you think!), to later-stage issues such as acceptances and even college transfers.

This book is a digest of some of the most insightful and helpful posts I participated in from 2016 – 2018 on the subreddit, r/ApplyingToCollege. The Reddit users cited in this book generously agreed that I could print their words here, so you get to see what others just like yourself are thinking and feeling on these topics and even see what help they offer each other. And then I chime in, too. I enjoyed writing this book because I got to collect all my thoughts on each issue in one place and expand on them a little bit, but the thing I enjoyed most was revisiting all the kids' posts and seeing the help y'all give each other.

Yes, I just said "y'all." This is not your average college admissions book. There's Gen Z style and Reddit slang (and a slang glossary for parents in the back), the occasional swear word (because sometimes with college admissions, you just need to drop an "f-bomb"), and sentence fragments. This book just wouldn't have made sense if I made all the Reddit posts look like English Comp essays, because that's not what r/ApplyingToCollege is about, and there's something wonderful about taking off our perfection goggles and being human together.

When you have a particular question, use the Table of Contents to find where another student asked the same question and we address that issue. You will probably find your favorite users whose stories you identify with, and just know that they came through it in the end, no matter how confused or upset they might have been at that time. You will, too.

about me

I was a teacher for thirty years. I know, I'm old. I taught freshman writing at a community college for the last fifteen of those years. During that time, I taught personal essay writing and often counseled my students on the college application process. Because of my addiction to all things education-related, helping students with college applications quickly became one of my favorite parts of teaching. When my youngest left for college, I decided it was time to officially give up my dry erase markers and move on to the next stage of my life. After helping my own kids and my students see applying to college as an exciting time of self-discovery, I wanted to share that experience. So I retired from my job as a writing professor and opened my private college counseling practice.

Today, I'm an independent educational consultant, and I work with private clients. I do this job for many reasons, including flexibility, my obsession with education and travel, and my love for teaching writing, but the most critical reason I became a consultant was the insane levels of stress. I saw families that were nearly shattered, children and mothers who'd stopped talking to each other, kids who were wearing their stress as badges of honor. I saw parents who literally could not talk about anything but college — starting when their kids were in 6th grade!

It disturbed me to my core. I want to change this culture of stress. Yes, you should work hard on applications and essays and college lists, but you (and this includes parents) should also relax, joke around, meditate, and breathe.

I don't believe in "packaging kids" for college admissions. I want you to think beyond the typical story. I want you to dig into the "Why" of your lives, not the "What." I encourage you to dig into your souls and bare them like never before.

Why r/ApplyingToCollege?

For many families, an IEC or admissions consultant relieves much of the pressure, but at a significant financial cost. Many people don't have the school or home support they need in this convoluted journey. Because I don't believe that money should be a barrier to college counseling, I knew from the beginning that my business would serve both paying and pro bono clients. So, I spent some time lurking on A2C, and then eventually, I realized I could provide some helpful advice at times. When I jumped on and began my lurking we had around 8000 members in our little community; today we have over 115,000, and we are still growing. To me that growth demonstrates a lot of need. I've found that it's important to be where the kids are, using their media of choice. On top of the 115k students we have as subscribers, we have around a million viewers on a daily basis, and sometimes that spikes up to 15 million viewers during critical application dates. That's a lot of kids from all over the world seeking advice and help.

my philosophy

The kids on r/ApplyingToCollege know I'm not what one thinks of when they think of a private college counselor. I'm a firm believer in searching for college fit and leaving rankings alone. I also believe that the purpose of education is to learn critical thinking and problem-solving and that college does not necessarily have to include job training. And most importantly, I believe that your health and wellness are more crucial than grades, extracurriculars, APs, SATs, ACTs, or the U.S. News & World Report.

I encourage you to be teenagers, to breathe, to laugh, to play, and, yes, to work hard. So, I probably have some philosophical differences about how to approach college with many of you reading this, and I respect that. Still, I hope you'll hear me out.

An admissions counselor at The University of Chicago told me that just when you think you've figured out what colleges are looking for, they're going to change their minds. So don't try to figure out what colleges want. Figure yourself out. Colleges want to see what you have to show them. Just present yourself. You are a unique mixture of personality traits, interests, and talents.

Do you. Be who you are. Open up. Peel back the onion layers. Bare your soul. Breathe. Laugh. Don't spend every waking moment trying to impress others. Colleges aren't looking for automated test-taking, grade-making machines who race to rack up extracurriculars. It's not about awards or being valedictorian or playing the flute since you were six (though good for you if you have those things!). I know it feels like that sometimes, but what they want is you — authentic, cool, nervous, funny, scared, confident, serious, personal you.

Stop worrying about what everyone else tells you to care about. Allow yourself time to reflect on what you genuinely care about. Look for the schools that are eagerly seeking students who bring your gifts. The best college for you could easily be one you (or your parents) have never heard of before.

If you glean nothing else from this book, I want you to know that this college admissions journey is stressful, no doubt, but it is also a fantastic opportunity to learn about yourself and grow into the person you can and will be. Don't waste it. There's a big, beautiful, badass world out there. Explore. Focus on yourself and what you want. Think about things you are thankful for. Take time to breathe.

I'll be here to guide you.

CHAPTER 1

Just the Basics

When you first start to research colleges, you should familiarize yourself with some basic components of the admissions process. That way, you'll ensure you have a firm understanding of the mechanics of this process, and you'll start out on firm footing.

You might be surprised at how many kids ask me for advice about application dates, rolling admissions, and college admissions vocabulary, but I'm not surprised. Many of these students have never been taught how to approach college admissions – let alone had anyone explain the basics. These kids are smart and capable; they just need someone to sit them down and give them a few pointers.

Consequently, in this chapter, I'll walk you through some straightforward but essential info about the nuts and bolts of the application process.

Basic Components of Most Applications

Application Platform – this is where you'll include all your official details. Way back in the olden days, when my oldest was applying to college in 2007, colleges required applicants to fill out applications on paper. But thankfully, many schools now use either the online version of the Common Application or the Coalition Application instead of those individual school forms. Even if the school still requires you to use their own online form, the application will ask for details like your name, date of birth, social security number, your parents' personal information, your school counselor's contact information, the contact information of the teachers who will be providing your letters of recommendation, your senior year courses, your personal essay, and a list of your high school activities. There is often an application fee involved, so be sure to see if you qualify for fee waivers if you need them or look for schools that don't have application fees.

Transcript – The transcript is the official document showing your grades throughout high school. Usually, your school is in charge of sending transcripts to colleges, but you need to know how to communicate which colleges you want to include. Be sure to check with your high school counselor to see what you need to do in order to get those transcripts sent.

School Profile – When your high school sends your transcript, they should also send a profile depicting key details about the school, like how many AP or IB classes they offer. Admissions officers rely on this information to evaluate the context surrounding your application.

Test Scores – Your test scores will include either the SAT, the ACT, or both. You will also include any Subject Tests you take. If schools require official test scores, you will submit them directly from the College Board, which administers the SAT and Subject Tests, or the ACT, which administers the ACT. This can get costly, so be sure to check and see if you can get fee waivers if finances are a consideration for you. Some colleges allow you to self-report, so you can simply list those babies on the application, and you don't have to pay anything extra!

List of Activities (Extracurriculars or ECs) – This section is where you will list all the extracurriculars and activities you've participated in during high school. Read the Extracurriculars Chapter for more information on what makes strong ECs.

Essay(s) – This is one of the most critical parts of the application because it affords college admissions officers a real opportunity to get to know you. Depending on the college, you might be asked to submit supplemental essays. Instead of stressing out, look at the essay section as a chance to show off your special brand of individuality.

Letters of Recommendation (LORs) – Admissions officers use LORs to paint a complete picture of you as an applicant. Traditionally, you should have at least two from academic teachers who taught you during your junior year and who know you fairly well.

Fee or fee waiver form – You need to include your application fee when you submit your application. If you meet the requirements for a fee waiver, you will need to include the fee waiver when you submit.

Sample of creative work – this is mostly required for students who are applying to a creative program that asks for a writing sample, art portfolio, or audition tape/CD.

FAFSA – The Free Application for Federal Student Aid is an application that determines eligibility for student financial aid. It is meant to be completed annually for both prospective and current college students. I'll talk more about this in the Financial Aid chapter.

The CSS/Financial Aid Profile – The College Scholarship Service Profile is an online application from the College Board that gathers information about non-federally sourced financial aid. I'll also talk more about this in the Financial Aid chapter.

Common Application vs. Coalition Application

anonymous

Are they equal? Common App and Coalition App

I'm looking at applying to JHU, and they accept both Common App and Coalition App. What're the advantages/disadvantages to each? It looks like most of the schools I'm interested in are covered by the Coalition App, so should I just do Coalition App essays and not even worry about the Common App?

Is there any difference? Thanks in advance!

> [–] admissionsmom
>
> When it comes to the Common Application or the Coalition Application, there isn't much difference. The Coalition App enables you to start keeping up with your information beginning in 9th grade in a "locker;" it also encourages you to limit your word count on your essay a bit more.
>
> I'd use the one that most of your colleges use. If you can do all of them on one app, go that way for sure. For the record though, you can apply to colleges using either app if they accept both platforms. You can also use the same essays and personal statements for the Common Application or Coalition Application. Just be sure to watch out for schools that have supplemental essays. [*AdmissionsMom's note:* For more on essays, see the Personal Essays and Supplemental Essays Chapters.]

What do all these letters mean? EA, ED, CA ....

u/allurredditsrbelongtous

Rolling Admissions?

This may sound like a dumb question but what exactly are rolling admissions, early decision, and early action?

> [–] admissionsmom
>
> Often, colleges that use rolling admissions do not have a fixed deadline. The idea is that the college's open slots fill

up as they accept students on the rolling basis, so that applying earlier to a rolling school can have benefits with acceptances and financial and merit aid.

Early Decision is a binding decision. If you apply by the ED deadline — it's different for each school, so check their websites — you will receive a decision of accepted, denied, or deferred (for some schools). If you're accepted, the decision is binding, and you must attend unless they don't offer the same (or better) financial aid they offer you with the net price calculator on their school website. So, before you decide to apply Early Decision somewhere, you must sit down with your parents and make sure the school is financially viable for you, and that you love it and can see yourself there for the next four years, and you won't regret not giving any other schools a chance for an acceptance.

Early Action is generally an earlier deadline for you to get your materials in to the college and then they can generally get a result earlier for you as well. It is not binding.

Should I get a head start? Prepping applications before they officially open

u/stuportrooper

Does anyone know when the common app goes live?

[-] admissionsmom

Common App usually opens up on August 1; but be aware that many colleges might not have their supplements out by that date. You can, however, start filling out basic information even before August 1 because that info will roll over.

u/warrior__princess

Is it possible to work on my application before the common app goes up?

I'm super excited and nervous about getting a head start on my apps. Can I start now in junior year?

[-] admissionsmom

It's never too early to get together important documents to assist you in your application process. I recommend that my juniors start to gather all their application details to get them out of the way in the summer if they're eager to get going. You can start filling out stuff like the basic info and getting your activities lists in order. Also, you can think about what kind of statement you want to make in your personal statement, but I don't recommend writing the real thing just yet. You can write practice personal statements and start getting the feel of what a personal essay is.

let me break it down

You can start to work on the main portion of your application, but you must be careful to avoid losing the work you've completed thus far. For the Common Application, you can "roll over" your account so you can work on the application before the official application becomes available. If you choose this option, certain data — the profile, family, education, testing, and activities — will roll over.

However, not all your Common Application information will roll over. You cannot roll over:

- Answers to questions from specific colleges
- Recommendation letter invitations
- Recommendation letter forms
- The Release Authorization and Family Educational Rights and Privacy Act ("FERPA") selection
- Answers to questions that have been altered or deleted from the application.

So, even if you want to use the rollover option, be sure to write all your information, especially your essays, in a Google Doc first.

Basic Admissions Vocab and Abbreviations

Sometimes it can feel like the college admissions process speaks its own language. Here are some helpful vocabulary words. I promise there won't be a quiz at the end of this chapter, or will there .....?

AA: Affirmative Action, a policy or practice adopted by many college admissions offices to improve diversity in the college's population. These programs are constructed to counter both past and present impacts of discrimination and bias seen in college admissions. Can also mean 2 year Associates of Arts Degree from a Community College.

Admissions Officer/Counselor (AO): An individual who works for a college or university to recruit student applications and accept appropriate candidates.

AP: Advanced Placement.

CC: Community College

College Admissions Consultant or Independent Educational Consultant (IEC): An individual who guides prospective students through the college admissions process, usually privately or through community-based organizations.

College Confidential, aka CC: A college admissions website that offers advice and forums upon which to discuss all facets of the college admissions process. It has a somewhat infamous reputation for encouraging an ultra-competitive, Ivies-or-bust perspective, but can be a helpful site for many kids and parents.

College Counselor: An individual who guides prospective students through the college admissions process; usually they work for a high school.

College Fit: The crux of my admissions philosophy. College Fit speaks to focusing on the school that will fit you instead of forcing you into a particular mold to attend a particular school. From the choice of major to climate to financial aid, College Fit involves a lot of factors aimed at making your college experience the very best it can be for you.

College List: The list of colleges you will eventually come up with once you've determined the college characteristics you care about most.

College Visit: A formal or informal in-person visit to a college.

Concentration: This could be the area you focus on within your major, but some schools like Harvard and others use the term "concentration" instead of "major." So, for example, one of my kids had a concentration in philosophy at Harvard, while the other was a philosophy major at Tufts. They mean the same thing.

Deferred: Sometimes if you apply early, you won't be accepted or denied, but the college decides to roll you into the regular decision round.

Demonstrated Interest: Independent of scores, grades, or extracurriculars, demonstrated interest is the degree to which an applicant shows to a school how serious he or she is about attending that particular school.

DE: Dual Enrollment. Often, while in high school, taking courses in a local college or community college

Direct Admissions: An admissions process whereby a student can apply and be accepted directly to a certain school that houses their intended major. For example, a prospective engineering student can be directly admitted to a university's college of engineering, but not directly to the engineering major. Can also be called **Auto Admissions** or **Guaranteed Admissions**.

EA: Early Action

EC: Extracurriculars

ED: Early Decision

EFC: Expected Family Contribution. This is the amount your family will be expected to pay after financial aid.

FA: Financial Aid

FERPA: The Family Education Rights and Privacy Act. This 1974 law protects students' privacy when it comes to education records.

IB: International Baccalaureate

Info Session: A structured presentation, usually held at a university's admissions office prior to a campus tour. The presentation covers a variety of topics including the admissions process, school highlights, and more.

Interview: The admissions interview is an additional assessment designed to help the school gather more information about a prospective student. An interview can be on or off campus, or it can be conducted in person or by phone or Skype. It can be with a current student, alum or admissions staff.

LAC: Liberal Arts (and Sciences) College

Likely Letter: Notifies some students (very few) that they should expect an acceptance letter. This is uncommon, and should not be expected.

LOCI: Letter of Continued Interest. Applicable if you are deferred for ED or waitlisted.

Lottery Schools: Highly selective schools where there is no way to predict if you'll be admitted or not, no matter how perfect and shiny your scores, stats, and ECs are.

LOR: Letter of recommendation. You will generally ask two academic teachers from your junior year to write these for you.

Major or Concentration: This is the subject that a college student officially commits to studying. It's not the same as your degree but completing all the requirements for your major and the core curriculum will earn you the degree in that subject. For example, once I completed the requirements for my English major, I earned my B.A. in English.

Merit Money: Monetary aid that is awarded to students without considering financial need.

Minor: A minor usually is a subject in which you take about 4 or 5 classes and is a focus secondary to your major. You don't receive another degree, but depending on the school or major, the minor might go onto your degree. For example, loads of students major in one subject but then minor in a foreign language.

NPC: Net Price Calculator. Every college has one on their website and you should use it to find out how much a certain college might cost for you.

OOS: Out of State

ORM: An acronym for "Overrepresented Minority"; refers to a minority group whose percentage of the college population is higher than their percentage of the national population.

Portal: Sent to you by a college once you have submitted an application, this is where you look to see if all segments of your application are completed, find updates from colleges, and check your admissions results.

RD: Regular Decision.

Reach Schools: Any school that admits fewer than 25% of applicants no matter how amazing your stats are, and schools where your stats are below the 50% marker for admissions.

Rolling: Schools that accept students year-round, with no specific deadline.

Subject Tests: Specific tests on academic subjects administered by the College Board.

Surefire Safety School: A school where you are guaranteed admissions based on your stats, is financially feasible for you, and you can see yourself attending.

Target Schools: Schools where your scores and stats fall above their 50th percentile.

URM: An acronym for "Underrepresented Minority;" refers to a minority group whose percentage of the college population is lower than their percentage of the national population.

WL (Waitlist): Neither a deny or accept. You will be notified if a spot becomes available for you. Best bet is to move on and bond with a school that has accepted you.

WLLLOCI: Waitlist Love Letter of Continued Interest. Applicable if you're waitlisted.

Words I Want Eliminated from College Admissions

From my years as a mom and an Independent Educational Consultant, I keep seeing the same words and phrases repeated ad nauseam. The worst part is that these words aren't all that helpful. They detract from healthy goals and often add to the stressful aspects of college admissions.

Seriously, I've seen countless kids and parents obsess over these words, and it's not worth it. Which is why we should go right ahead and squash them right now:

Dream School: No one school is ever going to be a "dream" because it's a real place, and real places aren't perfect. Also, instead of putting the focus on where you go, focus on what that institution can give you so you can become the best version of you possible.

Unique: Seriously, you are unique. No one else is like you. So when people tell you that they want "unique applicants," they're being redundant.

Passion: Instead of "Find your passion," let's say, "Explore your world," "Be involved," and "Develop your interests."

Spike: I don't want to see 14-17-year-olds so focused on one aspect of their lives that they don't develop other skills. That's not the point of any of this, and it's especially not the purpose of going to college.

Match School: Instead of worrying about a match, focus on the fit. Fit is stretchy like a sock. It doesn't have to check all your boxes for a perfect match.

Stand Out: Instead of worrying about standing out in your apps, worry about sticking with your application reader. Make sure they feel like they've gotten to know you and connected with you.

Reddit Basics

A2C: a community (or subreddit) on Reddit full of people who are interested in the college application process. Formally called r/ApplyingToCollege

Dox: to share someone's personal information—especially their address, personal phone number, and the contact information of their employer—on the internet without their consent; ex. "Did you see how that awful Twitter troll doxed that guy earlier? I bet they get fired by the end of the day."

F: a way to show respect and condolences

Karma: For Reddit users, karma signifies reward or positive feedback earned from other for popular or useful content, either links or comments. Having a post "upvoted" will earn a user karma; having a post "downvoted" will decrease a user's karma.

Lurker: someone who reads, but doesn't participate in the general thread discussions

Meme: an image, video, or snippet of text that signifies the understanding of some shared meaning or an inside joke among internet users. Can often be modified to adapt the piece of media to different applicable situations; ex. "I think one of my favorite memes of all time is 'On my way to steal your girl.' Fight me."

Mods: "moderators"; individual users who are appointed to volunteer their time maintaining their subreddit and usually have the power to delete inappropriate posts or ban individual users who violate the subreddit's rules; ex. "The mods are out in full force today, so be extra careful about following the subreddit rules."

OP: original poster; the individual who began the thread

Subreddit or Sub: community on Reddit

Threads: a line of conversation on a message board or internet forum; ex. "AdmissionsMom had a really good thread last night about getting summer jobs."

Tl;dr: the acronym for "Too long; didn't read"; used to communicate that a body of text might be viewed as too long or cumbersome to bother reading. The phrase is usually accompanied by a greatly streamlined summary of the text. "For the tl;dr crowd, just know that Early Decision is binding, so don't apply ED unless you're 100% going to attend the school."

For more Reddit lingo (as well as Gen Z slang), check out the Gen Z Slang Glossary at the back of this book.

CHAPTER 2

Prepping for College Admissions – Juniors and Seniors

I get a lot of questions from anxious kids worried about what they should be doing to prepare for college admissions and when. It's an understandable feeling, one fueled by a desire to do well and make the most of a stressful situation. Unfortunately, too many kids either freak out about prepping for applications way too early, or they don't know how to manage the process and end up scrambling at the end. What is already a challenging process can quickly become mega-frustrating, and I've seen kids put way more pressure on themselves than necessary.

To combat this epidemic of college-application-fueled anxiety and stress, I've put together my Admissions Journey Timeline. With this tool, you will have a clear schedule for how and when you can prepare for college admissions without dealing with much of the uncertainty and stress. Check out this student's question:

u/Seemeina_crown
a little help?
Rising junior here. Anyone got tips for what I should be doing for college apps? I haven't done anything because I'm not sure where to start?

Admissions Journey Timeline

Junior year is where your college admissions journey starts for real. Unlike freshman and sophomore year, you now have quite a few items to tick off your to-do list. But you can do this. Simply follow my guide.

Please note that my views about this might be different than advice you hear from other sources or even other students. My philosophy is that it's good to hear different thoughts and ideas, and then you can make decisions about what works best for you.

Rising Junior Summer

GET INVOLVED WITH STUFF
Yourself (Exercise healthy habits, engage in personal hobbies and projects, READ real books, or practice mindfulness and meditation).

Your family (Help with sibs, grocery shopping, clean up around the house, or take care of dinner one night a week).

Your community (Community service can be totally individual projects and/or organized group projects. Volunteer to play your instrument at a retirement home, coach a kids' team, make sand-wiches at a food bank, or drop off healthy snacks and water to the homeless).

GET A SUMMER JOB
Just getting an old-fashioned summer job will give you all sorts of skills you won't gain by volunteering and also demonstrate leadership, diligence, a willingness to step outside your comfort zone. A summer job also shows your determination. Make some smoothies or scoop ice cream or fold sweaters. It really doesn't matter what it is.

PRACTICE AND PREP FOR THE PSAT

You take it in October, and it helps you qualify for National Merit if you score high enough.

PRACTICE AND PREP FOR THE ACT and SAT.

Take a couple of practice tests and see which one feels better to you and which one you score higher on. Then move forward with that one. Consider taking one in December of junior year. Definitely take one in the early part of the spring semester. It's nice to have testing completed before you start senior year.

TAKE SAT SUBJECT TESTS

Especially if you are considering applying to highly selective schools. Take one or two in June or August that fit with classes you've just studied.

READ READ READ

Reading will improve your test scores and your essay writing. Read real books, magazines, newspapers, and more real books.

ENJOY YOUR SUMMER

This is super important. You need to take time to recharge your batteries. That's part of being involved with yourself. Be sure to take some time completely off from school and college admissions stuff.

START YOUR RESUME

If you haven't already, make a list of all your activities you've been involved in since freshman year. Keep in mind that basically anything you do outside of class time, homework, and test prep counts as an EC, so that includes old-fashioned summer or part-time jobs, home and family responsibilities, elderly and child care, personal projects and hobbies, independent research in addition to more traditional research, internships, and in-or-out-of-school clubs and sports. If you use the Coalition App, you can start on your application "locker." Keep this list updated throughout the next two years. Create the following categories: Education, Extracurriculars, Work Experience, Community Service, Interests and Hobbies, Awards, Honors

Junior Fall

Pretty much all of the summer stuff applies still.

TAKE THE HARDEST COURSE LOAD YOU CAN
Colleges say that your course rigor counts for more than your GPA and test scores. Remember they evaluate you in the context of your school. So don't worry about classes that aren't offered.

GET TO KNOW YOUR TEACHERS
Visit them at office hours. You will be asking them for teacher recommendations later.

KEEP UP YOUR GRADES

KEEP PREPPING AND PRACTICING FOR THE ACT AND SAT
Start testing in the late fall or early spring.

STAY INVOLVED
Keep up with everything I listed for summer. Also get involved with your school. Join a club or two that interests you. Create a club if you don't see one that interests you. Or simply do individual activities that add to your school environment. Sit with someone new at lunch once a week.

Junior Spring

LETTERS OF RECOMMENDATION
Ask two or three teachers who know you best to write your letters. I encourage you to ask junior year teachers who teach you in

core academic subjects. I prefer one from a STEM subject and one from a humanities subject, but some colleges have certain expectations, so be sure to read college websites.

COLLEGE VISITS

Start visiting colleges if you can. Look around in your city or town. Visit large schools and small schools. It doesn't matter if it's a college you think you might consider or not. Just go to start thinking about what feels right to you. Hang out on campus. You don't have to do a tour or info session if you're not ready for that yet. Then, if you can go on college visits to schools you might find interesting, do so. Be sure at this point to sign in and go on the tour and info session, but also wander around. Sit on a bench and eavesdrop on conversations. Do you like what you hear? Talk to students. Ask them what they'd like to change about their school. Or what they do on a Wednesday night. Don't be shy. They remember what it was like to be a prospective student and, even if they are annoyed by your questions, who cares? They don't know you and won't remember you. Move on and find a kinder person. Check out the dining hall and the gym. Look for the area near campus where kids hang out if there is one.

Lots of kids try to go on spring break trips to visit colleges if it's affordable. If you can't afford to visit out of your area, at the very least check out the colleges near you to get a feel for the kind of vibe that works for you.

COLLEGE LIST

Start thinking about what you want in a college and compile a big old list. Having a ton of schools on this initial list is ok. As you explore yourself and the colleges more as you go through the admissions journey, you will naturally begin to filter schools out.

COLLEGE FIT

Start seriously considering how colleges will fit you. This includes thinking about and potentially creating a spreadsheet for:

Financials: Will you need full financial aid? Will you qualify? Will you qualify for any aid? Do you need full merit aid? These are crucial considerations. You and your parents need to spend some time thinking about this and going through net price calculators on various college websites.

Geography: What areas of the country appeal to you? Open your mind here, too. I can't tell you how many kids say no to the Deep South or Midwest without really thinking about it, and in doing so, deprive themselves of some awesome options and merit aid. Also, do you want urban? Do you want rural? Do you want an enclosed campus or one that's incorporated into the cityscape? Do you want beaches? Mountains? Corn fields? Do you want to get out of your comfort zone here or stay with the familiar?

Weather: If you really, really hate the cold, then moving to Boston or Chicago or Maine might not appeal to you. If you have to have four seasons, then the Midwest or the northeast might have good options.

School Culture and Vibe: Are you looking for that stereotypical American big college experience with the big game on the weekends? Or are you looking for the quirky school? Or something that has it all?

School Size: Do you want a big ole state school with loads of options? Or are you looking for something smaller or even midsized? Do you want discussion-based classes where you can develop strong relationships with your professors or are do you want to be in big lectures where you can take notes or go to sleep?

Potential Major: If you don't have one, don't worry. You have plenty of time to figure that out, and it actually frees you up a bit. If you do think you know, research some schools that might be strong in your major. Maybe touch base with a professor or two.

Your Stats: Where do your grades and test scores fit in? Are they right there in the middle? I like my students to be well above the 50% for most of the colleges they are applying to.

This requires putting a lot of thought into what you want out of your experience and about who you are and who you want to be. It doesn't require pulling out U.S. News & World Report and listing the top twenty schools.

ADMISSIONSMOM'S BOOK CLUB
(I don't actually have a book club, just a list of books you should read.) I recommend *The Fiske Guide*, *Colleges that Change Lives*, and *Where You Go Is Not Who You'll Be*. See the back of this book for a full list.

NO COLLEGE-TALK ZONE OR TIME
Make a No College-Talk Zone or Time in your house. At my house, it was our dining room table. For other families I know, it might be all day on Sundays. This will help you and your parents keep your sanity during the next year.

NEW COLLEGE EMAIL ADDRESS
Make a new college-only email address to use for college applications and communications. Make it appropriate! I recommend this because then all your info from colleges won't get mixed up in your other emails. I encourage you to allow your parents to have access to it if you feel comfortable with it. Be sure to check your junk, trash, and spam inboxes, so you don't miss important info!

CHECK IN WITH YOUR HIGH SCHOOL COUNSELOR.
They have a lot of knowledge and can guide you along the way.

COLLEGE INFO SESSIONS
If a college comes to your town or close to your town or school,
go listen. Make sure you sign up and sign in.

COLLEGE FAIRS
Go to them! Talk. Ask questions. Learn.

Rising Senior Summer

All the same stuff as Junior Summer. (So, rising seniors, read the
junior summer info).
      Finish up testing. SAT, ACT, and Subject Tests

SUMMER JOB

BE INVOLVED

RECHARGE YOUR BATTERIES
Take time to care for your mental health and your body. Learn
more about meditation, mindfulness, or yoga. Get outside and
walk or run. Listen to music. Have dance parties in your room.
Breathe. Listen to books or podcasts. Hang out with friends.

WRITE
"Write like a motherf*cker," as one of my favorite writers, Cheryl
Strayed says. Write about yourself. Don't worry too much about
the essays just yet. Just write. Everyday. Get used to your voice.
Figure out who you are. Use themostdangerouswritingapp.com to
force yourself to get words on paper. This will help you get that
Personal Statement ready to go by October 1.

THINK ABOUT AND PRACTICE WRITING THE PERSONAL
ESSAY
Remember — no matter which prompt you choose or which kind
of vehicle or conceit you use to relay your message — the topic is

YOU. Focus on teaching the admissions officers about who you are. Don't worry about being unique; worry about who you are. Don't worry about standing out; worry about sticking with the reader. You do that by creating connections and bonds. Those are created by opening yourself up and letting them inside. Let the reader know what's happening inside you. They want to know what you think about, what you believe, and what you value. They don't need to hear a whole lot more about what you've already told them in other areas of your application. Focus on More Expressing, Less Impressing.

CREATE YOUR COMMON APP ACCOUNT
Start filling out the details like activities, family info, and educational background.

UPDATE YOUR RESUME

VISIT COLLEGES if you can.

START YOUR COLLEGE LIST
Start narrowing down your list — including a wide range of selectiveness. Make sure you have an SFSS (surefire safety school). This is one that guarantees you auto-admission based on your stats, is a financial fit for you, and is a college where you can see yourself. Don't take this lightly. This is a very important school — maybe even your most important one.

KEEP IN TOUCH WITH COLLEGES
Sign up to "request info" from the colleges if you haven't already. Also, I recommend that you follow the admissions offices on Facebook, Instagram, and Twitter for the colleges on your list or potential list. This might also be important for schools that look for demonstrated interest, so that you can show them you are keeping up with what is going on with their schools. They often put out a lot of helpful information for what's happening in their offices. I suggest following the Common App, too. Also, it's ok to contact

your regional college admissions officers or the general front desk with questions.

Senior Fall

All of the above....plus:

Finish up any college visits especially for EARLY DECISION POSSIBILITIES.

COLLEGE LIST
Continue to narrow your college list. Make sure you have one or two surefire safeties that you love and that will be good financial fits, as well as a collection of matches/reaches.

COLLEGE SPREADSHEET
Make a spreadsheet for all your colleges. Add application deadlines. Supplemental Essay topics — and look for overlap. Testing info. Contact info for your regional officer.

EARLY ACTION
Try to apply to as many schools by Early Action as are available. Make a calendar of deadlines and work through them one by one.

LETTERS OF RECOMMENDATION
Check back in with your recommenders. Send them a reminder email and stop by if you can. Be sure to give them a big thank you! (Also give them a resume and "cheat sheet" if you haven't yet.)

YOUR HIGH SCHOOL GUIDANCE COUNSELOR
Check in with your guidance counselor or college counselor if you aren't in regular contact.

SAT/ACT/SUBJECT TESTS
Finish up any testing you have left to do.

ESSAYS
Start writing your essays. Focus first on your Personal Statement. Then categorize your supplemental essays by due dates. How many Why College Essays do you have? When's the first one due? Then, organize the Why Major Essays and the Extracurricular Essays. Think about whether you want/need to write an Additional Info essay. And then group the others. Try to get the Personal Statement done by October 1.

INTERVIEWS
Be sure to check your email (and voicemail and trash and spam folders for interview invitations). Every school has a different method for signing up, so read the website carefully. For some colleges, you are automatically signed up. Others require you to sign up yourself. In most cases, they are optional and sometimes you might not be given the opportunity. Don't worry (as long as you've checked your trash and junk mails). I do suggest that you do them though — even if they're optional and you're nervous. Lean into your fear, admit it to them, tuck in your button shirt, comb your hair and wash your face, and go.

LOCI
If you are deferred Early Decision, be sure to write a LOCI (Letter of Continued Interest).

Senior Spring
FINISH UP APPLICATIONS

SUREFIRE SAFETY SCHOOL
Make sure you have a surefire safety school. If you don't, look for good fits for you that are still accepting apps.

KEEP THOSE GRADES UP
Being rescinded for grade drops is a very real thing.

TAKE TIME TO CARE FOR YOUR MENTAL HEALTH AND YOUR BODY.
Learn more about meditation, mindfulness, or yoga. Get outside and walk or run. Listen to music. Have dance parties in your room. Waiting for those acceptances can be brutal. Breathe. Acknowledge that once those little baby applications have flown away from your computer, you no longer have control.

EMOTIONAL PLANNING
Plan for the worst but hope for the best. Recognize that many colleges you might be interested in are extremely selective, and even if they're not, they might be holistic. Don't get too connected to any college except for your surefire safety.

GRATITUDE
Think about what you are grateful for. What are the good things in your life? Try to make a mental list every day.

ENJOY THESE LAST FEW MONTHS OF HIGH SCHOOL.
Connect with friends and family.

tl;dr

- Junior year is when the college admissions prep really kicks in, and you got this.
- Follow my guide while adapting it to suit your own needs.

CHAPTER 3

Course Rigor and
Class Selection

Few things are as frustrating or painstaking (but also exciting!) as selecting your courses during high school. There's always pressure to take the most honors, APs, or IB courses possible — like there's some magical combination of classes that will unlock your acceptance to the most fabulous college in the world — as if there were just one ;-).

However, I always tell students that, as with most things, they need to approach their course load with balance. Yes, they should challenge themselves, but they should also be realistic about how much they can handle. I also tell them that they need to consider courses that align with their interests because the world of college admissions is much wider than ticking courses off a list of what they (or their parents) think colleges want to see.

Once again, colleges want to see who you are and what you have to offer. If they want to see specific courses, they'll let you know in their admissions section of the website, so be sure to read that carefully BEFORE YOU OPT OUT OF THAT 4TH SCIENCE, MATH OR LANGUAGE CLASS

How Do Colleges Approach Course Rigor?

u/Checksallovame

Not sure which is better

I'm a freshman, and I'm freaking out over my classes right now. I'm not sure if I should go for harder classes and risk mediocre grades or settle for regular classes where I know I can make stellar grades. I want to take a bunch of basic freshman honors classes, and while I have an A average, it's not an A+ average. I have a friend who's purposefully taking easy classes to hold onto an A+ average. I'm worried my lower GPA compared to his will make me look less capable to AOs.

> [−] Atvelonis
>
> Colleges do take course rigor into account. You can see how heavily each school weights it in a table in section C of their Common Data Set. Stanford, for example, places course rigor in the "very important" column alongside GPA.

> [-] admissionsmom
>
> So, you're a freshman. My advice to you is to take the hardest and most interesting classes that you can take, make the highest grades you can in those classes, and still find the balance to be able to do activities, follow interests, and take care of your mental, emotional, and physical health. It's really all about the balance and learning to balance our lives is a skill you will always need. That means absolutely take honors, AP, and IB classes that work in your schedule and with your balanced life. Push yourself, but don't push yourself off the seesaw! (Do you kids even know what a seesaw is?)

my thoughts

As I also discuss in the GPA and Class Rank Chapter, schools with holistic admissions will consider your course rigor and grades in specific classes more important than your overall GPA. They want to see that you're taking the most rigorous course load available to you that you can responsibly handle *and stay mentally and emotionally healthy.* Other schools, especially many state schools, will be more willing to look at your overall GPA without significant emphasis on your course rigor.

Keep in mind that even if you had perfect 100 A plus plus plusses in every subject, every semester, every year on your transcript, your odds of getting into the most highly selective schools would still be low. So, the best way to approach this is to be an amazing student because you want to learn, not because you want good grades. Study hard. Learn, but learn for learning. Learn because you're fascinated.

However, that's not to say that lots of schools don't have certain expectations when it comes to course load.

OK, So what kind of classes should I take?

u/BioticAsariBabe

Community college classes vs. APs? Hey guys, homeschooler here. I f*cking hate APs. They're stressful and make me shit my pants, and I hate not having a professor to teach me/ having to do non-multiple choice for the test.

I can do up to 15 units per semester of community college by being enrolled at 2 at the same time and am considering going full blast in these — but I'm curious if admissions officers will see college classes as being "lighter" than APs.

Thanks.

[–] admissionsmom

You need to do what works for you. If you f*cking hate APs, clearly, they aren't working. Maybe you could try a blend if you'd like to experiment with that: mostly CC classes with an AP thrown in. Yes, some admissions officers will see community college classes as being "lighter" than APs. But, seriously, dude, is that worth ruining your pants?

u/kamillyswan

Not taking a Science senior year?

Just got my schedule, and I signed up for APES, but it wouldn't fit in my schedule. How bad would it be if I didn't have a science course my senior year? I'm mostly applying to schools for economics or a combination of the social sciences + computer science, and I would love some feedback...

> [-] admissionsmom
>
> You need to look at the websites for the colleges you're interested in and see what their course recommendations and requirements are. Many schools want to see four years of Science, but for most, you at least need a year of Bio, Chem, and Physics.

u/saada100

AP Chem?

I'm deciding my schedule for senior year, and I have to decide between taking AP Chem or Anatomy (which is a new course my school is offering). I'm hesitant to take Chem because I'm also taking AP Physics C and I'm worried I may overload myself. I'm taking AP Bio and AP Physics 2 now....any help?

> [-] admissionsmom
>
> Whoa. Hold on there. Even for a superstar STEM kid, that's a lot of science classes on your transcript. If you think AP Chem will overload your schedule next year, then as long as you already have a Chem class on your transcript, I think you need to put your stress level first. And before you jump on the Anatomy bandwagon, be sure that you have all the other classes your colleges will be wanting to see, like English, a History or Social Science, Math, and Foreign Language.

u/warrior__princess

Off period senior year?

Does it look bad to have an off period during senior year? Does it make you look lazy or incompetent? I have a bunch of challenging classes lined up, and I think an off period would be really beneficial for me, especially since I have an internship after school to worry about.

> [-] admissionsmom
> Just make sure you are taking your basic classes. You need a Math, Science, History type or Social Science, Foreign Language, and English. If you have all those, then you're in good shape. You should have at least 5 academic classes in my opinion – with some of those being honors, AP, or IB if they are offered.

let me break it down for you

A good rule of thumb to use when selecting your courses, especially if you want to apply to a highly selective college, is to follow the core curriculum. While you don't need to be enrolled in more than five academic classes at a time, you should make sure you have at least:

English (need all four years, and try to take AP Lang or AP Lit by senior year if possible)

History (or other Social Science)

Math (try to finish by taking Calculus (or beyond) your senior year, especially if you're a STEM kid or you are planning to apply to highly selective schools)

Science (most colleges want at least a year of Biology, year of Chemistry, and a year of Physics)

Foreign Language (the most highly selective schools generally like to see you take four years of a foreign language. I know. You don't want to. I hear it every day.)

Of course, this "rule" varies by college or university, so you should look up each of their course recommendations or requirements on their websites. Additionally, some colleges regard IB courses as more rigorous than AP classes, and AP classes are often preferred over Dual Enrollment ("DE") classes if students have these options. That being said, if you want to be a Humanities major, you should consider taking at least Honors or AP in those classes. If you think you want to be a STEM major, consider taking at least Honors or AP in those classes.

I hear each and every one of you about wanting to protect your physical, mental, and emotional health when dealing with a challenging course load. Reducing stress is an entirely valid goal. And no college expects you to take only APs, IBs, or Honors. Again, admissions officers want you to take the most rigorous course load you can comfortably handle, but that doesn't mean overload. I've heard them say that somewhere between 5 – 9 AP classes total throughout high school is enough, but as always... you do you. Remember the balance.

However, that doesn't change the fact that the most highly selective schools want to see these classes. If you can't find a way to square your concerns for your well-being with what Yale expects from applicants, maybe you should widen your school list to include colleges that want you for you.

You shouldn't run yourself ragged trying to get into a particular school. College is about much more than how you got in, and you are much more than your course load. Focus on what you can do maximize your best academic performance and put together your best application.

tl;dr

- Take the hardest course load you can handle, while holding on to your mental health.
- It's all about the balance.
- Focus on the 4x5: four years of each of these subjects, Science, Math, English, History, and Foreign Language.
- You don't have to take honors/AP/IB for every course. If Math isn't your thang, and English is...well, you do you. Take Honors English. Take regular Math.

- Check out the course recommendations and requirements for the specific schools you are interested in and for your major if you know it. Scour those school websites. They contain magical, important info.

- A note about Calculus: If you are interested in applying to selective schools, you really need to aim for taking Calculus by your senior year, if not before. If your school doesn't offer it, colleges will evaluate your application based on your school profile. I'd still recommend that you try to find a way to take it – either online or at CC.

- Talk to your high school counselor and teachers to see where they think you might best be placed for some of your classes you are questioning.

- Yes, I do think you need to take four years of Foreign Language.

CHAPTER 4

It's all about the GPA and Class Rank, or is it?

I get it. GPA and class rank can totally stress you out. No doubt, these are important metrics as they're often the only concrete things a student can point to in their college apps. And for a lot of schools, especially state schools, your GPA and class rank are determining factors for whether or not you'll be accepted. Yeah, this shit can be stressful.

But they're not everything. Actually, for many other schools, your GPA and class rank aren't as critical as you might think. They're pieces of a puzzle, parts of your whole application, and admissions officers know that.

So take a few deep breaths and read on about how colleges really handle your GPA and class rank. No really, breathe in. Breathe out. Now do it a few more times.

It's all about that GPA, right?

u/stuportrooper

Someone be honest with me. How bad will my Bs look?

I already have two Bs from sophomore year (I had a family death, and my grades took a hit). My GPA was already tanked because of that year, and I now have a B in AP Bio first semester senior year — fml. Am I gonna be able to get into college with this kind of mediocre GPA?

[-] admissionsmom

Here's what I want you to take away about GPA: most colleges that do holistic review do look at GPA, sure, but **your course rigor and grades in your individual courses in the context of your school are far more important.** Furthermore, many colleges recalculate your GPA using their own formula, so it's next to impossible to know how you'll compare to someone who comes from a school where they do things completely differently.

Having high grades in your academic classes is more important than your GPA to those schools who use holistic admissions. They look at the rigor of your classes. Is it a potential major class? Are you a STEM kid or humanities kid or both or neither? They can get lots of info by looking at your grades in your individual classes.

On the other hand, your GPA is important for a lot of public schools, who make admissions decisions with heavy deference to grades and stats. Even still, these **schools might recalculate your GPA with their own formulas.** It depends on the school.

let me break it down for you

At the end of the day, whether or not one C or a handful of Bs will keep you out of highly selective colleges will depend on the rest of your application. But know that the difference between a 3.68 and a 3.7 is negligible, especially if they recalculate grades.

Rather than obsessing about your grades, consider developing an authentic desire to learn and a thirst for knowledge. An avid reader who spends time self-studying a particular topic and then creates something or works somehow within that structure will most likely have a handful of grades looked over. A student whose whole schtick is only being a good student — probably not so much.

The fact of the matter is that admission to the most highly selective schools is ridiculously hard for everyone who's applying, no matter how perfect they are. All you can do is move forward and make sure you have a broad college list with a wide range of selectivity.

But while it's ok to slip up here and there in your classes, that doesn't mean you shouldn't give your classes your all. You should always try to excel in school. If you had some trouble early on in high school, you can turn the ship around. **Upward progression is definitely a positive in your applications.**

If you don't have the most stellar grades, please don't dwell on it. All you can do is move forward. If you need to explain the reason behind your not-so-great grades, you can and should address your grades head-on in the Additional Information section of the application. Be honest and upfront about what happened. Focus on what you've learned from your situation and how you'll manage overwhelming and stressful situations in the future (you can read more on how to approach Additional Info in that chapter).

In the process, you'll learn more from these bumps in your road than from anything else. Reflect on what happened, why you had these grade drops, and what you learned from them. Find the colleges that want you for who you are. Don't stress out trying to figure out how to squish yourself into the tiny boxes of the most highly selective schools. Allow yourself some room to expand and grow. You'll learn so much about yourself in the process of creating a list that fits you.

Class Rank — Looking at you, Top 10%

u/GeneriksGiraffe
My school just got rid of class rank at the end of our Junior year
RIP all that hard work and meticulous grade calculations I did to earn a good class rank.

Lots of kids are pissed at my school since we are getting rid of rankings entirely (and not replacing it with percentiles either). Why? Because the admins wanted to "reduce competitiveness" and "de-stress us." If anything, this stresses me out more because now colleges have no way of knowing how we stack up to the rest of our classmates. Feels bad, man.

> [–] admissionsmom
>
> Lots of colleges don't really consider class rank anyway, except for some of the bigger state schools that have direct-admit by rank like UT Austin. **Colleges with holistic review focus on your course rigor and your grades.**
>
> They know that class rank isn't the most meaningful measurement when they compare you to kids from all across the country, who came from a multitude of diverse backgrounds. How could they say that the #4 student at one school would be the #4 student at a different school?
>
> Honestly, it's truly not worth your time to worry about what is fair and not fair when it comes to class rank or the college process (or in life). You'll just end up frustrated.

my thoughts

Look, there's no way any of us can predict what the most highly selective colleges are going to do with your application. There are tons of kids out there with stellar grades and high rankings, so you have to be more than that. But, I don't mean "more" like how you're probably thinking. You can't *be* more than a perfect GPA or numero uno in your class. "More" means to dig down deep and discover what inspires you to learn, what pushes you to do, and what encourages you to be who you want to be. You have to demonstrate true blue authentic intellectual curiosity. A love for learning for the sake of learning. To read because you're enthralled by that book. To help because you see a need.

If a kid can demonstrate that they're more learning-driven than grade-or-rank-driven, that can often make the difference in admissions decisions.

tl;dr

- Colleges that do holistic review do look at GPA and class rank, sure, but your course rigor and grades in your individual classes in the context of your school are far more important.

- Many colleges recalculate your GPA using their own formula, so you actually don't even know what GPA they'll be looking at.

- If they do recalculate, they often only use your academic classes. Bye bye PE, Art, Health, and, of course, the proverbial Underwater Basket Weaving.

- If your grades are somewhat lackluster to date, then make every effort to turn them around. Upward progression is the bomb. Show them what you're made of from now on.

- Keep your grades up, but recognize that there is more to school than just grades. Learn to think for yourself. That's going to serve you far better in life — and college applications — than obsessing over some inconsequential decimal points.

CHAPTER 5

To SAT or ACT? — That Is the Question

Test anxiety is no joke. It's annoying and stressful, and nobody likes it. It all starts with that tough first decision: which standardized test are you going to take? You'll hear a variety of opinions about which test is better, which one is easier, and which one colleges prefer to see, but let's get some things straight. As far as I know, colleges don't really care which test you take — they just want to see you do well. So that means the best test is the one that works best for you. Read about the different tests, what they cover, look over practice questions, and consider which one matches your strengths.

anonymous
ACT or SAT
Rising senior here. My scores are 1350 SAT and a 30 ACT. I'm not sure which test I should focus on, but I'm aiming for the UCs (really want UCLA) or USC. People keep telling me that UCs prefer the ACT, but I'm not sure about that. Any advice?

> [−] admissionsmom
> Which test felt more comfortable for you? Do you prefer reading and writing or math?

> anonymous
>
> I like math way more, and I liked the SAT a lot more.

[–] admissionsmom

Then I think the SAT might be the way to go for you. I'm definitely not a testing expert, but from what I know and understand, the SAT is basically 1/2 math and 1/2 reading. The ACT is basically 3/4 reading and 1/4 math.

> anonymous
>
> Oh cool, hadn't approached it that way! Do you think colleges think of one as being better or more useful than the other? And thank you for your advice!

[–] admissionsmom
Nope.

u/SirBucketHead

Stressed about the ACT

With AP exams, regular finals, missing school for music festivals, and SAT subject tests, I have severely neglected my ACT studying. I'm probably going to get around a 32. I know this is objectively a good score, but it's disappointing to me personally. I already have a 1560 and 24 essay from the January SAT. Can someone please reassure me that it is okay to not do as well on the ACT? I'm feeling super guilty for not doing or trying my best, but on the other hand...I feel like I'll be okay without it. Any thoughts? Do I need to take a chill pill?

> [–]admissionsmom
>
> Why are you taking it? You have an excellent score on the SAT, so I'm not sure why you would want to even take the ACT. Yeah, I think you should take a chill pill for this one. Don't beat yourself up about this.

my thoughts

You almost never *need* to take both the SAT and ACT. If you qualified for National Merit, then you'll need to take the SAT to become a finalist, and if that's the case, then you're probably gonna get a kick-ass score on the SAT anyway. Otherwise, take practice tests for both. Read about the different types of questions. If you like math, consider the SAT. If you prefer reading, think about the ACT. Consider which test you'll get a better score on and say, *"Hasta la vista baby!"* to the other one. Most colleges accept both test scores, and they almost never favor one test over the other.

How many times should you take these tests?

Honestly, I get a different answer from every college admissions person I talk to, so I'll just give my take. I don't want to see kids giving up more than three or four Saturdays stressing out over these tests. That's a lot of your time you could be using to learn, study, explore interests, socialize, or recharge your batteries.

Since most colleges don't have a preference, how should you choose?

Ask yourself: Which test felt more comfortable for you? Do you prefer reading and writing or math? The SAT is basically 1/2 math and 1/2 reading. The ACT is basically 3/4 reading and 1/4 math. If you've taken both already, which felt better to you? And what are you more interested in?

Subject Tests. Wait. What? I have to take even more tests? !@%$&!

u/chanceme1234321
Do I really need subject tests, or nah?

u/TheHalima

Will Brown still review my app even though I can't afford SAT subject tests?

I have fallen in love with Brown upon visiting the school over spring break, especially their PLME program. I found out that Brown recommends SAT subject tests, sadly, and my family food stamps were cut off 2 months ago, and my parents only gave me enough of a budget to pay for SAT score reports, so I called the admissions office, and they said there was nothing they could do. I really, really want to go to Brown, but I can't afford the subject tests. What should I do?

> [–] admissionsmom
>
> Subject Tests are often recommended, but not required because of students like you. While they would love to see those tests, they also understand there are applicants who just can't afford to take them or who didn't even learn about them in time to submit their applications. First, check and see if you can get fee waivers. Talk to your high school counselor. And also, remember you get to send your scores for free when you take the test. If that still doesn't work for you, and you feel like it's important to explain to them why you don't have them, I suggest you do so in the additional information section, with a short paragraph explaining your situation.

my take

I think Subject Tests are important and suggest everyone take them if they aren't a financial burden — especially if you aren't particularly grade-driven, or you come from a high school they might not be as familiar with. Many schools use these tests when evaluating your application if you send them, even if they don't require or suggest them. And, by the way, I feel the same way about AP exam scores.

If you can afford it, you should take at least two Subject Tests. The reason they're often recommended and not required is because colleges understand there are students who can't afford to take the tests or who attend schools where the counselors don't encourage their students to take them. A lot of students don't even know these tests exist! But if you aren't low income or first gen, some highly selective schools will want to see those tests so study up and do your best.

For those of you just beginning your college application journey, you should start thinking about taking Subject Tests as early as your freshman summer. Maybe you can take Bio after freshman year or World History after sophomore year. If you do well in the classes, get the SAT Subject Test books or look around online for study materials. If you can take them early on in your high school career, it'll make your life a lot easier down the line.

Note — you can take up to three Subject tests on the same day, but you can't take a Subject Test and the regular SAT in the same session. And, as far as I know, the only school that really wants to see three Subject Tests is Georgetown.

Test Prep

u/warrior__princess
Need Help Prepping for SAT/ACTs
Guys, I need help. I have no clue where to start when it comes to studying for the SAT or the ACT (I haven't figured out which one to take yet). My parents just want me to "get them over with," and my college counselors aren't a big help, but I know I should study? Can someone tell me where I can even start?

u/robertobaz
Really want to improve my score. What is the most efficient way to get it up with a month and a half?
Hi, I am a very motivated student and my SAT scores kind of disappointed me. Granted, it was the first time I've taken the test, but I am really relying on my scores for admissions, and I would really, really want them to be about 130 points higher (got 1320, 690

English, 630 Math). English is my best subject, and in the practice tests I took beforehand I generally was in the low 700s. Math is more difficult, and I mostly focused on it in practices.

I will be taking the June one, and I realize I essentially have 4 chances to get my scores where I want them to be, but I am just not that close to a 1450 and want to at least get somewhere near it with the June one. What would be the best strategy for me so that I could use my dedication and maximize my time over a month and a half to do well? I appreciate any and all advice, I know there are practice tests available but am mostly interested in how to structure my time taking them and learning more of the material.

> [-] admissionsmom
>
> I'm no testing expert, but here are some of my basic test prep hints for studying: For the SAT, you should use Khan Academy and the SAT subreddit to help you. They're super helpful over there! For ACT, use the ACT subreddit and look at the official ACT website for some helpful test prep. Also, check out Applerouth Testing, CrackSAT, Erica Meltzer's books, and College Panda.
>
> If you're struggling with the SAT Math, I suggest you take an ACT practice test and see how that goes. When preparing for Subject Tests, be sure you get the Subject Test prep book. There are a lot of differences between Subject Tests and the regular SAT.

My Test Prep Tips:

- If you're struggling with the reading sections, then pick up a book and read! Read every day. Read lots of real books. Literature. Self-help. Sci-Fi. Fantasy. Whatever rocks your boat. But you have to read. The highest scorers in the verbal sections are readers.
- Take some timed practice tests. Be sure to adhere to the test conditions — time yourself, put your phone

away, and don't let anyone interrupt you. Check all your answers. Focus on the answers you got wrong. Try to figure out what you missed, and understand your mistakes.

- Do the "one page at a time test prep" a few days a week. I suggest taking the test one page at a time, checking the answers after you complete the page. If you get a question wrong or if you made a lucky guess, pause and figure out why the correct choice is correct. If you didn't understand the content, learn it. If you need to learn the strategy for a question, learn it. This way, you'll focus on your weaknesses and turn them into strengths.

- Cram hard for the two weeks before the test, but allow yourself a rest day once a week.

tl;dr

- Take practice tests to figure out which test feels better for you — the ACT or the SAT.

- Colleges don't care which one you take. If you already have a high score in one, there is no reason to take the other unless you need the SAT for National Merit.

- If you're Math-oriented, consider the SAT. If you're Verbal-oriented, consider the ACT.

- Ask your high school counselor about fee waivers to take the test.

- Consider taking Subject Tests throughout high school — for example, maybe take one after Bio freshman year and another after World History sophomore year. This can take the pressure off when you're trying to complete all your testing later in high school.

Bonus! AdmissionsMom's Last Minute Helpful Test Prep Hints

Don't cram the last night.

Get at least 8 hours of sleep the night before your test.

Do the Superman Pose the morning before the test. It's a thing. Google it! Stand in front of the mirror with your feet apart, your hands on your hips, and your shoulders back. Just stand there. Breathe. Feel your superpowers take over.

Eat fish the night before your test (grilled or baked, not fried). It's powerful brain food. I'm not kidding.

If you have a new calculator, make sure it's the right kind and program it the day before the test. Test it out and make sure it works and that you know how to use it. Don't wait until the morning of!

Put your ID, test ticket, extra #2 pencils, a pencil sharpener, a decent eraser that won't rip up your paper, and extra batteries for your calculator all in a baggy the night before — with some snacks and a bottle of water.

Take a sweater or a hoodie that you can take off if you get warm. Arrive 15 minutes early and make sure you know where you're going. You don't want to feel rushed.

CHAPTER 6

Test Scores — Report, Understand, and Make Peace with Them

It seems like everyday someone asks if they should retake the ACT or SAT or sometimes even both. Before you sign up for another testing day, take a moment to breathe and reflect. Then ask yourself:

How many times have you taken the test? And what's your breakdown?

If you've only taken either the SAT or the ACT once, first take a practice test of the one you haven't taken yet. See how you do on the other test before you pay money and dedicate a whole weekend to the test you already took. Say you didn't get as good a score on the SAT as you would've liked. Before you hunker down and sell your soul to the SAT gods, see how you perform on the ACT. It might be a better test for you! Then, after you've compared your experiences, prep for and take the one that feels best.

If you're not interested in the highly selective/lottery schools (and good for you!), look at the accepted students' scores for the schools on your potential list. Where does your score fall? If above 75%, then you're good. If above 50%, you're probably good, but I suggest taking the test once more to try to qualify for more of that sweet merit money.

If you're planning to apply to highly selective schools and you've only done one round of testing, then I suggest you try taking the test one or two more times to try and raise that score. After your third round of testing, then I think it's time to accept your score as it's not worth another whirlwind of stress.

u/Ultimatun

I took the ACT twice already and got a 32 the first time and a 34 the second time (with a 35 superscore).
But I'm applying for Computer Science, and my Math is only a 32 so should I take it a third time to improve it? I'm hoping to apply to competitive CS schools like Carnegie Mellon.

> [−] admissionsmom
> I can understand why you'd want to improve your score — even though I don't agree with you about the need, I won't judge you for the desire if that's how you want to spend your time. However, you have to be aware and admit that a 35 is an incredible score that most students can't even imagine making. Please be respectful of them and yourself. You did an amazing job.
>
> I'm gonna give you a bit of a testing intervention now. Take the test one more time and then move on. Maybe consider taking the SAT since you are strong in Math. There are many schools eager to admit you and many selective ones too. It's time to move on to other areas of your life and develop the person you're going to be.

u/warrior__princess

My test scores keep going down, not up! What's wrong with me?
My mom is freaking out because I started out with a 34 on the ACT. Then, I retook it to go for that sweet 36, and I got a 33. I took it again and got a 32! Like wtf!!! My score is going in the wrong direction, and I feel like giving up. My mom accused me of not trying

hard enough, and I feel like a failure before I even get started on this whole college thing.

I'm in the top ten percent of my graduating class, so there's at least something going for me, but I don't think it's enough. Without a perfect ACT score, I feel like I'm just going to get lost in a pile of other people who are average.

[−] admissionsmom

That happened to one of my sons. After three times of increasingly lower scores, he decided just to move on.

You can do the same — you have a solid score with your 34, and there are literally hundreds of colleges who will be eager to accept you, and don't forget the ever-increasing number of test-optional schools. Or you can try the SAT, or you can choose to keep focusing on the ACT to bring it up. Just remember that in doing so, you might be giving up some other aspect of your application (not to mention your life), so think about the balance there.

Also, I'm sorry your mom is saying stuff like that. Sometimes we parents say hurtful things. I'm sure she doesn't mean it. It's probably her way of trying to motivate you because she's scared about your future and doesn't exactly know how to talk to you about that. Maybe you can be the bigger person and tell her that her words are hurtful to you, and you understand that your college admissions future is really important and scary to her, and you appreciate all she has done and provided for you, but that you're doing the best you can and it would be amazing if you could have her support and supportive words right now.

Getting a perfect score won't outweigh your grades any more than the score you have right now will. You'll have a good application as long as you have good recs and essays.

my thoughts

There is no "good enough" application for highly selective schools. Making a perfect score won't mean much more to them than an already high score. Every year, Stanford likes to brag about how many perfect score candidates they deny, so it really isn't worth wasting too much emotional energy on seeking that 36 or 1600. Instead, work on understanding yourself and finding out what meaning there is to your life besides test scores. Be the best you — that's your best bet, and it'll help your application to highly selective schools as much as anything.

Should I send or self-report?

anonymous
Sending SAT scores?
I've heard a lot about sending SAT scores, but I am not sure what the best course of action is for me. I got my best super-score on the March test, so I guess I only have to send that one, but when? Should I send it with my application or as early as possible? I don't even know which colleges I'm applying to, so I didn't use the free score report option. Is that bad? I guess I have a lot of questions about the whole process and would like some clarification.

[–] admissionsmom
When you've completed your testing and you know which schools you want to send your scores to, you can send them at any time. I suggest you send them in the early fall of senior year when you have your college lists mostly complete. Be sure to check the admissions pages of your colleges' websites to find out whether they'll let you self-report your scores.

u/Mrkgamer

If a school requires all SAT scores, but I don't want to send any, do I still have to send them?

Hi. I am much better at the ACT and decided to only focus on that test. I got a good score on the ACT, so I decided to see if I could also get a good score in the SAT, even though I wasn't that good at it. I scored something that I'm not really happy with, and I'm not going to send it anywhere, but there are some schools that require all SAT and/or ACT scores. If I don't send any SAT scores to them even though I have taken one, is that a problem? Also, if I took 3 SAT Subject Tests, do I have to send all 3 to those schools?

They would have no way of knowing how many times you take it unless you tell them.

u/KaiserSand

Send all SAT scores although I only want ACT scores sent?

I've taken the ACT, and I plan on sending that instead of the SAT exam. However, I need to send in the SAT subject test scores that I've taken also. Some universities, like say UC, say to send all scores on the score choice option. But I don't want them to see my crappy SAT grade when I'm already sending them my ACT!!! Should I just send all but my SAT score? Help!

u/Ultimatun

Can colleges see if you took SAT subject tests?

One of my colleges recommends it (not mandatory), but I don't want to send it since I got a bad score. However, I'm afraid they'll see I took it and infer I got a bad score and that's why I didn't send it.

> [−] admissionsmom
>
> Here's what I've heard from most college admissions officers: They only see the scores that can help you. They don't even see — or they completely ignore — those that don't boost your

app. They totally get that everyone can have a bad day. If they don't require that you send them, I wouldn't, but if you feel like you need to, then go ahead — I don't think they'll affect your application. If they ask you to send ALL scores, you should.

u/TheHalima
Is it ok to self-report SAT scores?
So, I can barely afford to send the score reports on CB, do colleges allow you to self-report SAT scores?

> [-] admissionsmom
> After you use a fee waiver to take the SAT, you also get 4 free score reports on College Board. Try sending your scores through College Board, and see if it lets you send them without a charge. Be sure to send those to your four top schools! Also, many schools allow you to self-report your scores on the Common App and then send the official scores after you've been admitted. Make sure to read their websites carefully for this info.

APs are just for credit, right? Reporting APs for Admissions

u/allurredditsrbelongtous
Can my 5 on the APUSH exam offset my B in the class?
And should I even bother self-reporting my 3 in Calc BC?

> [-] admissionsmom
> Congrats on that 5! If you can afford it, I think you should send your high AP scores when applying. Otherwise, you can definitely self-report. You don't need to send or self-report anything lower than a 3. Those 3s probably won't hurt you, and your 4s and 5s might actually help you because some schools do use AP scores to help evaluate your application. That's why I suggest reporting or even sending strong scores. They can supplement and boost grades and other test scores that might not be as strong.

Lots of kids start taking APs as early as sophomore year. Some even as early as freshman year. I always encourage them to at least self-report 4s and 5s and to submit them if the cost isn't a financial burden.

The Importance of Scores — When is a high score high enough?

u/GeneriksGiraffe

As a possible journalism major, is a 730 on SAT R&W too low for Ivies?

I mean I feel that it's pretty low in comparison to my other stats/extracurriculars. Like, I got an 800 on SAT II Literature. Would that help balance it out, or should I consider retaking the SAT? My current score (1530) is about average for all the colleges I'm interested in. It's just that 730 seems low especially for an English-centered student at one of these schools.

u/Ultimatun

Is a 34 ACT with 35 superscore good for elite colleges like the top Ivies (engineering major at liberal art colleges)?

I know it's good, but I have a lingering doubt I'll be denied because of it. I chose not to take the ACT again and am kinda regretting it so need someone to tell me it's ok. It's pathetic I know lol.

[-] admissionsmom

Even if you have amazing, like almost perfect, standardized test scores, most colleges (with the exception of some state schools that admit strictly on stats) will look at and evaluate your entire application. Like any other part of your application, your test scores will not make or break your acceptance to any one school. It depends on the complete application. The impact of test scores also depends on the breakdown of the scores and your potential major. But, dude, seriously? Those scores rock – and you know it.

my thoughts

In the end, there are far more students with fantastic test scores applying to the most highly selective schools than there are spots. All you can do is present the strongest application you can, including your grades, course rigor, ECs, essays, letters of recommendation, and those awesome scores. Then, it's out of your hands.

There are some schools that prioritize test scores more than other parts of your application. As we talked about in the GPA section, state schools in particular care a lot about test scores. Many have formulas to show you your chances of acceptance based on your scores and grades. On the other hand, holistic review colleges, especially some LACs, are willing to balance your test scores with the rest of your application. It really sucks to feel like all your hard work comes down to a few hours on a testing day. That's why holistic admissions are a great alternative — because they'll consider all those other wonderful aspects you described. But, again, all you can do is present your best self on your best day and write killer essays.

There's no way to gain admittance by test scores alone, except for some state schools that use them for auto-admission. For the rest, there are too many other determining factors. Barring the most highly selective schools, anything above a 1300 is a very good score and might even get you admission with merit aid. And for many, many schools, that number could be above 1100 or even below. You can find those auto-admission numbers on the individual colleges' websites.

tl;dr

- A perfect SAT or ACT score won't grant you an admission ticket to a highly selective school, but it could help you gain merit scholarships to many schools who admit by stats.

- Some schools do consider your AP scores for admissions. Definitely self-report your 4s and 5s, and even consider submitting them from College Board if you can afford it, especially if they can offer a lackluster grade or another standardized test score a boost.
- Many colleges now allow you to self-report your test scores. Read their websites carefully and save yourselves some cash!
- Some schools let you apply without test scores altogether! Check out the info box for test optional schools.

There are hundreds of colleges that are test optional. Go to www.fairtest.org to see the list. Many of them are highly selective.

And, there are also lots of art schools, theater programs, music programs, and film schools that will care way more about any product you can show them.

CHAPTER 7

Activities, ECs, and Summers, Oh My!

"How good are my extracurriculars?" is one of the most common questions we get on r/ApplyingToCollege. Then I receive tons more about how many extracurriculars are necessary and whether a kid's chances will be hurt because they haven't performed at Carnegie Hall, been speaking Mandarin since they were five years old, or cured cancer.

I get it. It's an important part of your application. It's also a broad category, and as a result, there's a lot of room for creativity and individuality. That also means that kids feel a lot of pressure to have the most impressive, superhuman extracurriculars possible.

Be a Star

I mean colleges don't want you obsessing over the most impressive, superhuman extracurriculars possible. They aren't looking for you to have any particular kind of ECs. They want to know what gets you interested and involved. High school is a time for you to learn about yourself and what intrigues, interests, and excites you. Don't box yourself in, thinking that there are only a few things you should be doing.

As such — and I acknowledge I'm going against the grain here — my philosophy for helping kids with extracurriculars is all about being *star-shaped.* I don't actually recommend having one big "spike," meaning a single extracurricular you devote all your time to, though I recognize that's the trendy advice these days, nor do I recommend trying to pursue every single extra-curricular you can because you feel like you need to check off a laundry list of activities for the "resume booster club" so you can be "well-rounded." Instead, shoot for being kinda well-rounded with some spikes — like a star — by pursuing four or five activi-ties that interest and excite you. But honestly, you do you. Be who you are. That's what colleges want. And if being you means having one big spike or a being a perfectly round ball, then that's totally fine.

For real, though, what counts as an EC?

u/nomotho
Are my EC's weak? (Rising junior)

I always thought my EC's were good compared to everyone I knew, but after seeing all the strong ass EC's on this subreddit and /r/chanceme, I realized that mine are not even close to these other people. Can you rate them?

FYI the only thing I did freshman year was baseball and band.

- I have been a percussionist since 5th grade.
- 1 year marching band + 2 more. Section leader junior and senior year.
- 1 year pit orchestra + 2 more years.
- 1 year improv + 2 more years. Captain senior year.
- 1 year ultimate frisbee + 2. JV this year, Varsity the next 2 years. Maybe captain senior year.
- 1 year French honors society + 2 more.
- Member of the French club. 1 year + 2 more. I possibly will be the president senior year.

- National Honors Society for the next 2 years.
- This summer I am doing 2 college courses at a local community college: public speaking, and an intro to a college course.
- I was student director for a one-act play at our school. Definitely not gonna do that again but I'll put it on this list.
- I did baseball freshman year. I was on the freshman team. It was not fun, so I didn't do it again. Now that I tried ultimate frisbee, I'm not going back!

Thank you!

Edit: sorry. I knew these weren't "bad" in the first place. I originally was going to post this on chance me, where everyone and their endless list of strong EC's made me feel so underachieving. Now I sound like a jerk for saying this is bad.

> [–] admissionsmom
> For real? You're asking if these awesome ECs are good enough? So, what's a good EC? If you are passionate about it and do it because it resonates with you, then yes, it's a good EC.
>
> Ask yourself: Does it seem interesting to you? Is it something that you can get behind and feel like what you are doing is worthwhile? If so, yes, it can be good for your application. If not, then no. If you're worried about the amazing specialness of an activity or opportunity, it means you're really not that into it. The lack of interest is what makes that particular EC nothing special for you, and you'd be better off finding something else.
>
> An AO from the University of Chicago once told me, "As soon as you figure out what you think we're looking for, we're gonna change our mind." Colleges want to see the reflection of who you are and what interests you, not what you are trying to guess that they want you to do.

u/Allurredditsrbelongtous

Cooking/baking?

Not even joking, but I love to cook, and I've started baking breads and stuff recently to combat stress. I'm pretty good too. I blog about it (but no one reads my blog lol). Can I talk about that for my ECs?

> [−] TheRealClyde1
>
> Dude of course! Cooking may not be something structured like sports or debate or whatever, but you can talk about pretty much anything as long as you're passionate about it. Also, the fact that you're starting a blog shows that it's a serious activity and not just a casual hobby. So yeah, mention it in the Activities section of the Common App for sure, and feel free to talk about it in your essays if it seems relevant!

let me break it down for you

You gotta realize that extracurriculars are merely one part of your whole application. Do they guarantee admission to any particular school or set of schools? Are they the deciding factor between acceptance and rejection? No and no, because colleges that consider your ECs are looking at your entire application package and also at their own institutional needs, so there's no guessing what's going to appeal to any one school for any one year. If anything, learning about your activities provides an opportunity for admissions officers to get to know you better. That means you just have to keep doing you!

Keep in mind that it's not exactly about the type of ECs you do — it's more about your involvement. If you are enthusiastic, interested, and involved, then any EC is a good EC. They don't have to be unique. In fact, I'm not so sure there is such thing as a "unique" activity anymore. If it has added value to your life and helps paint a picture of high school you, include it in your application.

On that note, you might already have more ECs than you realize. Basically, extracurriculars are anything you do outside of class time, homework, or test prep. That includes jobs, family and household responsibilities, child or elderly care, and personal projects and hobbies, in addition to the more typical inside and outside of school clubs, sports, volunteer opportunities, internships, or even personal and independent research. There is no one right or wrong way to do your activities, and colleges understand when your financial, family, school, or community circumstances might limit what's available to you. Just be involved in some way. Find a way to be involved in taking care of yourself physically, emotionally, and mentally. Find a way to be involved in your family, your school, and your community if you can. Figure out what works for you in the context of your life.

Considering the opportunity that the Activities section of the application affords you, be proud of your extracurriculars! If you help out at your parents' business or care for a grandparent, include that! Do you work as a cowboy, like a real, working, horse-riding, rounding-up-cattle cowboy? Definitely put it down. Are you a professional speedcuber? Let colleges know. Do you like to read a lot? Show them. Do you moderate a subreddit? Do you spend a substantial amount of time running a meme page? Do you spend hours conducting your own Internet research about a topic you love? They want to know that, too.

Family Obligations

u/warrior__princess
Need advice with my EC's
Can babysitting my siblings after school three days a week, every week, really be an EC?

> [−] admissionsmom
> Yes. If it's a responsibility that takes up a good portion of your time, then that's important info. If you just occasionally babysit once or twice a month, not so much, but

some teens have to be at home every day after school to watch siblings while parents work. There's no way they can participate fully in extended ECs. Not only do your family responsibilities preclude "normal" ECs, but they also show your dedication, commitment, and responsibility. Colleges want to know about this.

my thoughts

Colleges know family obligations take precedence over more conventional extracurriculars. If your family relies on you to care for a relative, let colleges know. You can address this in the Activities section and then explain in more detail in the Additional Info section if you feel it needs to be addressed more fully in order for them to more fully evaluate your application.

Teenagers can't have jobs, can they?

u/Allurredditsrbelongtous

Does a job help or hurt me?
I work at a smoothie place about 20 hours a week because money is tight, and I pay for my gas/clothes/hanging out with my friends. I know it's not cool or impressive. Between that, AP classes, and other obligations, I don't have a ton of ECs with leadership. How will AOs consider my app?

> [–] admissionsmom
> Lots of admission officers love to see part-time jobs. It shows initiative, responsibility, and leadership. And they recognize that you are learning invaluable skills about customer service and working with and for others. Good on you!
>
> Also, here's a piece of unsolicited advice: don't worry so much about whether what you do is impressive or not. Just do what you need to do to live a life that you feel is worthy and satisfying. If you need this job for your finances or just because you like it and it helps you get where you need to be, that's

all that matters. Now, if you can live your life in this way and that shows through in your apps — that will be impressive.

my take

From scooping ice cream to chasing kids around at a daycare to working unpaid (or paid) at your family's business, jobs can only strengthen your application. By having a job, you are demonstrating initiative, responsibility, leadership, the ability to work with others, and a willingness to get out of your comfort zone.

A job can be anything. You could work at a restaurant, a retail store in the mall, an office, a gym, a bookstore, a garden shop, a public pool, a preschool, a summer camp, an artisanal vegan cashew cheesery — the possibilities are endless.

When filling out your list of extracurriculars and your resume for applications, be straightforward and honest about what your job entails. Simply say what you do. If you work at a pizza place, include the hours each week you work and your job duties. Do you work the cash register? Do you deliver pizzas? Do you make the pizzas? How do you interact with customers? Or if you work at a daycare, do you organize activities? Monitor children during playtime? Interact with parents? Facilitate the teachers with their lesson plans? Organize materials? Encourage literacy by reading books? Encourage problem-solving by playing with blocks? Encourage creativity by introducing open-ended art projects?

A job might seem like nothing special to you, especially when you go to it all the time, but it's often much more special than you might assume.

Following the Leader

u/23dagreatest

No leadership. How bad will this hurt me?
Not because I don't try. I just can't win the club/student body elections at my massive public high school.

[-] FeatofClay

I like to remember this: A leader isn't someone who is "in charge" of something or other people. A leader is someone who makes an effort to improve the space around them.

[-] admissionsmom

I love this. OP, leadership doesn't necessarily mean being the president of a club or the captain of a team. There are tons of other ways to demonstrate leadership. You can start a club, in school or out of school. You can coach a club or start a club in an elementary or middle school. Or maybe you have leadership within your family. Often siblings take leadership roles amongst themselves. You can get a job. You can work with senior citizens. I really feel what colleges are mostly looking for is initiative. Did you take on the role of being the leader of your life and figuring out how you can be a healthy person, physically, emotionally, and mentally? Did you do things that allow you to grow and learn? Did you allow yourself the opportunity to explore ideas and ways to give back? Do you help out with your family or community or church?

my thoughts

True, demonstrating leadership is key for many colleges, but you can show leadership in lots of ways besides being Class President. Just because you don't have a name tag or title that says "President" or "Captain" on it doesn't mean that you aren't a leader. Having a job shows leadership. Starting a club or project where you see a need shows leadership. Coaching little kids shows leadership. You can organize a volunteer effort for donating food/coats/other stuff drive or a clean-up effort, or be a mentor or big brother/sister to an elementary school kid if there's a program for that. Also, leadership can mean helping out within your own family by taking care of siblings, making dinner, being in charge of cleaning, or taking on some other household responsibility. Being a leader is not about having a title, but about being actively involved in improving your life and the lives of those around you.

Giving Back to your Community

u/GeneriksGiraffe

T20 acceptance without volunteer hours?
I feel kind of screwed since throughout my 3 years of high school I haven't really had the opportunity to volunteer to a significant milestone of hours and when the opportunity was presented to me, I rarely found it a valuable experience.

This seems to be the big hole in my application though, I have good ECs, grades, etc., but there's this blank spot on my application. I feel screwed for T20s; but at the same time not, unless I am fooling myself. It seems that many AOs weight community service organizations (NHS, Key Club, etc.) and lots of hours of community service not that high in terms of value on an application unless that person has a special story to tell or exemplary leadership. Would this be a deal breaker on my application or is it a smaller detractor and I still have a chance?

> [−] admissionsmom
> One of my kids got into some highly, highly selective colleges without listing a single community service hour — even though they'd done lots of them; they just didn't like the thought of doing them for "hours for college apps." Colleges are just exploring who you are — not who you aren't!

my thoughts

Volunteering in your community is awesome — and, to me, essential. I'm a firm believer in giving back to the community and tried to instill those values in my children, just as my own mother did in me. Not only do you get the chance to better your community and touch the lives of others, but you will also learn a lot about yourself.

If you want to pursue volunteer hours, go for it. Or, rather than pursuing hours as your goal, try focusing on helping others and doing things you find meaningful. Get involved in your community. Here are some ways:

- Help out at a retirement home or homeless shelter. My kids interviewed senior citizens about their lives at our local retirement home and then turned the responses into songs that they performed for the senior citizens a few weeks later. You could also write poems about them or make a story for them to share with their families.
- Make comfort bags for the homeless and pass them out to them on the street corners. In my family, we call these "Judy Bags" after my mom, who would always drop off food on corners for the homeless. Include water, granola bars, handy wipes, and anything else you feel could brighten their day and let them know someone is thinking about them.
- Walk dogs and play with kittens at your local animal shelter.
- Volunteer for an after-school program.
- Make sandwiches at your local food bank.
- Coach a kids' sports team.
- Tutor for the SAT or ACT.

There are multitudes of ways to be involved. Even just taking the time to answer questions for your fellow applicants on A2C can be helpful. Here's a mom reminder: "If you're ever at a loss with what to do with yourself, do something for somebody else."

If you don't feel called to volunteer, don't worry about it. Use the time you would have spent volunteering to cultivate the activities that interest you. After all, community service is not about college applications, and it's also not an absolute requirement for your apps. Do it because it makes others feel good, and it can also bring about some of those warm fuzzies inside you.

In the Good Ol' Summertime

u/TheBigDog420
Can you list summer programs as ECs?
I'm looking to attend a medical program over summer which aligns with my major to show interest.

> [–] admissionsmom
> Absolutely. Your summer activities, no matter what they are — research, internship, academic program, job, hobbies, or family responsibilities — can all be included in the Activity section of your application.

u/warrior__princess
Is summer research worth it still?
I've got a summer research/internship position with a professor lined up for the summer. I feel like a lot of people are doing this, so it's not a big deal or unique anymore. Should I scrap my plans?

> [–] Atvelonis
> Most people do not do research internships with a professor over the summer — it's still very much a "unique" EC. Remember that this subreddit represents a very skewed (toward the top end) pool of high school students. If you're genuinely interested in the internship, go for it.
>
> Still, the primary thing to focus on is ensuring that your experience in that internship will be a good one, and adequately reflecting how it helped you grow as a person in your essays. It's possible to make an otherwise fascinating EC seem boring to an admissions officer with a bad essay!

u/Chanceme1234321
My Summers are SOOOO Basic
My ECs are basically nonexistent, except for NHS and other honor societies. What should I do? Will doing a bunch of stuff this summer save me? And I see all these other kids getting research positions. How in the world am I supposed to do that? I don't have any connections or know any professors.

> [-] carmy00
> Instead of packing things in, I'd say to volunteer or intern in something related to your major/interests or get a part-time job doing anything. USC really cares about how passionate you are about what you do and the school and how you show that through your essays.

> [-] Mrkgamer
> I went to my local university's faculty page for the College of Engineering, Department of CS. I found a ton of professors and looked at the ones whose work I found really interesting and emailed them about possibly assisting them in the summer. I emailed at least 20 professors, and only one replied, and they interviewed me and had me in their lab over that summer. It's also noteworthy that you shouldn't seek this type of opportunity out if you don't enjoy it. I would have hated my summer if I didn't feel fulfillment in what I did every day there.

let me break it down for you

What to do, what to do? Summers are important, but there's no magical formula for what you need to do to get into any colleges — even the most highly selective ones. When it comes to your summer, please, please, please do something outside of school. Summer school is fine, sure, especially if you need it to graduate with all your credits, but try also to find something non-school to do that gets you out of the house. Even if it's just going to the gym, or, sure, you can help with research in a lab (you get those positions by emailing any and every professor you know or who you can find doing the research you're interested in). Or you can get an internship (you get those the same way as research). Or you can do a program somewhere on a campus or around the world. Those are all great ways to spend your summer. You can also do independent projects.

But definitely, don't forget the good old-fashioned summer job. You can actually stand out from the applicant crowd these days by making a smoothie, flipping a burger, or scooping ice cream. These kinds of jobs allow you to learn how to take care of many different types of people, how to organize your thoughts and time, and how to work with others. You'll have some experiences you might never have the chance to have again. Plus, you'll make some money, which is always nice.

Here's what William Fitzsimmons, Dean of Harvard Admissions, says about summer: "Bring summer back. Summer need not be totally consumed by highly structured programs, such as summer schools, travel programs, or athletic camps. While such activities can be wonderful in many ways, they can also add to stress by assembling "super peers" who set nearly impossible standards. Activities in which one can develop at one's own pace can be much more pleasant and helpful. An old-fashioned summer job that provides a contrast to the school year or allows students to meet others of differing backgrounds, ages, and life experiences is often invaluable in providing psychological downtime and a window on future possibilities. Students need ample free time to reflect, to recreate (i.e., to "re-create" themselves without the driving pressure to achieve as an influence), and to gather strength for the school year ahead."

You do you, Boo.

u/A2cthrowaway27416

Frustrated

How am I supposed to beat out some rich kid whose parents have put him in private school and violin lessons since he was 4 and who's had access to all the best tutors and extracurriculars money can buy? Just frustrated that no matter how hard I work or how many good extracurriculars I have, it won't be the same as those "great" ECs other kids can get.

> [–] admissionsmom
>
> Look, I know how challenging the process can be, just like I know the temptation to compare yourself to others is strong. If you are worried about where you stand right now, especially when you hear that the violin prodigy in your class is applying to the same school you are, know that you are not competing with this kid. You only need to show colleges who you are and what you've done with the cards you've been dealt. They aren't expecting anything more.
>
> You don't have to be homeless or super privileged to go to college, but I understand that sometimes it just feels that way. I promise you there are hundreds of colleges looking for kids just like you. And you do have a story. Everyone does. You are living it, so it doesn't seem like it's interesting, but whatever you have going on in your head that sparked your interest in coming on here to Reddit to ask this question is part of your story. Every thought you have when you're going to sleep is part of your story. Every chuckle you make when you're watching a funny video is part of it too. There's a lot more there to you than you're giving yourself credit for.
>
> So, instead of worrying about that kid and his music lessons, focus on what you have done with your life and what

you can and will do. Colleges want kids with all different experiences. They don't want a bunch of clones. Be you. Do you.

u/iZaxer

Why do colleges like to see an upward trend in GPA, but look down on increasing your EC load?

Raising your grades without a legitimate excuse for the bad start is just as much padding your resume as taking on extra leadership roles junior/senior year. How come EC loading is more frowned upon?

> [−] admissionsmom
>
> Colleges don't look down on increasing your EC load. They just want you to be genuine about what you're doing and not just participate for resume padding. If you want to explore what your high school offers and want to get involved, by all means, get involved!

Stepping Off the EC Hamster Wheel

anonymous

Stress regarding extracurriculars

I am currently a part of a speech and debate team, a gay-straight alliance/empower club, and a school art journal with a couple more minor clubs. I have an above 4.0 GPA and am an AP scholar as a sophomore, the year where my clubs typically have to be locked down by. The problem is that I really don't like speech and debate that much, and would much rather switch it out for a self-created animal rescue/shelter volunteer club. I am overly stressed out about this decision and am wondering if you guys think switching out my only competitive club that stresses me out in exchange for a noncompetitive club that I would start/enjoy more is a good move. I care way too much about small things like that, and this decision is a rough one. Does anyone have thoughts on how to proceed?

EDIT: I am planning on an ecology or veterinary field.

> [–] admissionsmom
>
> If you feel like you have too much on your plate, it's ok to back off on one or more of your extracurriculars. Trust me. Especially when this decision enables you to focus on extracurriculars you enjoy much more.

u/Stuportrooper

Don't have enough ECs

I only have 2 ECs — a seasonal summer job and my school's environmental club, which isn't as time-consuming as something like Model UN. I feel so overwhelmed by everything I see everyone else doing. What should I do?

> [–] admissionsmom
>
> This process is confusing. And you're making a great first step by doing some research and asking questions. Keep the research up and talk to your college counselors at your high school. It will become a little clearer. And, honestly, you probably have more ECs than you realize.
>
> Explore the wonderful world around you. It's never too late to start something new in your life in addition to your summer job. You could tackle a big fitness goal or walk a certain number of miles every day. You could learn a martial art. You could learn how to play an instrument or write music. You could create a blog or conduct personal research on a topic that appeals to you. You could start volunteering at a local assisted living facility or homeless shelter. Pick up that one activity you quit because you didn't think you had time for it even though you loved it.
>
> If you still feel like you need to do more with your extracurriculars, there are things you can do right now. Set goals for yourself. If you need a little help to take your current extracurriculars seriously, ask your parents to hold you accountable.

my thoughts

Most of all, enjoy high school! Explore and try stuff and take risks and change your mind if you don't really like doing something. This is the time for you to learn about yourself and what intrigues, interests, and excites you. Don't pin yourself into a box, thinking that there are only a few things you should be doing so that you — as a teenager — will become the expert. At the same time, don't feel like you have to be Captain Every Club or have to join a whole bunch of activities to fill out a crazy long list for college apps. Again, I encourage you to think about being star-shaped — having four or five points — rather than well-rounded or spiky. As frustrating, confusing, and scary as trying to figure out what to do outside school seems now, it can also be an amazing opportunity of self-reflection and learning if approached with the right mindset.

You might have noticed that I don't use that P-word here. That's because I think telling 14 and 15-year-olds, and even 17 and 18-year-olds, to "follow their passions" adds unintentional pressure. What if they're not feeling any passions yet? What if they're doing stuff that simply interests them? Or if they don't even know what interests them yet? That's why I encourage you to explore. Try new stuff. It's ok to learn what you like and don't like to do. There's no shame in starting something and then dropping it when you find something else that is more interesting or exciting to you. Plus, I don't think colleges are looking so much for that P-word in the way you guys imagine it anyway. They are just looking for authenticity — for you to portray who you genuinely are. Be your authentic self and try to lose the idea of who colleges "want you to be." You, the real you, are enough.

A Little Practical Advice

In addition to answering loads of questions about extracurriculars, I also see lots of questions on how to fill out this portion of the applications.

Generally speaking, you have a finite amount of space to tell colleges about your extracurriculars. First, you don't have to fill all the spaces. Second, recognize once again that your ECs are anything you do outside of class time, homework, and test prep, so you will probably have more extracurriculars than you think. Personal research is an extracurricular as much as after-school sports or waiting tables at your family's restaurant. Put it down. Be proud of it. Prioritize your activities in their order of importance to you. Put your most current and most important first, and then move down from there.

Also, don't forget that for some schools you can attach a resume or CV. Here you can include activities that either wouldn't fit in extracurriculars or didn't meet the bar for extracurriculars. For example, any activities or accomplishments that occurred before high school shouldn't be included in your Activity List, but you can consider adding those activities or awards to your resume, though I only recommend it if it's something on the national level or a long-term ongoing activity. You can also use the Additional Info section for adding more information about your ECs that might need more explanation, especially if the college doesn't have a "Why EC" supplementary essay.

tl;dr

- Think star-shaped for your activities: kinda well-rounded with a few points or spikes for special interests you might have.

- A summer job or after school job counts as an EC, as well as some other stuff you might not normally consider like family obligations, independent research, and hobbies.

- You do not need to cure cancer, have thousands of volunteer hours, be president of multiple clubs, or be in a sport. Those are all good activities, but they aren't a requirement.

Those Olympians, spelling bee champs, violin prodigies, computer wizzes, and cancer researchers are actually few and far between.

- Figure out what interests you. Try new stuff. Explore. And then dive in when something sparks you.

- Be your authentic self. As Jeff Schiffman from the Tulane Admissions Office says in his admissions blog, "Do whatcha wanna."

CHAPTER 8

Letters of Recommendation

Letters of recommendation, aka LORs, are often critical for your application. They demonstrate core aspects of your personality and ability as a student that grades, activities, and test scores can't. They're also one of the more nerve-wracking parts of the application.

Whereas you are entirely responsible for much of your application, including activities, essays, and general information, the letter of recommendation is an entirely different animal. It's the part of the application you have the least control over since you're not filling it out yourself. But that doesn't mean you can't take steps to increase your odds of securing kick-ass letters of recommendation.

After all, you are in charge of asking for the letters, and who you ask, how you ask, and the raw information you give them can make a big difference.

General Rules for Letters of Recommendation

u/szi8890

Rec Letters

How much importance is placed on recommendation letters and is it important to get them from a teacher who teaches in a subject related to your major?

[–] admissionsmom

I like to see you ask two teachers from your junior year. Some schools highly recommend that you have one humanities teacher and one STEM teacher, so I think that's a good rule of thumb to go by. Sure, if you have a teacher who teaches in a subject related to your major and who knows you well enough to write a strong letter for you, that could be an amazing choice, but it's not necessary.

u/Mrkgamer

Third LOR?

How valuable is a third LOR from a mentor like a professor for research? Also, are there any schools that really don't want 3 recommendations? Like I'm pretty sure Stanford really does not want its applicants to send more than two. Thanks.

[–] admissionsmom

You will need to read each college's website info carefully. If they say they don't want additional LORs, don't send them. If they don't say, sometimes adding that third or fourth recommender can really round out your application. You'll have to judge on a case by case basis. For that reason, I suggest adding your two academic recommenders that will go to every school on the application platform. For the additional recommenders, they may need to send by email or upload to the portal or even send by snail mail, so as to avoid some of the snafus I've seen happen over the years.

u/GeneriksGiraffe

Getting a Letter of Recommendation from a freshman-year teacher?

Hey A2C, I talked to my guidance counselor about potential teachers I should ask for a recommendation letter from. I have this one teacher who I have a fantastic relationship with. She was my freshman English teacher who I would love to have for a LoR. Only problem is that I haven't really been involved with her since then; I don't/haven't had her for any of my ECs or other classes. I've only talked with her and asked her to sponsor me in a couple contests the past few years.

My guidance counselor is advising me not to get a letter from her. She said that colleges would be concerned to see a rec from a freshman year teacher, even if I've had a great relationship with her because colleges would much rather see a letter from a junior/sophomore year teacher and would raise a red flag if not. Is this correct? I mean, I get the concern, but I feel like this letter would be great, so long as it doesn't raise any red flags.

> [−] admissionsmom
> You could use it as an additional LOR for schools that allow that, but for your main two recs, I think your counselor is right. The letters should come from junior year teachers if that is possible.

>> [−] GeneriksGiraffe
>> Thanks for the advice! I will definitely keep my English teacher on the radar for an additional rec then. I feel like she can really speak on my character in class and my growth through high school.

u/KaiserSand

Is a professor LOR better than a school teacher LOR?

Ok, here's my dilemma: Some colleges (like Stanford, USC, Princeton) only let me assign 2 teacher recommenders to them, so I can't submit all 3 of the teacher recommenders.

My recommenders are as follows:

English teacher: She really likes me and regards me as one of her best students. I've done a lot of stuff for her outside of class.

Calculus teacher: I've talked to him for a long time and discuss interesting math problems outside of class. He also knows a lot about me and my drive to get things done, so that might be good. I'm also the co-president of the math club, which he advises.

Physics professor: I took a summer program at UC Davis. He really likes me because I discussed a lot of cool computational physics problems with him. He has said, multiple times, that I am one of the most creative students that he's had in the program.

The problem is that for schools like Stanford, I can only submit 2 teacher recommendations and 1 "Other Recommender." I can't submit a teacher as an "Other Recommender." Do you think I should submit the physics professor instead of one of my teachers? Do you think the professor should be an "Other Recommender"? In that case, Brown, USC, and Yale wouldn't accept Other Recommenders and only teacher recommenders.

Any thoughts? Should I ask the professor to submit the LOR twice, once as a teacher and once as an "Other Recommender"?

Thank you!!!!

> [−] admissionsmom
>
> I think your two high school teachers should be your recommenders and your prof should be your other.

let me give it to you straight

Many schools allow applicants to submit only two letters of recommendation. **Some might allow you to submit a third "additional" letter or perhaps even more, but the two mandatory letters are the most important.** In nearly every case, these two letters should be academic in nature, meaning that your teachers wrote them.

For your two academic recommendations, I recommend that you ask junior year teachers. Many colleges will even specifically say that. Sometimes colleges will accept a third recommendation, which is appropriate for either teachers from your freshman or sophomore years or for non-teacher individuals.

I also recommend asking one STEM teacher and one humanities teacher because many colleges request or require that. Again, that means a teacher from your academic subjects - think Math, Science, History, English, or Foreign Language. If the college doesn't specify, and you aren't applying as a STEM major, you might be fine with two letters from humanities teachers, and vice versa (if you are applying as a STEM major).

Keep in mind that the letter doesn't have to come from a teacher whose class you aced. It needs to come from a teacher who knows you well and will be able to speak about your character and perseverance as well as your ability to do well in class.

Asking For and Submitting Letters of Recommendations

u/allurredditsrbelongtous ·
asking for rec letters
Do I have to do something special to ask for a letter of recommendation from my teachers?

> [−] admissionsmom
> I suggest you ask the teachers in person and then follow up with an email. Or you can start with an email and then follow up with an in-person appointment. In the email, include a "cheat sheet" (sometimes known as a brag sheet) and a resume that includes all your activities and interests. In your cheat sheet, be sure to include what you enjoyed about the class and what you learned the most about. Talk about what you struggled with and the specific projects or units you feel you learned the most in.

u/Mrkgamer
Can I send my MIT application before all my LORs are submitted?
I know the Common App lets you do this, but does MIT? Thanks.

[-] TheRealClyde1

PSA: Teachers can send letters of rec after the application deadline in most cases.

Unless they completely forget to send them, there's no need for you to worry about teachers sending your letters of rec. Just make sure you have all of your materials in by the deadline. That is all.

Edit: This is true in ~95% of cases. If you want to be sure that there's a grace period, or you want to know how long it'd be, contact the admissions office, as appropriate.

u/stuportrooper

LORs when I'm a bad student?

I'm not going to lie...I really didn't work as hard as I should've. Turning in stuff late, sleeping in class, generally not giving a shit until I realized I was screwing myself. What can I do to still get good LORs? Anything?

[-] admissionsmom

Hmmm. You could apply to colleges that don't require a LOR. I was just at a Common App info session yesterday, and they said that greater than 50% of the colleges don't require a recommendation. I think you can do a filter for that. Also, I know many state schools don't require them. Look for schools that focus more on stats and who don't do holistic evaluations.

Also, check in with your counselor and see what they say. They might have some suggestions for you. **Also, don't hesitate to talk to some of your teachers who might respect you for who you are. Just because you didn't ace the class, doesn't mean the teachers don't have positive things to say about you.** Talk to them and see what they say.

here's what you need to know

As far as asking goes, lots of students request LORs in the spring of their junior year. In fact, many high schools require that students request them in the spring.

Asking for letters of recommendation is not that complicated. You simply ask your teachers if they'll write you the letter. While it's perfectly fine to ask your teachers in an email, you should also ask to make a follow-up appointment to meet with them, so you can thank them and talk about the letter.

When they say yes, follow the directions from your high school college counselor, but generally, you submit the teachers' names and email addresses to the application platform for your schools. They receive an email from the application platform with instructions on how to submit their letter. Then they write the letters. They each write one letter, which will be sent to all your schools that take letters.

For schools that have their own application, you do the same thing — give the school the teacher's name and email. And then they contact the teacher. Your teachers write one letter of recommendation each that goes to all your schools.

The Handy Dandy LOR Cheat Sheet

u/chanceme1234321

Info for teachers writing my LORs

What should I put on the cheat sheet/list of activities for my LORs? Should I give them a resume?

here's my take

While I'm sure your teachers remember you better than you think, they might need a little bit of help while writing your letter. That's where a cheat sheet (aka brag sheet) comes in.

A cheat sheet is a reference sheet for teachers who will write your recommendation letters. Even if they know you very well, your teachers probably don't know all about your other classes or extracurriculars simply because teachers have a lot to keep track of already. So the cheat sheet is a handy dandy tool that helps them provide more context to your recommendation letter.

Basically, the cheat sheet allows the teacher a peek into your perspective of time in your class and other circumstances and gives them reminders about areas to address in their LOR.

The cheat sheet should include stuff like:

- Your favorite activities in school
- Major awards
- Why you liked their class
- What was hard about their class
- What you learned in their class
- What aspect of their class will you remember most
- What you like to do outside of school
- Your favorite activity/project/essay topic in their class and why
- The high school accomplishment you are most proud of
- What struggles you have overcome in and out of school
- A one-page "highlights" resume.

However, this is not an excuse to bring a laundry list of all your accomplishments, like every award, report card, or SAT score report. **The cheat sheet isn't supposed to be a rehash of your achievements because the letter isn't supposed to be that at all. The letters are meant to describe you as a student, to provide insight into who you are as a person that only a teacher can really provide.**

LORs for Scholarships

u/warrior__princess
How to get a copy of a LOR?
I want to repurpose a letter of recommendation for scholarship applications. Can I ask my teacher for a copy?

[−] admissionsmom

I hope you signed the FERPA saying that you have agreed not to see the letter, so it will be up to the teacher if they want to give the letter to you or not. I would ask the teacher for a letter for scholarships. Maybe they'll give you the same one. Maybe not.

Remember to Say "Thank You"

u/gulfcoast_babe

Gift for recommender

Are gift cards good? How much money?

what you need to know

It's always a nice idea to thank your teachers or recommenders after they submit their letters of recommendation, but there's no need to go overboard. It's enough to make sure that you let them know how much you appreciate their taking the time to write you a letter.

As a result, I like letters and cards. Emails are nice too. If you want to go beyond that, don't spend much money. I have gotten and enjoyed Starbucks gift cards and small succulents. Both are nice gifts.

tl;dr

- For your two main letters, ask for recommendations from teachers you had for academic subjects - Math, Science, History, English, or Foreign Language
- If you have the option for a third letter, you can ask a non-teacher recommender for a letter
- Submit a cheat sheet to the teachers who have agreed to write your letters
- Don't forget to thank your recommenders for their time and effort, but don't break the bank. A simple card or small gift will be just fine.

CHAPTER 9

Why Include a Resume?

u/roouel

Pros and Cons of sending a resume to colleges?
I've been hearing a lot of conflicting things about resumes. If a school has resumes listed as optional, what're the pros and cons for sending in one? (Granted that it's one that's not too long, like 1 - 2 pages at most).

> [–] admissionsmom
> Remember there's really no such thing as optional in college admissions. If they give you space to submit one, I think you should.

u/soft_kittywarm_kitty

Is a resume worth it for an interview?
Will they even look at my resume? Isn't that what the activities list is for?

> [–] admissionsmom
> I think unless a school specifically says not to bring a resume to an interview, you should bring a highlights resume. I have no idea if they will look at it. Some will and some might just put it aside, but it gives them a platform to ask questions from, a place to take notes, and they can refer back to it to remember you better when writing up their notes.

let me break it down

A resume can provide further details about your accomplishments that may not fit into another section of your application. For example, if you won an Odyssey of the Mind competition or the National Spelling Bee, or if you were a serious athlete before high school, a resume could show that.

However, a lot of colleges don't ask for resumes, which means you have to include all your best and most relevant stuff in the application itself. As a general rule, you should put your top 10 most noteworthy activities in the application, and then include those and everything else you've done on your resume.

Unless a college explicitly says not to include a resume, a resume can only help your application. Also, I encourage you to bring a one-page, just-the-highlights resume to your interview unless the college or interviewer specifically say not to bring one. The very worst that can happen is that they don't read it.

Don't worry about awards.

u/carmy00

No awards?

So I have no awards. Academic awards are not given until May of senior year. I debate, but my team does not win any awards. I also am president of the school newspaper, but there is nothing truly notable about it. We don't win any awards, and I am not published in a local paper. Since I'm a junior, is there anything I can do at this point? I really don't know what to do about awards.

> [−] admissionsmom
> You are who you are. You can't be anyone else. So there's no use looking back. Most applicants don't have a list of awards.

this is the truth

So many kids think they don't possibly have a chance at getting into college because they don't have any awards. And you know what? Those same kids still get into awesome colleges all the time.

Awards are great to have, and you should include them on your resume and on your application if you have them. But by no means are they necessary, and a college acceptance will not hinge on whether or not you got the History Award your junior year.

No need to freak out about not having any awards. You cannot control which kid a teacher will nominate for a book award, just like you can't control whether or not your senior art portfolio places at a local competition. Colleges know this. They also know that your grades, test scores, extracurriculars, and essays are all things you can control. That's where you should spend your time and effort.

Resume Tips

u/23dagreatest

Polish my resume?

I need to up my resume game. Does anyone have a good sample resume or a list of steps?

here's my take

When putting together your resume, don't overdo it. It doesn't need to have a super fancy format or wild ink colors or superfluous language. Just make sure you have listed all your accomplishments clearly and that you correct any errors.

A good time to start compiling your resume is in the summer when you have time to think about how to fit everything you want to share about you.

And the best part is that these tips will help you with resumes throughout your life. It's not only colleges that want a simple and easy to read format free of mistakes.

AdmissionsMom's Fresh and Clean Resume Tips

Use a simple, easy-to-read font. Generally, resumes are one-to-two-page documents, but some colleges like UT Austin want to see an extended resume, and those can often be as long as five pages — see more info below.

For the heading: put your full name, ID # for that school, address, email, and phone number. Be sure to center all this information in the heading.

I recommend starting with the EDUCATION heading and putting your high school name and years attended. Add your high school GPA, class rank, and test scores (SAT, ACT, SAT Subject Tests, and AP or IB) here if you like and if they'll help your cause.

Then add these categories:

EXTRACURRICULAR ACTIVITIES

WORK AND SUMMER EXPERIENCES

COMMUNITY SERVICE

HONORS AND AWARDS

SKILLS AND INTERESTS.

List the activity, give a brief description, and put hours per week, weeks per year. Obviously, this is you distilled into one or two pages, so brevity is key.

Extended Resumes

u/stuportrooper

Extended resume for UT Austin?

UT wants a really detailed resume. I know most colleges want only one page resumes, but UT says they want an extended resume. What does that mean? How can I make it more detailed? How long should it be?

[−] admissionsmom

Some schools want extended resumes, like UT. If a college asks for an extended resume, it should definitely be longer than 1-2 pages. Many are 3-5 pages. List everything you've done. And really expand on what you do and how it has impacted you and how you've grown from the experience.

tl;dr

- A resume isn't required unless a college specifically asks for one or recommends it.
- If you submit a resume, make sure that you list your top ten activities/accomplishments from your application with the same positions and hours.
- For resumes, clear and easy-to-read is key
- Don't submit an extended resume unless the college explicitly requests one.

CHAPTER 10

What to Study? Choosing a Major

Another huge concern on r/ApplyingtoCollege is majors, future careers, post-graduate paths, and what to pursue. There's a lot to unpack from these concerns: what to major in to get a great job, how a major could affect a student's admissions chances, what's the best major for grad school, and on and on. These are natural questions to ask, especially when there's so much pressure to define the course of your life from the jump. Many students feel like they have to figure out what to do with the rest of their lives as teenagers, and one of the essential components of that decision is what to study.

But guess what?

You have time to figure this all out.

And you can change your mind!

Only a handful of majors and some colleges (usually fairly large public ones) require you to declare your major when you apply. Many other schools allow you to pick your major your sophomore year. Additionally, most graduate degrees, like medicine or law, don't require specific majors as prerequisites.

That means you get to explore a bit. The purpose of college is to learn how to think, learn, problem-solve, use your creativity, and understand history and the world around you. In doing so, you will learn all sorts of skills that will help direct you towards a career, or you may learn you are the kind of person who is perfectly suited for grad school. Approach your college education as an opportunity rather than a track you have to lock yourself into. In other words, college (and life) is an open world, not linear.

Majors and Minors — and We're Not Talking Chords Here

u/TheBigDog420

Majoring in a social science (psych) but with all stem classes

All of my honors classes are STEM-related (2 AP math, 1 AP and 1 honor science) but I am planning to major in psych. In fact, I haven't even taken AP psych yet. Will this look odd to AO since my courses suggest that I am attracted to the STEM field? I have an EC - tutoring - that makes me want to pursue psych, however.

> [–] admissionsmom
> While it can help paint the picture of who you are to have your classes relate to your potential major, most AOs recognize the likelihood that you will just change your major anyway. I'm fairly certain they won't be concerned about the fact that you are strong in STEM and want to apply for psychology.

u/CatOwlFilms

How much do majors matter?

I'm rather undecided, but I do have some subjects I like. Will applying undecided affect my chances at admission?

> [–] admissionsmom
> On the whole, you don't have to know what your major will be when applying unless it's engineering, computer science, or nursing. Most colleges in the US, except for large state universities, don't even let you pick a major until the end of your sophomore year, giving you lots of time to "try out" different majors. So, you can explore and enjoy the learning process instead of engaging in vocational training from the get-go. Not that there's anything wrong with that.

But please realize that you have time, and there is no need to feel like you have to decide right now what you want to do for the rest of your life. However, I do suggest that you apply with a potential major – something you think you might be interested in.

u/chanceme1234321

Is there a way to up my chances by switching my major to something rarer?

I want to go to MIT for mechanical engineering, but everyone wants to go to MIT for mechanical engineering. If I apply as a music major or something like that, will that help me get in? And then I can switch to engineering?

> [−] Atvelonis
>
> It's often difficult to change your major to engineering (very competitive) after gaining admission if it's in a different college at your school. If you're the best in the state at an instrument and genuinely enjoy it, a music major wouldn't necessarily be a bad idea. The job market isn't as good as an engineer's, but there are more jobs than just performing (recording/production, editing, etc.)

my take

Do you know what the two most popular majors are? A few years ago, at an info session at Georgetown, the admissions officer told us that they're "Undecided" and "I'm Gonna Change My Major."

I do encourage you to pick a major for your application because I think it helps clarify the application and at least will lead you in a direction but do so knowing that it's highly likely you'll be one of those change-my-major majors. I'm all for changing direction if needed.

Know, however, that many universities have schools that you apply to within the application. And it can be difficult — but not impossible — to switch into one school from another. Within the colleges of science and liberal arts at the universities, it's usually fairly easy to move from one major to another. At many universities, it's especially difficult to move into engineering, business, and computer science. So, if you're interested in those subjects, I would apply to those programs first, since it's easier to transfer out of them if you decide it's not for you.

That being said, I don't recommend applying with a specific major that you have no intention of pursuing. Don't bank on getting into a highly selective program by saying you're going to study some other obscure subject when you really want to pursue computer science. Colleges are on to that game.

A WORD ABOUT THE HUMANITIES

u/23dagreatest
What are the majors to avoid?
Are there any majors that are worthless? I don't want to be an engineer or accountant, but then, I want to have a job when I graduate. My parents tell me that if I major in English or Philosophy like I'd like to do, I'll end up working in a coffee shop for the rest of my life...

> [-] admissionsmom
> I hear you. I was an English major, and it's not like I didn't hear some of those same arguments way back in the 80s. It's unfortunate, but I see a lot of students thinking they should avoid the humanities and go straight to a "good" degree that will guarantee them a "stable" job in the future. The idea is that majoring in something like Philosophy or Linguistics or English is limiting and worthless, that employers want workers with skills that are immediately suitable to the business's needs. These kids — and their parents — ask, "What could I possibly do with a humanities degree?"
>
> Well, I think the bigger question is what CAN'T you do with a humanities degree? You can't be an engineer or a

scientist in a lab (at least not right out of college). What else? Coding doesn't work here because you can learn to code while pursuing a humanities degree. But what else can't you do with basic problem solving and creative thinking skills?

What can't you do with learning to write well?

What can't you do with learning how to analyze your thoughts and organize them into cohesive sentences that express them in such a way that others can understand?

What can't you do with learning how to parse and analyze texts?

What can't you do with reading the thoughts of others and giving yourself a deeper understanding of the world around you and the depths of its history?

Philosophy majors help with data management systems. Google hires Linguistics majors for a host of multi-million dollar projects essential to its continued success. English majors can find their services in high demand as technical writers for lots of industries. And that's not even touching all the applications your humanities degree has.

Furthermore, giving yourself the gift of a humanities education adds depth to you as a human, so that no matter what job you decide to pursue, what job skills you might need, you will be prepared to think and question and analyze and problem solve and understand and create.

my thoughts... and a warning: mini-rant ahead

I believe that if our populace is not truly educated, meaning if we don't have a deep understanding of philosophy, history, literature, psychology, and yes, math and science, then we put our country at risk. And I'm not being melodramatic. We need people who understand how to question and analyze and not just follow orders and rules. We need people who understand how to solve problems creatively and not just follow directions.

I'm sure with a STEM-based or business-based education, that type of education is surely possible. And God knows we need computer scientists, engineers, entrepreneurs, and businesspeople — but first, educate yourselves. Truly educate yourselves, then get your job training.

Please don't confuse a university education with job training. I fear that by creating a generation of children who feel that they can only be successful in life if they train for a specific job, we are limiting the creativity and problem-solving abilities you all can contribute. And you're limiting yourselves.

Thus, there aren't really any "bad" majors, unless they force you into a job that you find unsatisfying. If you learn to think and problem-solve and ask questions and analyze information, then you can get a job. If you're taught well and you learn, you can develop skills that you can transfer.

Look — job skills are learned on the job. Except for engineering, computer science, and nursing, the vast majority of majors are going to work for just about any path you want to take. My first son, who majored in History, is a surgery resident who is performing research on traumatic brain injuries. My second kid was a Philosophy major who teaches welding as an art form and works as an artist, creating welded sculptures. And my third child was another Philosophy major who had a summer internship with a big broadcasting company in New York and is now living in Los Angeles interning with a documentary film company.

So, at the very least, all you STEM-loving, computer science aficionados, and business-leaning kiddoes, please do yourselves — and the rest of us who will be growing old as you begin to run our country — a huge favor and take as many philosophy, literature, and history classes as you can. You can't truly understand Kierkegaard, Sophocles, Hume, or Shakespeare without the guidance of a scholar and the questions and comments from your fellow learners.

Learn to think, learn to question, learn to solve problems, and then go forth and make your piles of money. I promise the two are not exclusive!!

Your Major, Grad School, and Your Future

u/77kev89

Accepted to a few schools for Undergrad. Question about Grad School later on.

Does the university I get my BS degree from weighing heavily on being accepted to grad school and selected for TA programs?

Hello all, I looked through the threads briefly and couldn't really find an answer. I applied to a few different schools and got accepted to all of them. I do eventually want to end up going to Grad school (Ph.D.), possibly from a different university. From what I hear, the cost of grad school is covered mostly by the school if you end up taking a teaching or teaching assistant position (i.e., grading/tutoring for undergrad students). My questions:

In regard to the acceptance process for grad school, how much of a factor is the school I get my BS degree from? Does it make a difference if I get my BS degree from a "more prestigious" university? Or, do they just see: BS degree, good grades, you're in?

I am returning to school after 6 years in the Navy, and I have years of supervisory experience.

> [-] admissionsmom
>
> First, thank you for your service. Liberal Arts and Sciences Colleges (known as LACs) have high success rates with grad school as a generalization. One of the reasons is bc they are focused on undergraduates, so you can get lots of research time and get to know your professors well for stellar recommendations.

u/Mrkgamer

Can you major in CS, but take pre-med courses at the same time?

I am really set on majoring in computer science, but pre-med is now seeming like something I'd also really like to do. Since it's not technically a major, I thought I could major in CS, and take pre-med courses at the same time. The problem I am thinking of is that CS is very rigorous at the schools I'm looking at, and I don't want to ruin my GPA/quality of life by overloading myself. Has anyone done this before? I'd just like to hear what would the work be like or if it's even possible. Thanks.

> [–] admissionsmom
>
> One of the awesome things about being pre-med is you can major in anything you want as long as you take the pre-med required classes. So, major in Computer Science, Gender Studies, English, Astronomy, or even Musical Theater! It will definitely make you stand out as a med school candidate should you ultimately decide to go in that direction.

let me break it down for you

I don't believe in deciding on a major solely to get a job later. Yes, college is almost a necessity to find a well-paying job these days, but getting a job shouldn't be your only goal in life. If you pursue that path, you won't find fulfillment.

That being said, if you've figured out what you want to do with your life, that's awesome! And you should do what you can to follow that path.

For example, if you want to go to law school, majoring in Political Science, Philosophy, or English could be helpful but isn't necessary. You need good grades, a high LSAT score, strong essays, and a genuine desire to learn the law.

On the whole, medical schools love humanities majors, and they also love graduates of liberal arts and sciences colleges. As for Pre-Med, you can major in anything, but you need to take the medical school prerequisites as well as have high grades, a strong MCAT score, some research, doctor shadowing, and maybe some medical volunteer work.

For other graduate degrees, it depends on the individual programs. Some have some specific prerequisites; others don't. Some require particular degrees while others don't care. Do your research. The information is out there, waiting for you to soak it up.

This is why it's useful to consider liberal arts colleges (LACs) for your undergraduate degree. As I explain in the chapter on Liberal Arts (and Sciences) Colleges, these schools foster an intimate learning environment where you can take advantage of favorable professor-student ratios as well as get the kind of attention undergrads at big schools dream about. Even better, LACs offer lots of marvelous opportunities for undergraduate research as well as forging close bonds with your professors. Those experiences will help you stand out on your grad school applications and help your professors write you amazing letters of recommendation.

tl;dr

- Many colleges and universities don't require you to declare a major until sophomore year.
- Some universities, especially large public ones, do require you to apply by major, so read websites carefully.
- The most popular majors, according to some Admissions Officers, are Undecided and Change My Major, so you're not alone if you don't know what exactly you want to do at 17 or 18 years old.
- It's ok if your high school classes don't perfectly line up with your potential major.
- I do recommend that you apply with a major that you might be interested in to give your application some direction.

- Don't eliminate the Humanities because you're worried about job potential. Read my mini-rant about that above.
- If you plan to major in some of the most impacted majors like CS, Business, or Engineering, apply as that major. It can often be difficult to transfer into those programs, so check out the schools' websites to see what their policies are.

CHAPTER 11

Rankings Schmankings

Title says it all. Forget about rankings! Some applicants are raised on the absurd idea that they have to go to certain elite colleges, that if some website doesn't list a school in its top 25 then that school isn't worth the money or the time. These kids spend their whole lives stressing over this ridiculous notion but let me tell you now: **the ranking of a college does not mean it will be a good one for you**. One college can be a great fit for one student and a lousy pick for another. Applicants shouldn't focus on what school has the best ranking, but rather they should look into **what school is the best fit for them**.

My absolute biggest philosophical problem with the admissions craziness, which I feel leads to rampant anxiety and stress, is the fact that children are being curated and crafted to attend certain colleges because of how they are ranked. In the process, they often lose their childhoods, including their teens and early twenties.

This makes me sad and really frustrated.

I get it. There are a lot of unknowns in the college admissions journey, and it's hard to know how to choose a college that's right for you. It's only human nature to take the advice of "experts" and think that — even though they've never met you before — they can evaluate a college in a way that will tell you what you need to know.

But let's make one thing clear: the good people over at the U.S. News and World Report don't know you. Rankings like this work via projections. They consider some statistics that they think applicants will care about and run them through a formula. They wholly ignore other statistics you might care about. And, sure, you probably do care about some of the numbers they take into account, but do you really care at all what another college's dean thinks of its reputation? If I were you, I'd focus on the things that can't be measured by a simple percent. Like how the school chooses to educate its students, what real-world opportunities the college provides, or what the vibe on campus is like. **Rankings don't show you everything.**

If you're gonna consider rankings at all, be sure that you take them with a heaping serving of salt.

anonymous
Just deal with the fact that I'm hardcore T20 or bust
I need people to be impressed with me, and where I go to college will make that happen. It really pisses me off when people tell me I "have value" no matter where I go to school. I'm sick of people telling me to "fall in love with my safety" and other bullshit like that. Let me be with my hardcore T20 or bust — that's where I find my fit.

> [-] admissionsmom
> I don't usually read all these T20 posts bc I recognize for the most part that it's just y'all letting off steam, but I do want you to recognize that while it might be your choice to be a T20-or-bust kinda guy or gal, it also might be completely beyond your choice or option to attend one. We see it happen time and again here, unfortunately: kid works their asses off creating what they — or their parents or some other well-meaning adults — think colleges want to see. Those kids show up with sparkly shiny stats and on

point essays and ECs. They feel that they've checked all the boxes. And then bam! They are slammed in the face with rejection bc they've forgotten that colleges have their own interests and institutional needs and those are completely beyond the control of any of us here on the other side of the admissions office. Once your application is submitted, you have no control over what happens to it — it's a hard fact.

But you do have control over how you respond to admissions decisions. And one way to respond that won't have you crying in a dark corner for days on end is to recognize that there are hundreds, and I mean hundreds (and this isn't an exaggeration although I do love to exaggerate :)), of schools that will allow you to have that same amazing, possibly better, intellectually challenging, hardcore intern placement, prestige-seeking experience that you think you'll only find at a T20. We see kids come back from college freshman year and beyond and rave about the safety school they thought they'd never like or bemoan how miserable they are at the school they only attended bc it was a T20 but not a good fit for them.

So yeah, keep up the hardcore T20-or-bust mentality if that's what you need to do because you know I'm always gonna say "you do you" in the end, but I hope way back in the far recesses of your brain there's a tiny little eeny weeny hint of a voice reminding you that you can only control what you can control, and college decisions aren't one of those things you can control. But you also know that life has a weird, wonderful way of working out and there are hundreds of incredible non-T20 schools for you to be excited about too.

Now, go on get back to your T20 or busting. I won't interrupt any longer.

I guess rankings can be useful...

u/warrior__princess
Where do I get the most trusted lists for college reputation?
Title says it all.

> [−] TheRealClyde1
> Friendly reminder that you shouldn't base the schools you're applying to solely on rankings. "Fit" is much more important, and the more you show that you love a school, the more the school will want to accept you. Rankings can be used to narrow down options for sure - in fact, they're actually really helpful if you want to know what programs are strongest in each school. But like I said, it shouldn't be the only criteria you use for choosing schools. For instance, you wouldn't just apply to every T20 and call it a day.
>
> And idk if it's just me, but I'd want to go to a school that I know I'd be happy to attend. In that case, "fit" would be very important. Some people are truly fine with anything, and that's alright. But if you're a bit pickier, you're gonna have to do more research on schools than just browsing the rankings.

my thoughts

To be clear — I don't think prestige is utterly unimportant. I'm not a total hypocrite. I agree that prestige matters to a certain extent, and **I definitely agree that the quality of the education matters**. I have to admit that I don't know much about rankings for specific programs like CS or Business or for those who want to work on "The Street" or make it to the Supreme Court. I see people saying all the time that undergrad rankings matter for those paths. I'll leave that advice for those who are more knowledgeable than I. I just don't think that random rankings matter.

Full disclosure: my kids went to highly selective schools: Harvard, Vanderbilt, and Tufts, and I was happy to support their choices. They were encouraged to follow their own paths. But to me (and I hope to them, too), it wasn't about the bragging rights, bumper stickers, or even their future earning potential; it was about the education they would receive, the rich campus life they got to experience, and the academic opportunities that were available to them. As they grew up, I made sure they knew there wasn't only one path to success, and they knew that if they chose a new path, I would support them all the way. Hell, I actually thought one of mine was gonna skip college altogether.

Trust me. **There are many, many, many more prestigious schools out there than you probably know**. I talk to employers all the time. I've been in the education world for thirty years. I live in a community of highly educated people, and the list of schools where kids of well-educated and highly successful people around me go is loooong. Simply put, you don't have to go to a T20 school to get a great education.

anonymous
What about Community Colleges and Rankings?
What's the best community college for me to go to in order to get to a T10 school?

> [–] admissionsmom
> Keep in mind that community colleges don't have the same type of rankings. Community colleges traditionally provide a means for students to transfer to their state universities. For example, the California community college system seems to be very successful at transitioning students into its schools. I know from my own experience that my community college in Houston was mostly successful at helping students transition to UT Austin, the University of Houston, and, very occasionally, Rice.

So, if you're looking for a list of prestigious and well-known community colleges that will get you into a highly selective college via transfer, I'm not sure such a list exists. Or that it even should exist. You're much better off focusing on finding the learning environment that will support your learning and development so that you can put together the very best application you can once it's time for you to take the next step.

...but rankings don't guarantee success.

u/chanceme1234321..

Harsh truth about college reputation

For everyone saying that ranking isn't a good indicator of anything, what do you say to the high correlation of prestige to college and how that affects things later on? Tons of people who go to top law schools went to Ivies first. Tons of CEOs for Fortune 500 companies went to the Ivies. Most of our presidents went to Ivies. It just seems obvious that there's something going on there.

> [-] admissionsmom
>
> Whenever anyone loves to trot out arguments about how college reputation is indicative of future success, and that success is confined to certain institutions, I like to share some details about my life.
>
> Two of my immediate family members went to Harvard: my father and my middle child. My father ended up selling insurance for most of his life, supporting himself, sure, but there wasn't any mansion-living or yachting in my childhood. My middle child is pursuing an art and stage career and currently works at an art studio doing social media and creating welding sculptures. She and many of her best friends from Harvard all lived at home after graduation, trying to figure out what they wanted to do in life, which is totally fine.

The perceived prestige (or lack thereof) of a college has little to do with how much success a person will enjoy in life. Yes, a student with access to the Harvard alumni network might have specific connections not available to a student from The University of Iowa or New Mexico, but those advantages are nothing if the student doesn't actively choose to use them. Even then, those advantages are no guarantee. According US News (my favorite news source :/), in 2018, only 16 of Fortune 100 CEOs went to an Ivy or Stanford; 84 did not.

A super-motivated kid will take advantage of whatever facilities, professors, and education she has at her disposal. It's not going to matter where they go to school. An unmotivated student isn't going to have any more of the stereotypical success at an Ivy than she would have had at any other school. (In fact, I feel like that student would be better served at a smaller, more individualized college.)

let me break it down for you

Success depends on the student. It's as simple as that. If a student has drive and is willing to take risks, they're going be more "successful" in the terms I'm sure you're thinking of. I know many kids from all kinds of colleges, both selective and not, who went on to achieve "success" and get jobs that made money. It's all about the person. Not the school.

I have no problem with people making money. But, let's be real, I don't think it should be the goal of education. Rather, I think people should receive education to gain a deeper understanding of the world, and if they happen to make money as a side-effect, then great!

I have visited over seventy-five schools in the last few years, and I've talked to kids at all of them. Do you know how many genuinely remarkable and brilliant students attend large public universities or the small regional LAC by choice? At every single school, without exception, I found amazing, ambitious, interesting, smart kids. The kind of kids that people assume belong at highly selective schools, yet there they are happy and thriving elsewhere.

Understand that whatever happiness you might derive from the external validation of rankings is tenuous. It's like walking on thin ice and waiting for it to break. Instead, focus on finding that internal validation that comes with finding the right fit at one of the many schools where you belong.

tl;dr

- **There is nothing official about rankings.** The USNWR isn't published by a public government committee. It's a private magazine that makes money by getting people to read their rankings. And it plays off your and your parents' insecurities.
- Can we please just drop the whole T-anything stuff?
- Highly selective schools can be amazing and lead you to great success.
- There are also hundreds of amazing schools in the US that can lead you to great success.
- The name on your diploma or the bumper sticker on your car does not define you as a person.
- You are the determiner of your future success, not the number beside the name of a college in a magazine or website article.

CHAPTER 12

I Don't Believe in Dream Schools – Finding Your Fit

How many times during those early fall days do I read a post from yet another kid talking about their dream school? I know you've been taught to "dream big" and to "follow your dreams," but if you ask me, **it's not about finding the school of your dreams; it's about finding the you of your dreams.** Find the best version of you. When you're drooling over that perfect school with a perfect campus and perfect classes, you're not dreaming about any one particular school. No, you're dreaming about who you want to be and where you can become who you want to be, and there isn't only one "dream school" where you can do that.

Consider your college fit when you're thinking about where you can discover Dream You. What're you looking for as far as financial aid, geography, distance, weather, school size, and vibe?

It's all about Dream YOU, not Dream U

u/madeleine24

Help me I am so sad :(

Guys how do I get over not getting to go to my dream school (that I got into but couldn't afford). I keep crying every time I see its name, and I full-on started sobbing when I sent in a form letting the institution know I won't be attending. How do I get over this? WHEN will I get over this?

> [−] admissionsmom
>
> First, you have to recognize that it's ok and normal to have these feelings. It's a sense of loss. Then, after giving yourself some time to deal with your disappointment, I want you to recognize that what you imagined at this school was the dream you — not the dream school. So, think about everything about that school that you loved and think you will miss and then realize that it was all about you. And you are amazing, and you are going to college with yourself wherever you are.

anonymous

Can somebody please make me hate NYU?

Ever since I read about NYU on their website and saw pictures of it, all I can do is imagine myself hanging out in Washington Square, riding the subway in NYC, and taking all those crazy classes. It's my dream school, but I know that I'm never gonna be able to afford it — even if by some crazy ass chance, I do get in. Help! How do I make my dreams come true???

> [−] admissionsmom
>
> I think instead of being in love with NYU, you're actually in love with the you that you see there. Yep, I'm suggesting that the dream is not actually the school, but the you that you imagine doing all that cool stuff. I invite you to think deeply and figure out what it is about NYU that makes you love the "you" that you see there. What do you see yourself doing, being, and becoming at that school? What is it about that campus and the way you see you that you've fallen in love with? Think about how you imagine yourself there. What about YOU have you fallen in love with there? Figure out what you love about those aspects of you, and that will lead you to discover other campuses where you can find your you. Then find all the schools where you can find that you. I guarantee that your dream isn't out there in the form of a college, it is in YOU.

Making YOUR College List

u/warrior__princess

Does anybody have any tips on how to create a college list?
My stats are pretty good, and I have dedicated ECs I enjoy. But
there are so many schools that I get overwhelmed. I don't know
which ones to apply to.

> [–] admissionsmom
> When you're thinking about applying to college, it can be
> easy to feel bogged down by the thousands of colleges you
> have to choose from. As with most important tasks in life,
> the most critical part is just getting started.
>
> Start by thinking about what you think you might want in
> a college and compile a big ole list. It's ok to have a ton of
> schools on this initial list. As you explore yourself and the
> colleges more and as you go through the admissions jour-
> ney, you'll naturally begin to filter some of the schools out.

let me break it down for you

Starting your college admissions journey with the basics simpli-
fies the process of finding the school best suited to your academic
and personal needs. Everyone has their own needs, wants, and values, and what's important to you may not matter to someone else.
I've created a step by step guide to help you create your college
list by finding you're your fits, not the other way around.

5 Steps to Create Your List by Finding YOUR Fits

STEP 1: Gather Resources and Begin Research
I really like these websites and books you can use to begin your
search:

- *Colleges That Change Lives* by Loren Pope, book and
  website

- *The Fiske Guide to Colleges* by Edmund Fiske
- *The Insider's Guide to Colleges* by Yale Daily Review
- *Where You Go is Not Who You'll Be* by Frank Bruni
- *College Match* by Steve Antonoff
- *The Best 384 Colleges* by Princeton Review
- Niche.com
- Common Data Set
- College websites and mailing list newsletters
- College Admissions Offices' social media accounts: SnapChat, Instagram, Twitter, Facebook, Tumblr, and Pinterest
- Student newspapers and college news feeds

I am so excited to add my new app, College Vizzy, to this list. Check it out on the app store or at www. collegevizzy.com.

Helpful Hint: I can't emphasize enough to all of you to read each college's website. They tell you the kind of kids they're looking for. There's no secret there. Are you that kid? For real? Don't try to squish yourself into their mold. Figure out who you are and then find the many schools that you — the real you — fits into their shape. Also, make sure you give yourself some room to grow and expand.

STEP 2: College Visits
Start visiting colleges if you can. Look around in your city or town. Visit large schools and small schools. It doesn't matter if it's a college you think you would consider or not. Just visit to learn what feels right for you. Hang out on campus and try to get a feel for what kind of campus feels right to you. See my College

Visit Chapter 14 for more information on getting the most out of your visits.

Helpful Hint: I suggest using a spreadsheet to track your research and give yourself a visual overview of how the schools stack up. This is information I track as I'm making lists based on research:

- Travel distance (one flight, two flights, 3-hour drive, in my town, nearby, just around the corner, etc.)
- Surrounding area (city, shop-lined cute street, rural, far from any shops restaurants, etc.)
- Name and email of your area counselor
- Cost on net price calculator
- Application Platform (Common app? Coalition? School?)
- Average Standardized Test Scores
- Weather
- Urban or Rural
- Social and Cultural Vibe
- School Size

STEP 3: Develop Your List as You Think about Fit
Before you apply to a college, it's essential to know if that college fits your needs and if you'll enjoy your time there. So, you need to do your research! As you read books, investigate colleges, and possibly even get to visit them, think about these seven kinds of "fits," and what you think will fit you:

Financial — Can you afford this college? Will you need full financial aid? Will you qualify? Will you qualify for any aid? Do you need merit aid because you don't qualify for enough financial aid, and if so, does this school offer merit aid? These are crucial considerations. If you're unsure how much a college costs, google search "net price calculator" followed by the name of the college or university and then you can find your EFC, expected financial contribution. You and your parents need to spend some time thinking about this and going through net price calculators on various college websites. If you can't afford the price of the school, it's not a fit.

School Size — Do you want a big state school with loads of options? Or are you looking for something smaller or mid-sized? Do you want discussion-based, seminar-style classes where you can develop strong relationships with your professors, and it will be noted if you don't attend class? Or do you want large lectures where the professor might never know who you are and where you can sit anonymously taking notes?

Social Atmosphere — What kind of social life are you looking for? School spirit? Greek life? Quirky kids playing video games in their rooms? Huge raging parties? Stress culture? Laid back? Work hard, play hard? Football games? Are you looking for that stereotypical American big college experience with the big game on the weekends? Or are you looking for the quirky, creative kind of experience? Or something that has it all?

> *Helpful Hint:* The best way to learn about a college's social scene is to visit the school or download the College Vizzy app. Other ways to research a college's social atmosphere — besides reading their websites and the college guides — include reading the college's subreddit, following the college's social media accounts, and reading the student newspaper.

Geographic — What areas of the country appeal to you? Don't be dismissive right off the bat. Some kids say no to the Deep South or the Midwest without really thinking about it, and in the process, miss out on some fantastic options and merit aid. Do you want urban? What about rural? Do you want an enclosed campus or one that's incorporated into the cityscape? Are you a ski bum? A beach bum? Or do you thrive in a concrete jungle? Do you want a college town? Corn fields? Do you want to get out of your comfort zone or stay with the familiar? How many plane flights will it take to get home? How long is the drive to and from home? And what about those travel expenses? Think about your daily routine and the activities you enjoy for fun or leisure. Think about the routine you might want in the future or the activities you've always wanted to try but never had the chance. If a school doesn't offer you the opportunity to do those things, it may not be for you.

Climate — Can you tolerate long cold months? Does hot weather bother you? Do you want to experience each season? Do you see yourself walking around in rain boots for months on end? Does cold dark weather affect you? For many Southern and Western students, going to the Northeast or Midwest can be a shock to the system in the depths of February. Think about that. For many, it's no big deal and getting a dose of seasons is exciting and fun. But, if you really, really hate the cold, then moving to Boston or Chicago or Maine might not appeal to you. If you have to have four seasons, then the Midwest or the Northeast might have good options. And if hurricanes aren't your thing, maybe avoid coastal areas.

Potential Major — If you don't know what you want to major in, don't worry. You have plenty of time to figure that out, and it actually frees you up a bit. If you do think you know what you want to study, research some schools that might be strong in your focus. Maybe touch base with a professor or two. Does the school even have the programs you think you might be interested in? Does the school offer lots of other stuff in case you change your mind?

Your Stats — Where do your grades and test scores fit in? Are they right there in the middle? I like my students to be well above the 50% for most of the colleges they're applying to.

STEP 4: Find Your Sure Fire Safety School

Make sure you have at least one Sure Fire Safety School. A Sure Fire Safety School is a school where your stats, scores, and grades qualify you for automatic or direct admissions OR where you've already been admitted AND where you would like to go AND they are a financial safety. Any school that uses holistic admissions is not a surefire safety until you've already been admitted. I think kids should apply to at least a couple of schools with rolling admissions early on so they can have that safety out of the way. You must LOVE your safety. Research it and imagine yourself there.

STEP 5: Add Some Safety/Match/Target/Reach Schools

These schools are colleges where your test scores and grades are above 50th percentile range, they use holistic application review, and their admissions rate is above 25%. Once you see that you fit the academic profile of these schools, make sure they fit what you're looking for in a college. Apply to a few that you've researched that are a good fit for you and where you have a strong chance of getting accepted.

STEP 6: Wildcard Lottery Schools

Lottery schools are all the highly selective colleges. They're highly selective no matter how shiny and sparkly and beautiful your application is. This group of schools also includes places where you're in the lower half of their stats. That doesn't mean you shouldn't apply. If a school feels right for you, go for it; we all know stats aren't everything. As always, research each school you apply to, reach out to their admissions officers, talk to your college counselor at your high school, and visit if possible. Include a couple of these wildcard lottery schools that are crazy stupid highly selective if that appeals to you. Each college accepts loads of students every year. One of them might as well be you — or not (if you're not feeling it.)

my thoughts

Creating this list based on your fits requires putting a lot of thought into what you want out of your experience and about who you are and who you want to be. It doesn't require pulling out USNWR and listing the top twenty schools. Think of your fit like a sock, not a shoe. It's stretchy. That sock can fit on lots of feet, just like you and your fit can fit on lots of colleges. Be open-minded but think critically about what will work best for you.

tl;dr

- Focus on discovering Dream YOU, not having a dream college.
- Consider the Seven Basic Fits: Financial, Geographic, Climate, Size, Social/Cultural Vibe, Potential Major, Your Stats
- Research, Research, Research
- Visit as many colleges as you can, even if they're the local ones where you know you don't want to go.
- Figuring out what you don't want is often as helpful as figuring out what you do want.
- Your Surefire Safety School is THE most important school on your list.

The AdmissionsMom Create a College Challenge!

IT'S ALL ABOUT DREAM YOU, NOT DREAM U

Many of you really have no idea what you want other than a "top" school" or a "t-something," so I have a task for you — *if* you are up for the challenge:

1. Think about fit. What're you looking for? Where do you see yourself? Consider school size, if you want large lectures or small discussion seminars, geographic areas, weather, cultural and social dynamics, and vibes: Intellectual, Academic, Sporty, Quirky, Serious, or ...?

2. You can draw this out, write about it in an essay, journal format, make a photo diary, bullet points, or claymation it. Whatever.

3. Get creative. Make the perfect college in your mind. When you imagine your life for those four years, what do you see? What're you doing on a Saturday afternoon or a Wednesday night? Who're you surrounded by? What does the setting look like? What're you involved in?

4. Make sure to put yourself in the action. That's the dream part!

5. Remember: Map it. Draw it. Write it. Film it. But don't rank it!

CHAPTER 13

Liberal Arts Colleges: The Best Little Schools You've Never Heard Of

Psst...there's a well-kept secret in college admissions that thousands of students don't know about.

This secret is for those of you who are leaning towards a smaller environment where you can explore where your intellectual curiosity might take you, for those of you who'd like a little more time to decide upon your major, or for those of you who are interested in pursuing a graduate degree in law, medicine, or a doctorate.

What is it? Liberal Arts (and Science) Colleges, commonly known as LACs.

These schools are wonderful choices for students who crave a more intimate learning environment with favorable professor-student ratios, who want attention as undergraduates that they may not receive at larger schools, and who are less concerned with "vocational" or "pre-professional degrees." They focus on how to learn earnestly, how to think critically, how to solve problems creatively. And they do this with subjects that are widely applicable to a range of occupations.

u/shoulderofgiantx

A Hard Hit of Reality for Being One of Many Ducks

I've spent the first few weeks of summer weirdly genuinely excited to apply to colleges. I wasted hours looking up videos of beautiful Princeton and Stanford campuses, Brown vocal groups, and Yale dormitories. And although I'm a bit ashamed to admit it, I started to really develop a stronger desire for the "name brand recognition of a T20."

I wanted my hard work to pay off-something so that my parents could finally be relieved that immigrating to America would pay off. Something that my dad could look forward to even after working twenty years as a minimum wage truck driver in a foreign country with different cultures and customs. In a way, I wanted to use an admission letter as a way to repay him for all that he's sacrificed, to allow him to claim that little bit of prestige in an endless cycle of work and lack of economic fulfillment.

I worked my ass off in school with test scores and grades and work and fell in love with biology and music. Most of my life, my clubs, and my free time center around those two topics, and I couldn't picture myself being without those two influences...

...I'm scared of looking like the rest of my doppelgangers aiming for a Biology degree at a T20.

> [-] admissionsmom
>
> If you want to be a doctor, consider a Liberal Arts College, where you can create bonds with your professors in your small classes and get to do the actual research. And many of them have the most beautiful campuses, cool acapella groups, and lovely dormitories. I think you would find that the "vibe" is very much what you imagine when you fantasize about your colleges. And, I can guarantee to you that there are at least 50, maybe 100 of them, that would love to have you if you can give them a great application demonstrating to them that you are serious about applying to their school.
>
> Keep in mind, everyone, that often the best fit for you might be a college you haven't heard of yet.

u/23dagreatest

Can someone explain to me why people on this forum don't really talk about liberal arts colleges?

I get that small size isn't for everyone, but is there more to it? Is it limited resources? Some people I know have gone to LACs, and they love it. Just confused.

[–] Atvelonis

In regard to your point about the limited resources at many smaller colleges, it's also important to consider that some LACs are in consortiums with other nearby institutions.

For example:

Five-College Consortium: Amherst, Hampshire, Mount Holyoke, Smith, and UMass Amherst

Tri-College/Quaker Consortium: Bryn Mawr, Haverford, Swarthmore, and UPenn

Claremont Colleges: Claremont McKenna, Harvey Mudd, Pitzer, Pomona, Scripps, and Keck

Students can register for courses at other schools in their consortium, which gives them access to a greater variety of resources while still maintaining a small school atmosphere.

[–] admissionsmom

I do! I like to talk about LACs! At LACs, you get the opportunity to get to know your professors well, and you'll need them for LORs if you are applying to grad school of any kind. And you get to do hands-on research, not just the grunt work the grad students don't want to do at universities, which can be helpful again for grad school apps and even job hunting.

As such, LACs are perfect for kids who are interested in more than sitting anonymously in the back of the class and taking notes from lectures, since you will have more discussion-based seminar classes, get a ton of research opportunities, and get more individualized attention from your professors. And contrary to popular perception, there are many LACs that have substantial merit and financial aid available. Be sure to check out *Colleges That Change Lives.*

let my fellow Redditor break it down for you

Liberal Arts Colleges are uniquely positioned to offer students a world-class education with hands-on experience, though there are some trade-offs. Redditor, u/mmmya explains it this way:

In general, LACs are focused on the study of "liberal arts." This is a historical definition based on what people of antiquity believed were subjects that were "essential" to free people in order for them to participate in civil society. As such, the focus of education is not generally on trade or profession, but on building fundamentals.

1. What is referred to as 'liberal arts' has changed throughout history, but today they commonly include **literature & composition, mathematics, social and physical sciences**. The general theory is that this builds character and skill sets that help them be better prepared for life (and graduate school).

    Having said that, many top universities, despite their name, also claim a 'liberal arts education.' Harvard, Yale, Dartmouth, Brown are all examples of this.

2. **Most LACs are undergraduate-focused.** Yes, some LACs do have graduate programs (Williams), or more commonly a strategic relationship with a university that has graduate programs (Barnard-Columbia, Wellesley-MIT), but in general, they are created for and designed around undergraduates. This theoretically leads to a lot

more opportunities for research, internships, etc. (though this will depend on individual LAC schools). The reason for this is simple; students don't have to compete with grad students for these opportunities. This is one reason why pre-med students like LACs...because medical schools require so much research/lab time.

3. **LACs will generally have more 'teaching professors' vs. 'researching professors.'** Obviously, this is a blanket statement and not always true. But it is true that LACs do heavily recruit and prefer to retain professors that are great teachers first, and researchers second. Professors at LACs 'know' their students and the schools absolutely encourage closer relationships.

4. **LACs are small.** Harvard college has 6,700 undergrads. Williams has 2,000, Amherst has 1,800. This leads to a much tighter community. Not only do you get to know your professors better, by the time you graduate you'll probably know everyone at school. This often leads to a strong school spirit...which leads to the following point:

5. **LACs, especially the higher ranked ones, have rabid alumni networks.** And it's not just limited to a single school. LAC grads will often go out of their way to help not only people from their own school but also students from other LACs. Alumni support of top LACs is easily comparable to that of most Ivies. This leads to:

6. **Huge endowments.** While the Ivies generally have the largest raw endowments, if you look at it from a perspective of the endowment by student, then of the top ten, five of them are LACs. This leads to:

7. **More opportunities for students, and generally an attractive tuition assistance program.** Most top LACs have incredibly generous need-based programs. Amherst does not even distinguish aid based on nationality. And

with aid given to 50%+ of students, this is something a lot of other universities can only dream of.

8. **Excellent post-grad school matriculation rates.** This may be the same with other top-tier schools (e.g., Ivies), but in general, LACs are famous for their ridiculous acceptance rates into higher education; med, law, MBA + Ph.D. programs. The reason behind this is a combination of all the factors listed above; strong educational foundation, reputation among AOs, powerful alumni, research/internship opportunities, supportive professors + in general (not always) a strong support system at school.

tl;dr

- Liberal Arts Colleges focus on teaching undergraduates.
- Professors are more teaching oriented than research oriented, giving students an opportunity to get to know their professors better.
- Undergrads may have more research opportunities because there are no grad students to work with professors.
- Med Schools love LAC grads because they want their students to be truly well-educated and know how to think and problem solve, not just memorize.
- Many LACs have extremely strong alumni networks, helping with connections in the intern and job market.
- Classes are normally discussion based, rather than lecture.
- The focus of LACs is on educating the mind to learn, think, question, and problem solve. The focus is generally not on learning specific skills for a job (vocational training), but rather to train students to learn skills that can be useful for many jobs — and for life.

CHAPTER 14

Look for the Vibe and Find Your Tribe: Campus Visits

If you can afford to and are able to visit a college, I strongly recommend that you do so. When it comes to getting a feel for a college, nothing beats a campus visit. In this day and age, every college has slick websites with professional photographs that make their school look like the best place in the world. I'm not saying they're not, or that you wouldn't love those schools, I'm just saying that there's a lot more to a school's vibe than how it looks on a screen.

While I do think there are benefits to the tour and info session, I think it's even more beneficial to explore the campus and soak in the vibe.

This is your chance to feel what it's like to walk the campus, to see what the dorms look like, to get to know how crowded the main hall gets between classes, to tour the classrooms, dining halls, gyms, or whatever building is essential to you. More importantly, a college visit is your chance to talk to current students about their experiences with the school. You get the chance to interact with the campus, students, and professors and see how you would fit in as a student. When you're figuring out where you're going to spend the next four years of your life, that's a pretty f*cking big deal.

Making the Most of Your Visit

u/23dagreatest

How do I do college visits?

I'm going to visit UMass this weekend with my parents. Any tips for what I should do besides the tour? Is it ok to wander away from the tour?

> [-] admissionsmom
>
> One of my fellow moderators on r/ApplyingToCollege, u/ BlueLightSpcl, shared an article from the *New York Times* titled, "Skipping the College Tour." The author argued that college tours might "hinder students' ability to pick a college that will further their interests and goals" because "whatever students see or experience during a brief campus visit...will inevitably stand out and have a disproportionate effect on their decision-making."
>
> The article suggests that prospective students shouldn't be taken in by the gleaming gym facilities and refurbished dormitories, but rather they should approach current students with questions like "Why did you consider attending this school? Are you happy to be here? Knowing what you know now, would you make the same choice? Would someone like me be happy at this school?'"
>
> I wholeheartedly agree with the second part, but I don't think you should totally blow off tours and info sessions. When I visit campuses, which I often do, I try to go on the tour and attend the information session.
>
> But, even if I can't make the timing work for the tour or info session, I always make sure I have time to wander around — to get lost. I ask students for directions. I eat in the student union or the cafeteria. I buy my magnet in the bookstore. I visit the library and sit and read a little. I sit on a bench in the middle of campus and watch. And listen. I investigate what's going on around campus and just off campus.

here's my take

I tell students that it's great to take the official tour and attend the info session. I also tell them that it's equally important to spend time wandering, which is an excellent way to get a true feel for a campus — especially when the tours and info sessions start to bleed together for various schools.

Self-guided tours are great too. All you need is a map with some points of interest marked, and then you can take things at your own pace and experience life on campus more naturally. If you still have questions about the school after, you can always go to the admissions office and they'll be happy to give you answers.

Whatever you decide to do, here's my game plan for the ultimate college visit:

- **Sign in at the admissions office.** Make sure you do this as soon as you arrive.
- **Go on the tour and to the info session.** If you can't, no biggie. But if you can, then you should make appointments for them. Check online for a schedule.
- **Do the bench test.** Sit on a bench in the middle of campus. Put your phone away, and listen. What kind of conversations are you overhearing?
- **Wander into an academic building of your interest and see if you encounter any professors.** Bonus points if you say "Hi!" to one. Crazy bonus points if you have actually made an appointment to meet with one.
- **Sit in on a class**, if you can.
- **Visit the gym.** Do you see yourself working out here? Do they have intramural activities or amenities you care about?
- **Visit the dining hall.** Get some food. Listen to the conversations.

- **Visit the library.** Walk around. Can you see yourself studying here?
- **Go to the student union.** Walk around. What's it like there?
- **Go to the bookstore.** Are there kids shopping there? Maybe buy a tchotchke or a t-shirt. I like to add to my magnet collection, but maybe you'd prefer stickers or snow globes.
- **Hang out outside a dorm for a few minutes.** Do the kids seem happy?
- **If you have learning issues, go to student support services and ask questions. This is essential.**
- **If you experience mental health issues, go to counseling services and ask questions. This is also essential.**
- **Make a spiritual visit to the religious facilities** — Hillel, a chapel, a meditation room...if you have a spiritual side.
- **Find the wall or post with posters and flyers about club activities plastered all over it.** Do you see something fun and interesting to you?
- **Find a coffee shop nearby**. Sit and observe.
- **Wander aimlessly for a while.** Do you feel comfortable? How many kids are wearing college gear? Are kids walking alone and staring at their phones? Or are they interacting and smiling?

Try to imagine how you'll fit in on the campus. What's the vibe? How does it make you feel? Can you easily picture yourself here, happy and excited? Your college visit is about you, so you do you. If you see something interesting, follow your instincts. Watch the kids toss a ball around or read on the quad. It's all about feeling it out and seeing if the vibe fits with how you like to spend your time. I can't tell you how to do that. I can only point you in the right direction.

You should also do your best to **talk to kids on campus.** This is a big one! You'll find that most kids are open to the conversation because it wasn't that long ago that they were in your prospie shoes. If the first or second person you approach isn't available, then ask someone else. Here's a list of questions to ask. Pick a few people and ask them one or two of these questions that interest you:

- "What do you like about the school?"
- "What would you change?"
- "What do you think prospective students should know about the school?"
- "What's close to campus that's walkable for you to do?"
- "What's the general vibe?"
- "What do you and your friends do on a Wednesday night?"
- "What about a Saturday night or Sunday afternoon?"
- "How late do people stay in the library when it's not midterms or finals time?"
- "What kind of student support services do they have? Mental health? Tutoring? Health services? Does it cost extra?"
- "Do students wear college name stuff?"
- "What's your favorite cafe or coffee shop nearby?"
- "Where do you go to study when you don't want to use the library?"

What if you can't visit?

u/allurredditsrbelongtous

What should I do if I can't do the college visits?

How am I ever going to pick my schools? I want to visit, but it's going to be hard for my family to fly me all over the place. How are my parents supposed to be expected to pay for visits all over the country, ffs? But, aren't visits important for demonstrated interest? Am I screwed?

> [–] admissionsmom
>
> For lots of schools, visits are important to show demonstrated interest. You can check the school's common data set to see whether or not they value demonstrated interest. They're also a good way to gather intel and start learning more about what you're looking for in a school and its vibe.
>
> Many colleges, like Dartmouth, Swarthmore, Tufts, and Hamilton (and many more) offer free overnight visits to their schools for low-income or first-gen prospective students. These give you a chance to experience life on campus, partake in sessions with and get tips from admission officers, and frequently can be a great way to give your application more attention.
>
> I've found these sources helpful when looking for info about fly-in programs:
>
> Scholar Match: https://scholarmatch.org/for-students/online-resources/fly-in/
>
> College Greenlight: http://blog.collegegreenlight.com/blog/2018-fly-in-programs/
>
> Get Me to College: https://getmetocollege.org/what-colleges-look-for/2018-fall-diversity-visit-programs
>
> Even if you get rejected from the fly-in, don't be too sad. Simply putting in an application for a fly-in will count as

demonstrated interest for those schools who consider interest. I know of kids who've been rejected from fly-ins and still gotten admitted.

let me break it down for you

College visits can be tough to figure out. If a college is within a one- or two-hour drive or an easy train or bus ride, I suggest you make every effort to get there and visit. For those schools that are further afield, sometimes you just can't make the trip. And that's ok. Maybe your family can't afford it, or you have an accessibility issue, or you simply can't fit the visit into your schedule. If you encounter this obstacle, don't freak out. There are still ways to find out more about how you will fit in with a school's environment. One thing you should definitely do is visit all the schools near you so you can get a feel for what kind of vibe feels right for you. Try to visit large schools and small schools, rural schools, and city schools. That way you'll begin to know what's right for you.

For more information about a specific college and its vibe, the internet is your friend. Specifically, you should:

- Watch all the videos about the school you can.
- Read niche.com, Princeton Review, and the Fiske guide. They all have helpful information.
- Dig deep into the colleges' websites.
- Read the online college newspaper.
- Follow the colleges and their admissions offices on social media. Most are quite active on Twitter and Instagram, as well as Facebook and Snapchat.
- Go to the college's subreddit and read what the students are writing about.

Keep an eye out for my new app College Vizzy. It's an experience sharing app to help kids who can't visit colleges feel the vibe from kids who can and do visit. The app should be out by summer 2019, and I hope you'll check it out — www.collegevizzy.com

And yes, colleges that want to see demonstrated interest like to see that you've visited, but that's not the only way you can show demonstrated interest. I go over this more in the Demonstrated Interest Chapter. If the school considers demonstrated interest at all, you should email your regional admissions officer and let them know why you couldn't visit and ask any questions you might have. If they don't consider demonstrated interest, it really doesn't matter, but it won't hurt to reach out to your regional admissions counselor.

tl;dr

- **If you can, you should visit the colleges you're interested in.** At the very least, visit some of your local colleges to get a feel for what college campuses feel like.

- When you visit, go on the official college tour but also leave time to wander around without the tour guides. That's your chance to talk to students, sit on a park bench and soak in the atmosphere, and check out parts of campus that the tour doesn't cover. Be sure to think about the amenities or qualities that you want a college to have.

- If you can't swing a visit, research online. Find videos, read the online college newspaper, follow the college on social media, reach out to current students online, and watch for my experience sharing app College Vizzy, dropping soon!

CHAPTER 15

EA, ED, RD, SCEA, REA

Let's pause for a moment. As you are getting your list of activities together, requesting teacher recommendations, and drafting your essays, there's another important thing to decide as you develop your list: *When will you apply?* This decision has a lot of far-reaching effects, from minimizing stress during your senior year to boosting your chances of admission to ensuring you get the very best financial aid package available.

Basics of Application Timeline

There are five main kinds of college application deadlines:

- **Early Decision (ED)**: A special round of admissions that allows you to apply much earlier to your first-choice school for schools that offer ED. Early Decision applicants agree that they will attend the school if they are accepted during Early Decision. This is a binding contractual agreement, so Early Decision is not for uncertain applicants. Obviously, you can only apply to one school Early Decision. In order to apply ED, you must run the net price calculator for that school to make sure it is a financial option for you; then, you, your parents, and your counselor will have to sign the binding agreement before you can submit your application.

- **Single Choice Early Action or Restricted Early Action (SCEA, REA)**: With SCEA or REA, you are indicating that the only Early Action/Early Decision application you intend to file is that school (with the exception that you are still allowed to apply to most public schools), but you are not bound to the decision by the school. Each school has their specific policies and guidelines, so be sure to read them carefully on their website.

- **Early Action (EA)**: Similar to Early Decision in that applicants can submit applications before the Regular Decision round, but different because Early Action applicants are not bound to attend schools that accept them. You can apply to any number of Early Action schools.

- **Regular Decision (RD)**: This is still the most popular time to submit applications. Applicants are not bound to attend a school that accepts them.

- **Rolling Admissions (Rolling)**: For schools that do not have Early Decision, Early Action, or Regular Decision rounds, Rolling Admissions allows students to apply at any time during a large window. However, admission (and often financial aid) is granted on a first-come, first-serve basis.

College application deadlines, including Early Decision, Early Action, and Regular Decision, generally follow this schedule:

Decision Type	Application Deadline	Notification from the School
Early Decision I (ED I)	Early to Mid-November, often November 1	Early to Mid-December

Single Choice Early Action, Restricted Early Action (SCEA, REA)	Early November, often November 1	Early to Mid-December
Early Action I (EA I)	Early to Mid-November, often November 1	Early to Mid-December
Early Decision II (ED II)	Early January	Early to Mid-February
Early Action II (EA II)	Early January	Early to Mid-February
Regular Decision (RD)	January 1 – Mid-March	March – April 1
Rolling Admissions (Rolling or RA)	September through July	Ongoing Basis

Of course, you will want to consult with the official deadlines for your colleges on their websites, since each school does things a little differently. It's an excellent idea to include application deadlines not only on your college spreadsheet but to make a calendar of deadlines and work through them one by one. You can never be too organized during this stage of college admissions.

Let's dive a little deeper.

Early Decision

u/TheBigDog420
What are the pros and cons of applying early decision? Furthermore, what is the point of it?
Some people said that applying early shows that you have prepared early. Also, is it harder/easier to get accepted early? (A certain

college admits from my hs stats – early 3.8, regular 3.7.) Can I get any other general info on this topic, please? Thank you!

> [-] admissionsmom
>
> Many schools have much higher acceptance rates for ED. I think there is a benefit if you are dead-set, absolutely certain it's your top choice, and it's where you want to be for the next four years and the financial aid they are offering on their own net price calculator works for you and your family. Many schools also see an ED application as the clearest demonstration of interest.

u/thehalima

Should I apply EDII?

I would like to apply EDII for some schools, and I want to know if I can get out of financial circumstances because I come from a low-income family. If for example, Emory doesn't meet the demonstrated need can I get out of EDII?

> [-] admissionsmom
>
> Be sure to do the Net Price Calculator on the school's website, which you can find by googling "Net Price Calculator" plus the school name. If the EFC number they give works for you and your family, then you can safely apply to the school. If you don't receive at least that amount for financial aid, then you can be freed from the ED binding decision.

anonymous

Hey so I have kind of a weird question – if I'm applying to a sort of low-profile college, should I let my classmates know I'm applying ED? The school is really selective, just not super known where I live, with a few kids every year applying there each year. Seniors who graduated from my school the past few years don't even remember this college, lol.

The problem is that a lot of friends/classmates/randos keep asking me where I'm applying. I am really anxious about them finding out where I'm going, applying there, and ruining my chances of admittance. Everyone is so cutthroat and Type A at my school. I am absolutely sure that the people fishing for info have better grades than me.

If that happens, and these kids apply ED as well when almost no one from our school applies there, will this tank my acceptance odds? (Yeah, I know this is paranoid and selfish, but whatever, kids at my school are so competitive, and I get asked every. single. day. I don't want to add more stress to my plate.) Thanks in advance!

> [-] admissionsmom
> ok - and even good - to keep your admissions journey private. It's personal information.
>
>> anonymous
>> Cool, cool, I feel like I'm on the right path! :)
>
> [-] admissionsmom
> Just say that you haven't decided yet. Or that your parents asked you not to talk about it because they recognize that it's unhealthy for teens to be obsessing about college all the time. Also, this means that you don't ask others about their plans, right?
>
>> anonymous
>> It's only fair! In general, I try to sidestep the issue because things get so stressful and hard for everyone. But of course, everyone wants to know about everyone else, ugh. I'm almost there, praise Xenu.

here's my take

If you absolutely, positively, 100% know that you want to attend a particular college, and you can get the financial aid you need from that school, then apply Early Decision because if you get in, you're going.

In addition to finding out if you're going to your first-choice school before your winter break, Early Decision very often (although not always) gives applicants a slight edge in the admissions process. Just look at the stats for the schools, which you can easily find out from their data sets. According to my research and a lot of schools' assessments, it seems like there's a clear benefit to applying ED.

However, as mentioned above, Early Decision is binding, which means it's next to impossible to get out of. You need to make sure that your Early Decision school is where you want to go, period. If you can afford it, visit. You can even ask your regional admissions officer if they will fly you in for a visit. If you can't swing a visit, ask questions. Go to the college's subreddit. Ask the kids there what the school is like. Ask your regional officer if there are any students you can talk to. Look online for virtual tours.

You must also consider the impact Early Decision will have on your financial aid. Early Decision is binding even if you don't get all the financial aid you need. While lots of students get financial aid during Early Decision, the problem is you can't compare packages because you've signed a contract and committed to going there if accepted. However, if you do the net price calculator and that school's calculator gives you a financial aid number that works for you and then you don't receive that amount of aid from them, you can get out of the contract. As such, if you've done the FAFSA, you want to apply early, and you're not sure if your top-choice will give you the most financial aid, applying Early Action is the better way to go if it's an option.

(Side note: If you are deferred Early Decision, be sure to write a LOCI, a Letter of Continued Interest. I'll discuss these in the Deferred/Waitlist chapter).

Early Action

u/allurredditsrbelongtous
EA/ED or Regular decision
I've heard that if I need financial aid, I shouldn't apply EA or ED to schools. Is this true?

let me break it down for you

Early Action is different from Early Decision because it is non-binding. This wiggle room gives applicants plenty of time to compare financial aid packages and then select the best option.

Early Action can be a great deal for applicants looking for financial aid. Financial aid and merit money can be much stronger earlier in the year. (That doesn't mean you're screwed if you don't get them in early, though.)

In general, Early Action is a compromise between Early Decision and Regular Decision. It isn't binding, admissions readers have fresh eyes, and you get to relax and enjoy more of your senior year by completing your applications in your fall semester. That's why I have my students apply early action for all schools it's available for, so they can start hearing about merit aid and their acceptances.

So, to me, if you can apply Early Action, you should.

Rolling Admissions

u/23dagreatest

Does submitting my application early (but not EA or ED) help my application get read sooner?

what you need to know

It depends on whether the school has Rolling Admissions or not. For some schools, there is definitely a benefit. For others, there isn't. As a general rule of thumb, I think you should apply as early as possible during the Rolling Admissions window.

Regular Decision

u/conceptalbums

Is there any advantage to applying early on RD?
Just got my ACT score and I am definitely trying the Ivy League now! Columbia is my absolute top choice, but I can't apply ED

because I need to be able to compare financial aid packages. Is it still advantageous to submit my application much earlier than the RD deadline, like if I have all my materials ready?

Or since I have no choice anyway should I take my time and make sure everything is perfect by the RD deadline? I guess it would be better to have more time to work on essays, and I may have some more ECs/awards under my belt by then (but nothing major). I'm also a gap year student if that changes anything, maybe they want to know more about activities I've done during my gap year.

> [-] admissionsmom
> First, did you run the Net Price Calculator from Columbia on their webpage? If that number works for you and your family, then you could get out of the binding agreement if they don't meet it. But, since you seem ok with working on RD, it seems like you have a great plan in place. For some schools, they care about when you apply during the season, and the earlier, the better for demonstrated interest. But for many other schools, including the most highly selective colleges, it makes no difference to them whether you apply on the deadline or three months earlier.

my thoughts

If you just couldn't get it together on time or your colleges only offered Early Decision, and it wasn't your clear first choice, then you will need to apply Regular Decision, and there's nothing wrong with that. Period. So don't feel bad if you didn't get your application in by the Early Decision or Early Action deadline. It's not at all the end of the world.

tl;dr

- After you've made your college list, create a calendar and spreadsheet with all your application deadlines, be they Early Decision, Early Action, Regular Decision, or Rolling Admissions.

- Early Decision is binding, so make sure you want to go to that school, and you can get enough financial aid. Do the Net Price Calculator on the school's website to make sure it meets the needs of you and your family.
- Early Action is non-binding and the best time to apply, if it is available.
- There's no problem with applying Regular Decision, but for many of the highly selective schools, the admissions rate is much lower than Early Decision or Early Action.
- Apply as early as you can for Rolling Admissions to receive your decision and financial aid offers early.

CHAPTER 16

Figuring Out the Finances

I need to start this chapter with the fact that Financial Aid is not my specialty. So, you won't find a lot of info on filling out the forms or the best ways to look for scholarships. There are tons and tons of sources online for researching financial options for college.

What I do know is that I'm a firm believer that college should be about learning for everyone. In my opinion, the purpose of your education should be just as much about getting an education and learning to think, being creative, solving problems, and understanding the world you live in as much as (or more than) it is about your job training. However, with the skyrocketing costs associated with college, the focus naturally turns to the salary one can earn upon graduation to counter balance potential debt.

I don't think it should be this way. Students shouldn't feel the insane push-pull between going to college and racking up hundreds of thousands of dollars in debt.

First, that significant debt will keep you treading financial water for the rest of your life. You will feel yourself being pulled under, and that is scary.

Second, significant debt also prevents you from taking risks after you graduate, like starting a business or writing that screenplay or focusing on your idea for an app or traveling the world. You might think right now that there is no way you'd want to do any of that, but you don't know future you, and future you might be a little unhappy with the amount of debt you are incurring for them.

Because of these reasons, I would never recommend to a student that any significant amount of debt they would incur is worth the cost, no matter how prestigious a college they attend.

Bottom line, the cost cannot be ignored or minimized while applying for college. It should be the first factor and one of your college fits, along with the School Size, Social Atmosphere, Geography, Climate, Potential Major, and Your Stats fits. It's crucial to know if you will qualify for aid and if it will be enough for your family. **You need to talk to your parents and get your financial status out in the open.** And if you don't qualify for aid, figure out how much your family is willing to pay and/or how much merit money you will need.

Life Pro Tip: Don't be afraid to reach out to the financial aid offices at your colleges and establish relationships with them.

I've seen too many kids get burned by going through this process and then ending up with only acceptances they can't afford. Don't do this to yourself. Find at least one school where you can get aid. If not financial aid, then merit aid.

Just the Basics

anonymous

How do I know if I can afford the cost of a school or not?
I really want to attend either one of the Ivies or my flagship state school, but I'm not sure what the cost of attendance will be? In fact, I want to apply ED to either Brown or Penn. My parents make pretty good money. Does that mean I won't get any financial aid?

> [–] admissionsmom
> You need to check out the Net Price Calculator. Every school has one. You can find it by googling the school's name and

"Net Price Calculator." Then, plug in your numbers. If your EFC (Expected Family Contribution) is within a range that works for you and your family, then you can apply ED and be comfortable that you will probably receive that amount. If it is more than your family can comfortably pay, then you shouldn't apply ED.

u/wilandhugs

Worried about financial aid options at my top schools (ED)

So I've narrowed down my top two schools to be CMU and JHU after visiting both and doing a looot of research, so I'm going to decide ED between the two of them. My issue, however, is over the accuracy of the financial aid estimate of the NPCs at each school. Based off of everything but price-wise I'm leaning more towards CMU for my ED. However I fear being misled regarding their FA. FWIW the NPC on college board told me that at both schools I would basically be paying 16000$ a year (without work-study). For some generic background info on my financial situation:

I come from a middle-upper class area in NY, and my household is roughly in the 25th percentile for income in my area.

I have a sister going into her junior year of college and a twin brother who will be enrolling in college at the same time as I will

We don't own any property (other than our home), have much in savings, don't have trust funds or anything of the like, and the amount of money I make at my part-time job is negligible.

> [–] admissionsmom
>
> Do the net price calculator on their websites. Talk to the financial aid departments. It's not too early to develop a relationship with them. Reach out and make an appointment for a visit or a phone call and go over your concerns.

u/warrior__princess

How do I file the CSS with divorced parents?

Advice for how to handle talking about sensitive financial documents with parents that don't get along? Yaaaay me.

[-] memeoneco

If your parents are divorced, you need to fill out the non-custodial parent form regardless, especially if you're mainly living with one. Tell your parent to fill out the main CSS (ignoring the info for the other parent), and send another email to your noncustodial parent filling out noncustodial CSS (don't fill out the info for the main parent as well). That way, I assume that they can fill each of their forms individually and won't need to be in contact. Although that does mean your noncustodial parent also has to pay the $25 fee for CSS though, RIP.

> [-] warrior_princess
> How do you do that?

[-] memeoneco

do what? For your noncustodial parents to fill out the noncustodial CSS? Just log into CSS, scroll down, put your noncustodial parent's email in and tell them to fill it out by creating another College Board account with your info.

You fill out the CSS info with your custodial parent, ideally. Your noncustodial parent would fill out the form by themselves. They match the CSS's based on your DOB, SSN, and name. Go to the College Board CSS page, sign in, and just start filing.

u/TheBigDog420

do u fill out the FAFSA and the CSS Profile or just one of the two for financial aid

u/thehalima

Do I have to submit both FAFSA and CSS profile?
I already submitted FAFSA, and I am planning on submitting CSS soon. Do I have to submit both in order to receive aid from the schools I am applying to?

[-] admissionsmom
Every college has different needs for financial aid. You will need to carefully read the financial aid sections of their websites and find out which forms they need. Also, pay careful attention to their deadlines. They are school specific. In general, nearly all schools require the FAFSA, and many private colleges require the CSS Profile.

here's what you need to know

I see a whole lot of the same general questions being asked on r/ApplyingtoCollege. To give you peace of mind (and show you that a lot of kids and their families are in the same boat as you), here is that list of frequently asked questions:

What is the FAFSA?
That's the financial aid form you will use for all colleges.

Who fills out the FAFSA?
If you live with only one parent, then your custodial parent fills out the FAFSA for your household.

What is the CSS?
CSS form is the additional one many private colleges require as well.

What is the EFC?
EFC stands for Expected Family Contribution, and it's a central component of your FAFSA filing. The FAFSA takes into account the number of siblings in college as part of the equation for your Expected Family Contribution.

Who fills out the CSS?
For CSS, you have to include both parents' incomes, whether you live with them or not.

What is a financial aid calculator?

A financial aid calculator is a tool you can use to estimate your expected family contribution before you file out the FAFSA.

When applying to a college, you should research online and do the financial aid calculator. Look for that specific school's Net Price Calculator to calculate your EFC — your Expected Family Contribution. Talk to their financial aid office. See what that price looks like for you and find out where you might fit into their acceptance pool.

How much debt is too much?

A rule of thumb I've seen and read about is that your total debt shouldn't be more than your first year's salary out of college. Of course, if you can get it lower that's even better.

Is merit-based aid across the board?

Ivies, and some other schools like Tufts, don't give merit aid at all. They only have need-based financial aid.

Application Fee Waivers

u/allurredditsrbelongtous

Fee waiver

My family doesn't make much money, only ~40k a year. Can I get application fee waivers?

> [−] thehalima
> My family makes the same amount, and I applied to 20 schools for free.
>
>> [−] admissionsmom
>> Can you explain how you did that? And also, what did you do about sending test scores?
>
> [−] thehalima
> My hs counselor sent in fee waivers for all schools, and I did pay for some of my test scores to be sent — aside from the 4 free, I got 4 free extra since I already had fee waivers. Wow, I'm broke lol.

let me break it down for you

Applying for college can get pricey, especially when you're applying to a long list of schools. Some application fees can be upwards of $75, and between those fees and testing fees and fees for reporting your tests, you could end up spending a lot of money. This is why fee waivers are important for students who don't have access to unlimited financial resources.

A fee waiver is pretty straightforward. Essentially, this waiver allows you to apply to college without paying an application fee. You can ask your high school counselor and email your regional officer or the general admissions office to ask them for fee waivers. Additionally, if you register for the SAT or a Subject Test with an SAT fee waiver, you can receive up to four fee waivers.

If you can't qualify for fee waivers and you're worried about racking up costs, you can always find schools that don't charge application fees. The Common App makes it easy for you to sort schools in this way. I know the "Colleges That Change Lives" schools don't have application fees, and there are many more.

Looking for Merit Money

u/saada100

Scholarship opportunities for rising senior
does anyone know of any scholarship opportunities for a rising senior, any help would be greatly appreciated

> [-] admissionsmom
> Honestly, the best places to get scholarships are the merit scholarships through the universities. Also, look for local scholarships.

u/Skrapman2

Scholarships?
Also, lots of financial aid would probably be needed (lowest income bracket)

[–] admissionsmom

I need you to get going on some important research today.

Look into:

QuestBridge

Posse Foundation

Jack Kent Cooke Foundation.

Those all offer awesome scholarship foundations that are competitive, but you should apply early.

[–] Skrapman2

Thank you, I will look into this when I get home.

What if you get that sweet acceptance letter, but the financial aid just isn't enough?

anonymous

Question regarding the financial aid appeal process and how to approach it at Ivy Leagues — my first choice is slightly out of reach.

Hello all! I was lucky enough to get accepted into Yale EA, but the financial aid package is teetering on the edge of affordability, especially because I have a twin sister who has gotten into a few expensive LACs for acting and will be attending college at the same time that I am.

I will definitely be writing an appeal (and attempting to set up a physical meeting), but a bit of a timeline would be helpful. As I see it, I only get one written shot plus the meeting. However, the Yale financial office is pretty difficult to work with and hard to contact from what I have heard. Should I wait for the round of Ivy decisions to see if I get a comparable offer should I get accepted somewhere else? Alternatively, I could send a letter explaining my situation now, an official appeal following Ivy Day, and the meeting in late April. I just don't want to get my appeal entirely ignored or swamped in the sea of other appeals.

What steps (unofficial or official) should I take and in what order should I do them? Literally, any aid they are able to provide could make the difference if I attend or not. Thanks!

> [−] admissionsmom
> When you finally hear back about financial aid, be sure when you're reading through all your financial aid coverage to see if it covers living expenses, books, and travel. Books and traveling back and forth to home (if far) can be expensive. Books could be as much as $1k a semester. Food alone can cost money. Some colleges don't provide meals all weekend long or during the holidays.
>
> Always try to negotiate the amount of aid with the financial aid office. Say that you would really like to attend their college, but you can't without more aid available (if that's true), so you are hoping to be able to negotiate the financial aid packet. If your financial aid situation has changed, explain it to them.

u/PM_ME_UR_GAMECOCKS
College did me dirty
I was really excited about getting in yesterday, right? I have a 3.8 GPA, 34 ACT, decent ECs, all that stuff. Based off what I've read, I thought I'd be competitive for some scholarships there.

Nah fam, today they released financial and merit aid on their portal, and I got a grand total of $7k. Apparently, it wasn't even a merit grant; just something they gave to kids who didn't receive any other aid.

My family is pretty well off with my dad's doctor's salary, but nowhere near rich enough to afford around $60k a year. It's a damn shame cause I really liked the school too, but I have to turn it down. This is a great way to keep yield numbers low.

> [−] admissionsmom
> You might want to send other scores or updated info if you have them and contact them about renegotiating your merit money if you seriously would go there. Wait and see

what you get from the other schools and then you'll have some leverage power. Congrats on your acceptance, btw!

> [–] PM_ME_UR_GAMECOCKS
>
> Hmm, that's useful info. In the common app section where you can self-report scores, I put down both my ACT and SAT. I didn't put my subject test scores in Chem (750), Literature (740), and Math 2 (740) because I was only in the 50-80th percentile for them, which I thought would detract from my application.
>
> What would be a good way to go about negotiating merit aid? I've considered it, but I don't know if there's any certain protocol or specific way to go about it with colleges. I've heard of them renegotiating financial aid, but never with merit aid.
>
> Once again, thank you so much!! I deleted my old account here a month ago due to being doxxed, but although it's a new username, you've helped me greatly in the past, and I truly appreciate it!

[–] admissionsmom

When you get all your acceptances and aid packets, you can take them and use the info to evaluate your options. If there are schools that you'd like to attend, but you can't for financial reasons, you should talk to them. The worst thing that can happen is that they won't increase your aid. I've seen it work for more than a few kids... And, you're welcome! Glad I could help :)

Looking for Merit Money

u/chanceme1234321

Too rich for need-based, not rich enough that it won't suck

How can I get merit aid? My parents are well off, but they don't want to clear out savings to pay for college, which is where a lot of their money is.

[−] admissionsmom

You are not alone in this predicament. Loads of kids are lucky enough to have parents who make more money than will allow them to qualify for financial aid. This means you need to start searching for colleges who provide merit scholarships. Look for schools where your stats are in the upper 75% of their accepted classes and who provide merit money.

my take

If seen this happen way too often — kids with affluent parents end up struggling to figure out to pay for college. Yeah, their lives, in general, are probably much easier and less stressful when it comes to money, but when it comes to paying for college, it really depends on the family structure, savings, values, age of parents, deficits, and a variety of other factors. Maybe their parents make money, but they have so many other expenses that there's no money for college. Maybe there is a super awkward family situation, and while the money exists, one parent doesn't want to pay for college. It sucks. It's unfair. But it happens.

Just because some parents *can* pay for college if they want to sacrifice their savings and retirement doesn't mean they *will*, and then those kids are basically screwed when it comes to financial aid.

This is why merit money has become important. **Even if you don't qualify for need-based aid, you can still qualify for merit aid.**

Some schools will want you to have filed the FAFSA and CSS profile to give merit aid. Others don't care. I've had clients wait and see if they knew they wouldn't qualify. It really is up to you and your parents. Some counselors will tell you that everybody has to do the forms. I haven't found that to be true.

In particular, there are tons of liberal arts colleges and state schools that give plenty of merit aid. A good way to find them is to search for liberal arts colleges where your test scores are above their 75% percentiles, which will increase your chances of receiving a robust merit aid package.

tl;dr

- Get familiar with these terms and abbreviations: FAFSA, CSS, EFC, NPC, IDOC, NPC, COA
- Make sure you understand the difference between Merit Aid and Financial Aid. Many schools only offer financial aid and no merit. Some have better merit aid and not-so-great financial aid.
- Even if you don't qualify for financial aid, you could still qualify for merit money.
- Check the Net Price Calculator of a college to see if it is in a workable range for your family by finding your EFC, Expected Family Contribution. You can find the NPC by googling "Net Price Calculator" and the name of your college.
- Reach out and establish relationships with the financial aid offices at your colleges.
- Talk to your parents about the amount of financial or merit aid you will need. Get your financial status out in the open.
- Financial Fit should be one of your top priorities in your list of Fits as you create your college list.
- Be careful with how much debt you incur. A rule of thumb I've heard is that your total debt shouldn't be more than your expected first year of salary.
- The prestige of a college cannot make up for saddling you with years' worth of debt.

CHAPTER 17

The Personal Essay Topic? You.

Here's the thing about essays: they don't need to be incredible pieces of literature. Of course, you shouldn't have glaring grammar mistakes and sloppy style, but what's really important is that they're sincere. So many kids focus on finding the *unique*, presenting the *incredible*, or trying to show the *amazing* that they forget to write the *real*. They forget to be honest and open about who they are.

When I read an essay (and I've read lots and lots and lots (and lots) of essays), I look for a connection. So how do you write an essay that someone can connect to? Well, take it from the admissions officers themselves. I hear AOs say time and time again that the best essays are those that give a window into who you are. You see, **the whole point of the college essay is not to stand out to admissions officers, but to stick with them,** and you do that by creating a connection with them. You create that connection with them by opening up about who you are. You have to dig deep within yourself and ask yourself some questions — what do you believe? What do you value? What do you think about before you go to sleep? What comforts you? What's one item that reminds you of home? What's your superpower? What's your secret sauce?

My advice is to write something about yourself that they won't find elsewhere in your application. Look to the inner you. Let them get to know who you are and what you value and believe. It doesn't have to be about something you're good at. It should be something they can connect with. You're not trying to show off; you're just trying to show.

Peel back your onion layers and start reflecting on the essentials of your you-ness. Learn as much about yourself as you can and then teach what you learn to the admissions officers. After all, you are the expert on you.

How do I even come up with a topic?

u/ninja542

I know that writing a college essay about your grades and academic achievements is a really bad thing, but is it bad to write an essay about an extracurricular at school that means a lot to me?

> [–] admissionsmom
>
> You're right. Make your personal essay about you, not an activity you do. If your prospective colleges require supplemental essays, you will often have to write about an extracurricular. So, write your personal essay about a different aspect of you that they won't necessarily find in your application already. If you write about something you believe in or something that defines the essence of who you are, then you might use your involvement in this EC as an example or as part of your story, but I would advise you to shy away from the EC as the vehicle you use to relay your story of YOU.

u/thehalima

I made a brand-new essay, and I decided to write about how my mother's illness made me more passionate about my ECs.
Which common app prompt would this be?

[-] admissionsmom

Here's a secret. You don't really need to worry about the prompt too much. You always have the option of the free choice prompt. Instead of focusing on the prompt, remember to focus on the topic. And the topic is always YOU. Inside you. Thinking you. Developing and growing you.

u/KaiserSand

Every essay topic that I think of is utter crap. I'm kinda hopeless right now.

Haven't started my supplemental essays either.

[-] Ninotchka

My favorite bit of advice is that you've probably read a lot of things about writing the perfect essay and your mind is focused on perfection. What you need to do is give yourself permission to write a terrible essay.

Just sit down and do it. Write the worst possible college essay. Make it trite, make it stupid, make it arrogant, make it profane. Put in everything you think college admissions doesn't want to hear. There is a bunch of crap that you think about yourself that is getting in the way of the good stuff. One way to get that out of your head is to write it down.

Then, put aside that terrible essay and do something to clear your mind. Run around the block, put music on your headphones and dance, do some stretches and yoga, do some household chores that require at least mild physical exertion, rearrange your room. The trick is to get your muscles moving and your blood flowing faster and a bit of mental distance.

Then go back and reread what you wrote. Do a dramatic reading. You may surprise yourself – there may be a nugget of something in there that's shocking and interesting and can be turned into a very good college essay. Or it may be crap, but you may have cleared enough mentally to write the good stuff.

For extra credit, give it to your parents when they ask how the essay writing is going and watch them try to pretend that it's good

> [-] admissionsmom
> I love this advice so much!

[-] admissionsmom
That isn't true! And you know it. Write it and make it great — not crap, but the only way it's gonna be great is if you write it. And let's define what great is: it's getting your words and your thoughts out there. It's taking a chance on opening up your mind and sharing with others. It's you making a connection with someone else. That's all. Try writing on themostdangerouswritingapp. com and practice throwing some words down. Answer these questions:

What do I believe?
What do I value?
What makes me laugh?
What frightens me?
What do I think about first thing in the morning?
Last thing at night?
What are my superpowers?
My secret sauce?
What comforts me?
Who are my superheroes and why?

Take those questions, go to that website, and as my favorite author Cheryl Strayed says, write like a mother f*cker. Then edit edit edit. Abraca-effing-dabra! You've got an essay. Now, giddy up! Get going. You got this.

[-] KaiserSand
Hahahaha :D

Your feedback has helped me greatly (which is why I decided to write something completely frank). Yesterday after writing this post I talked to my English teacher. He started asking questions about my past and my life in Iran and Norway, and I realized that I have so much to talk about. So much raw information that couldn't be contained in 650 words. Writing for the sake of being creative and sounding poetic makes me look pathetic, which is why I'm going to tell my story in detail - in simple English simply. Thanks for all your help :) Will show you the essay later on!

my thoughts

You know, I've been reading college essays for a long time and have honestly only come across a few that were utter crap. Well, guess what? Those essays were written by kids who were trying too hard to impress and refused to have open minds. They chose to write about what they do (the easy part) and not who they are (the hard part).

Here's a helpful hint: it doesn't matter what prompt you choose. Your topic is you. Choose a vehicle through which you can build a connection. Now, any subject can be kickass when it's approached by a stellar writer. But, let's be real — most of y'all aren't stellar writers (yet), so take some time to consider the vehicle — or subject — you use to get your topic across. Remember the topic is YOU.

Cringe or Snooze? Tips on Essays to Avoid

When deciding on the vehicle, here are some tips about subjects you might want to avoid. They're not taboo, but the following essays cause me to sleep. Or cringe. Or toss them to the side.

Recapping how amazing you are at your extracurriculars	*cringe*
A narrative without a clear message. Just a long boring story that's trying to capture a moment — like you read somewhere you're supposed to do — but really there's no point to it	*snooze*
Details about the specifics of an extracurricular	*snooze*
An essay that focuses on another person or persons	*set aside*
"Here's what I learned from sports/ mission trips/volunteer work."	*Classic Admissions Officers' Pet Peeve*
Pedantic and trying too hard	*cringe*
Trying too hard to be clever and gimmicky	*cringe*
Anything describing private bathroom or bedroom behaviors	*cringe*

If you feel soooo strongly that you must write about your amazing EC for your personal essay, and you just can't bear the thought of writing about anything else, well, go ahead and go for it. It's your essay after all. You do you. But be aware that if you're focusing on an extracurricular (or your grandma or your service trip or your sports injury) and not yourself, then there's a pretty high chance that you're writing an essay AOs have already read hundreds of times. However, if you focus on yourself and your beliefs, thoughts, and values, then your essay is going to be one of a kind — there's no way they've read it before. My advice is to make the topic you (what you believe, what you think, what you value) and then you can possibly bring in your EC that you love so much as an example or part of an anecdote to get YOU across.

At the same time, don't stress about being unique. The fact is **you are unique. There is no one else like you.** You also don't have to have exciting life experiences or extreme struggles. Admissions officer aren't looking for a feature-length biopic of your incredible life; they're looking for a window into your head, a sneak peek into what makes you—you.

How can I possibly talk about myself?

u/PeperoniTrainOld
Personal statement/essay question
I'm a shy and extremely introverted person, and I know people say to be genuine for personal statements and essays, but would mentioning my shyness have a negative effect? Colleges seem to prefer people that are outgoing and see them as better leaders. I guess what I'm asking is that although being shy is a huge part of me, would it be terrible not to mention this?

> [−] admissionsmom
> I think instead of writing about a characteristic of you, you should think about writing about something you believe in. Or what makes you—you? I bet that although you are shy, you have some really deep thoughts. So, sure, of course,

you can discuss being shy, but I'm sure you are so much more than that. Think deeper about yourself. They are looking to get to know the internal you. This is your chance as a shy person to let your voice be heard.

my thoughts

Again, for the kids in the back, you're not trying to impress admissions officers. Your resume and application take care of that for you. **In the personal statement, your goal is to make them want to hang out with you, or, well, at the very least get to know you.**

Many of the admissions officers I've heard at conferences or whose blogs I've read say that in your personal statement they want to hear about the you they can't get to know in the rest of your application. So, while doing Science Olympiad is cool and all that, it shouldn't be the focus of your essay.

Think of it this way: Would you honestly sit and brag to your friends about your ECs? Your SAT scores? If you're munching on a slice of pizza at lunch would you really describe to your buddy in poetic detail how, although you lost in that championship game during your junior year, you learned a great deal about the importance of grace in defeat and grew as a person? Of course not! That would be weird. You're not a character in a cheesy teen movie. You want the admissions officer to get to know the person behind the shiny ECs and stats. Ask yourself, what makes me a great friend, a desirable roommate, or a solid classmate?

There is so much more about you for them to get to know, so in the personal statement write about another aspect of yourself. Think about those questions that I repeat time and again: What do you believe? What motivates you? What's your secret sauce? Who are your role models? What's your comfort food? What scares you? What do you think about first thing in the morning? **Think about the you that's deeper than you've ever really explored.**

anonymous
BORING and NORMAL
I'm just a totally normal, boring, middle-class kid. I can try to figure out what the schools are looking for and write that shit down,
but there is no way I'm ever going to be able to stand out in the
admissions process. I feel like thousands of kids can write the exact
same essay I can. I just don't know if I'll ever be able to write a
good essay. What did y'all do?

> [–] musicman0910
> Write a lot. After a while, you will find your story and your
> voice so that you know how to slant everything in the direc-
> tion you want to go. You can be as mundane or as out there
> as you want. Don't do anything for colleges to like you. Live
> your life the way you want to, and when it comes the time,
> tell them your story. At the end of it, you'll be left with a
> few good options, and life will be ok.

> [–] iphsyko
> Not everyone will approach college admissions the same
> way, but I didn't really try to "stand out" with my applica-
> tions in any way because I have no idea what the AOs are
> looking for. I just did my best to show who I am, and if they
> reject me, well, maybe I wasn't a good fit for that cam-
> pus. You can try to do research on what makes applicants
> stand out and build your application like that, but others
> will agree with me that being unapologetically authentic is
> the easiest way to create your college application because
> all the AOs are really trying to figure out is what kind of
> person you are. /u/admissionsmom, thoughts?

>> [–] admissionsmom
>> I think you expressed that perfectly! Yes. All you
>> can do is present who you are, what you bring,
>> and how you see yourself. The trick is you have
>> to really dig in deep and think about those impor-
>> tant aspects of yourself. If you can do that and can

portray a sense of who you are, then I think the AOs can identify with you and connect with you. And honestly, if they don't connect with who you are, why would you want to be there? Find the school that does truly want you.

let me break it down for you

To those of you writing your essays now and searching for advice, please don't take it personally when I push you to dig deeper and learn more about yourself. That's part of the process.

In addition, please know that your essays need to be as well-written as possible and that they definitely need to be grammatically correct, including correct punctuation and spelling. Please also know that just because you technically write well, that doesn't mean I would want to hang out with you or get to know you better from only reading your essay. Tons of kids complain that they don't stand out. My answer? Forget about it. Write an essay that *sticks with*. Focus on building that connection. *That's* your goal. You want the admissions officers to *want* to meet you.

So, to help you engage in some of that soul-baring you need to do, I've put together a list of tips to help you write the very best essay you can. Keep in mind that some of the best college essay writers are actually the ones who have the fewest amount of preconceived notions about what a college essay should be, so if you're feeling unsure about what to write or you're questioning your ability to write a "great college essay," then take a deep breath. Ok. Maybe you're not a great essay writer now, but writing is a muscle. If you reflect, practice writing, and are patient, then you'll have a damn good essay in no time.

Before you get started, check out my two favorite websites for the personal essay: www.thecollegeessayguy.com and www. thisibelieve.org. College Essay Guy has an awesome website, as well as a great book. Thisibelieve.org has great examples of the personal essay; I particularly like this site because they aren't college essays, so the pieces come across as much more personal and real, which is what colleges are telling us they want.

One last thing: practice writing. Here's a great website to get your writing juices flowing: themostdangerouswritingapp.com

---

My Quick and Dirty Tips for Writing and Editing Essays

Let your voice shine through by sharing what you believe and how that belief affects your life. My students who do this have the most success as we work on getting to the nitty-gritty, soul-sloppy belief that really defines who they are.

Show your very best you on your very best day. I get it that I'm asking for a lot of soul-baring from you, but that doesn't mean it's time to air all the dirty laundry around here. This is not sob-story time or let-me-show-you-how-shitty-my-life-is time. Find the good parts of who you are – and you have loads of them, and then let them get to know that you.

Make sure your essay sounds like you and feels like you. Do the thumb test: If you hold your finger over your name at the top of your essay, would your mom know who wrote it? Would your best friend or a close teacher? Would they recognize your special sense of humor or sarcasm? Or your serious nature?

Eliminate most (read ALL) adverbs. Especially really, very, and so. Yuck!

Use contractions. They sound friendlier and more personable and casual.

Slang is fine. As long as it's not inappropriate or disrespectful (no fuccboi) and the readers will be familiar with the words, feel free to use your casual language. Emoticons can also be ok if used sparingly. It should fit the style of the writer, and it should make sense :).

Don't start your essay with a quote. You want to catch their attention and draw them into who you are as soon as possible with YOUR words. Starting with a quote or even using a quote can be a waste of precious word space.

Practice, practice, practice. I encourage my students to practice writing everyday way before they sit down to write their essays. That being said, I encourage you to wait until the early fall or late summer of senior year to start the actual essays themselves. I know I'm going against the college counseling grain here, and you do you, but I think and have seen in my years of experience, that you still have a lot of developing to do and experiences to gain during junior year and summer vacation. But, for sure, practice writing every single day. Even a sentence or two of writing about yourself will help. Put this into action by writing in a daily journal or challenging yourself with daily prompts. Daily gratitude thoughts can be a good way to get started.

Edit, edit, edit. Read your essay *out loud* at least twenty times. Read it to yourself, to your mom, your dad, your teacher, your dog, and maybe a friend. Then, ask them to read it to you. **Be on the lookout for bumps when you're listening, and feel for those bumps when you're reading. That's where you need your edits.** Also, read the essay backward while you're looking for typos and basic mistakes. Another trick is to print it up and read it. Sometimes you find things on paper you wouldn't see on a screen.

I'm so lucky to have three extremely talented, problem-solving, creative kids, two of whom helped out quite a bit with this book. Some of you have met one of them, u/AdmissionsSon, because they've been helping me with essay stuff on A2C for the last couple of years. I wanted to include their advice because I felt like it was important info for you all to hear. Enjoy the creative mind at work.

u/AdmissionsSon

On the Importance of Specifics

Be careful about writing from what I call a hot air balloon perspective. Currently, a lot of you are taking the reader on a pleasant journey over the landscape of your life where they can see all these features and facets of you in broad, general strokes. That's great. But while a hot air balloon ride is more than fine for orienting the reader in the big picture of your life, it's also not the most exciting way to experience a new place. We, the readers, want to get down into the muck with you. We don't want you to only point out the jungle from above, but lead us on a gripping trek through the underbrush, with you our intrepid guide machete-ing us a path deeper into the unknown. What I'm trying to say is: I want more specifics!

To use another metaphor, broad, general themes and observations are often the meat of the essay, in that they provide a unifying focus and give the reader something to chew on, which is good but can also be bland. Specifics are the spices — they make the essay worth eating. Or reading. You get it. Instead of saying that you are practicing "the audition pieces," tell me specifically which ones. Was it Mozart's Concerto No. 23 in a minor? Was it Carly Rae Jepsen's "Call Me Maybe?" I want to know! Instead of saying that you are "in classes," tell me which classes — Physics? Welding? AP Bio? Semi-Professional Clowning? If you don't tell me, I'm forced to assume, and the reader is going to assume the most boring option every time, which means the more assumptions you leave us to make, the more boring the essay. And seriously, if you take Clowning classes, you cannot leave that out. I need to know that.

Any time you find yourself talking about something vaguely — classes, pieces, peers, siblings, books, devices, volunteer opportunities, employers, whatever — consider using a specific instead.

EG:

> *My curiosity about the devices the character used in a book series I read sparked my interest in technology*

Vs

> *My curiosity about the supersonic jetpacks and laser-powered lockpicks that Captain Amelia Proton used in "Galaxy Gal," which was my favorite book as a kid, sparked my interest in electrical engineering and computer science.*

Sure, it's twice as many words, but it also communicates a whole lot more and in a much more interesting way. Plus, if you write the first sentence, you will probably need to add more sentences that say, "I am interested in electrical engineering and computer science," or "I've always been interested in space," while those two bits of info are already communicated in the more specific sentence, so it can often even save you words to write this way. And perhaps more importantly, the second one is just more interesting to read and helps me feel like I know you much better than the first, vague sentence does.

So yeah. TL;DR: Be specific!

Writing, Editing, and Critiques

u/riverdanced

I don't even know what my essay is about anymore

Y'all, I have read my UChicago essay so many times I'm not even sure what it means now. I don't know what good writing is anymore. Does this make sense? Does that sentence sound jarring? Does that flow well? Who knows. Not me. Words have ceased to have any meaning.

I think it might be time to submit. Either that or start over completely.

u/ninja542

Overediting vs. under-editing essays: Is there a point where editing your essay removes personality from the essay? How do you tell?

> [-] admissionsmom
>
> I think it's ok to edit, edit, and edit your essay some more, but that's with *your* edits. Where there can be a problem is if you t-rex (**thesaurus** rex, that is) that essay to death. Use vocabulary you use. Keep your voice. If it sounds like you, it's all good. Then, put it away for a few days and come back to it. Edit some more. Then, eventually, you gotta let that baby bird fly away.

u/roouel

Advice on taking advice from friends for essays?

If I do a rough draft, it seems that when I share to a close group of friends, the majority will like it but one or two may not. I know I can't please EVERYONE, but what's the general advice with sharing essays to friends and receiving varied, often conflicting critiques.

> [-] admissionsmom
>
> Don't. Just don't. When you've finished writing your essay, the only question you should ask your friend is if it sounds like you when you read it to them. Would they recognize it as yours if they picked it up off the floor in your high school hallway? If the answer is yes, then it's all good.
>
> Though it's valuable to have someone read it over, first to make sure you're making sense and later to help with proofreading, I don't suggest that you pass it around to everyone and anyone you know and water down your voice so much so that you can't be found in your own words.
>
> So, unless you have a friend whose specialty is writing personal statements, I'd advise you to say no thank you.

u/USS-Enterprise

Contractions in College Essays

Hi, this is a dumb question, but I was wondering if contractions are appropriate in college essays? I'm going to guess they are, but I don't want to do anything too informal. Thanks!

> [–] admissionsmom
>
> Yes, they are! And I even suggest using them for a few reasons: they make the flow of the essay smoother, they give the essay a more casual, conversational feel, and they eliminate words. You want the reader to feel like they're having a nice chat with you to build those bonds. Contractions are one way to accomplish that. I encourage you to write like you'd be talking to a slightly older cousin you look up to.

Even More Helpful Advice from AdmissionsSon

Way Too Long Essay Advice #2. Be casual! Be weird! If you want to, that is.

For this post, I want to talk about formality vs. casuality, which seems to be a bit of a point of contention on A2C. I'm pro-casual, which won't blow anyone's mind on here, but I wanted to share my reasoning for why I think leaning into casuality can help you. Bear in mind these are just my personal thoughts and that there are no rules for what a college essay Should Be. Some of you will disagree, and that's fine. But here's my two cents:

Stop thinking about English class. This ain't English class, and nobody wants to read a five-paragraph analytical essay. You can use the Second Person (you can say "You")! And please, y'all've just gotta use contractions! You could even cuss if you want to be a badass — just, you know, be smart about it. College essays are not a black-tie affair. It's more like you're writing an email to an old friend you haven't seen in a long time. You like them, they like you, and you're just trying to get them reacquainted with the person you are today.

In most cases, I prefer to read essays that are conversational and informal, but if formality is your natural writing voice, then that's 100% ok. The biggest reason I push for students I work with to be sillier and more casual in their writing isn't because casual writing is inherently better, but because I think it helps free them up to have more fun with the process, to trust their instincts more, and to get more of their unique personality into their work. College essays are, after all, personal essays. If there were times while writing where your instinct was to go a little looser or weirder or sillier or more casual, but you felt the need to keep the essay nice and buttoned-up because that's what you thought an essay *should* be, feel free to go back in and have some fun with it. Take off its glasses, let down its ponytail, etc. Again, you don't have to do this if you feel that a formal essay is the essay that best represents you. If it is, then that's great. I'm just saying that it is ok to be weird or casual if you want to be.

Here's the bottom line: if you didn't enjoy writing your essay, I'm probably not going to enjoy reading it. If you have fun writing it, I'm more likely to have fun reading it.* Of course there's a limit to this — for example, I would find it very fun to go off on an extremely long tangent about the Great British Bake Off right now, but that wouldn't do much to serve my overall point, so I'm not going to do that. As for where that line is, I can't give you a hard and fast rule. I'm sure you've had lots of times in your life when you didn't make a joke you found hilarious because you knew the people you were talking to wouldn't appreciate it. Or maybe you wanted to talk about this sweet dream you had, but you knew nobody else would give a shit, so you kept it to yourself. You kind of just have to try to be self-aware.

My advice to you is that, while you are drafting these essays, you should err on the side of saying "yes" to whatever weird or silly ideas or word choices bubble up in your head. Then, when you get a friend or teacher or parent or counselor to read your essay, they can tell you if you went too far in that direction. You'll be surprised how often people will actually like what you thought for sure was a dumb idea, and it's always easy to dial it back if it ends up being too much. Contrariwise, if you don't try out your ideas, nobody will be able to tell you whether or not they would have been good or worth putting in the essay. By not putting them in there, you deny yourself and the reader a lot of potentially good and fun stuff.

*Not everyone writes fun essays, and that's ok. The same general principle holds for more serious or somber essays. If you feel emotionally affected writing it, then I will be much more likely to feel that emotion as I read it. If you are bored or overly detached from the emotional content of your essay while writing it, then I'm probably not going to have any emotional attachment as I read it.

TL;DR: Feel free to be weird and casual. Have fun while drafting. It's easy to edit out anything that pushes a bit too far past the boundary, but it's very hard to know whether an idea would have worked if you never try it.

How do I handle Essay Writing Hell?

anonymous

My essays are super basic, and I'm lowkey freaking out. How many examples of accepted essays should I look at before writing my own? Every. Single. Accepted. Essay. Is. Fire.

I am so screwed. How am I gonna write that kind of essay? I'm not even creative at all. It makes me not even want to write an essay because there's no way my essay will ever stand out.

[−] admissionsmom

I say just Say No to the "Accepted Essays" books, websites, and blogs. To me and in my experience, reading other people's essays can be harmful to the creative process. It puts in your head what an "accepted essay" is supposed to look like, but the truth is that there is no true right way to do an essay. But one way to do it wrong is to try to replicate someone else's. Not because that's cheating or anything, but because it can and often does stymie the creative process. And yes, you can be creative. Everyone can. Just work that creative process muscle. Also, forget about trying to stand out in your essay. That's not the point. The point is to stick with the reader. Build that connection.

let me break it down for you — with some help from u/BlueLightSpcl

One of my fellow r/ApplyingtoCollege moderators, u/BlueLight-Spcl (aka Kevin, Founder of Tex Admissions LLC), who has experience as an admissions officer, made a great Reddit post about writing essays. He always has awesome advice, especially when it comes to writing essays without losing your mind by obsessing over those "magic" and "perfect" admitted college essays. Here's what he has to say:

> Very few people write naturally well, especially about themselves. I certainly don't.

> Students want that silver bullet essay topic that will ensure them admissions to UT honors programs or most selective universities nationwide. Questions like 'What is the best essay you have ever read? What's the best topic to write about? What topics should I avoid? What is the most memorable essay you have seen?' These miss the point. I answer, 'it depends.'

Instead of focusing on what students write, you should inquire how successful applicants approach college essays and why they choose to write on one topic rather than another. Process matters more than the final draft. A topic or writing style useful for one student may not be effective for you. There is no substitute for authenticity and hard work. Colleges nationwide are seeking sincere and passionate students who write thoughtfully. Essays are as much about editing as they are writing.

When you see a selection from 'Best Harvard Application Essays,' you don't see the rest of the author's application. You don't have access to their supplements, resume, transcript, or recommendation letters. You don't see early drafts and dead ends. By trying to isolate the essay from the rest of the application, you might, at best, write a strong essay, but it may not be an effective college essay. The best essays complement the rest of the application, provide details, introduce nuance, and elaborate on things that a reviewer can't assume from your transcript or resume."

I totally agree with Kevin and this approach. That's why I suggest avoiding any admitted essays books or websites. It's too easy to get caught up in what worked for someone else. A personal essay needs to be what works for you.

Digging deep and getting to know yourself and who you are will help you much more than reading other people's essays. I've seen kids get frozen many, many times by reading others' essays. Instead, focus on those questions like who you are and what you believe. Think about them. Walk with them. Shower with them. Free write about them.

And besides, the fact that someone was admitted somewhere could very likely have nothing to do with their essay.

Words of Writing Wisdom from a Member of our a2c Tribe, u/iphysyko:

My personal advice: personal essay writing is not something we students are typically doing every day. We're usually analyzing a fictional character's feelings or someone else's action. It takes practice to figure out how to talk about your feelings and your actions—to discuss your life and give a glimpse of your personality to the admissions office in under two pages of text. So practice! Whenever you feel strongly about something, take out your phone, open your Notes App and just type what you're feeling. Type about why you're feeling whatever emotions you're feeling and what you feel the need to do in that very moment. After some practice, you might notice that you do indeed have a unique voice in your writing and there are things you value that you might want to tell admissions officers all about.

tl;dr

- No matter which prompt you choose or which vehicle you use to tell your story, the topic is YOU.
- Dig in deep and become the expert on you. Then teach that lesson.
- Your purpose is not to stand out, but to **stick with** the reader. You do that by building connections.
- Just say no to "Accepted Students" essays.
- It's totally cool, and even recommended, to use contractions and your normal, conversational, casual voice.
- Keep that slightly older cousin you respect a lot in mind as you write your essay.

- Don't become a Thesaurus Rex by making your essay sound like you swallowed a thesaurus. Use your vocabulary and your words.
- Read your essays out loud to someone else and listen and feel for bumps. That's where you need to focus your edits.

Personal Essay Exercise

See if you can have a sentence that begins with each of one of these in your essay somewhere. If not, then I have a feeling your essay just isn't personal enough.

- I think
- I feel
- I believe
- To me,
- I mean
- You see,
- You know,

CHAPTER 18

Supplemental Whaaats? More Essays...

Just when you think you've reached the finish line and put that bad boy — the Personal Essay — to bed, you realize you've now got even more essays to write: the supplements. Each school has their very own special brand of awesomeness when it comes to these babies. True, some schools take pity on you and don't have any — and those schools deserve a special place in our hearts — while others are looking for your quirky souls and hope to dig in and find them in their offbeat topics, which can often turn out to be hella fun to write and read. Many will have some version of the "Why Major" or "Future Career" essays, others will have "Tell us more about your background and perspectives," and lots have the "Why College" and "Why EC" essay supplement.

Why Major, Interest, EC, or Career?

u/KaiserSand

How to write supplemental essays if I have no energy left?
I'm really struggling. I'm a prospective CS guy who has done some amazing stuff — yeah I know I'm bragging, but saying it for the sake of context. I just don't know how to write the "why is CS your main interest?" essays. I don't know. I just like it because it was my way of sticking it in the face of all the cool kids at middle school

and now I just enjoy creating things. How do I answer the essay without being all cliché? How do I stand out?

anonymous

The challenging "why major" essay.

To a very large degree, my common application brings up my passions and my future plans. It should be obvious to just about anybody who knows me that my passion for ecology is driven by a love for the natural world — whose isn't? Rather than repeat how much I love animals and whatever, am I able to talk about specific college programs and why they help make that major best for me? I feel like repeating my interests is the wrong approach. Thanks!

> [–] admissionsmom
>
> Here's what I want you to keep in mind about these supplemental essays. They are all about you and what you can bring to their college. So, don't go off the deep end on tangents about the details of the major, EC, career, or interest. Stick to the basics. You. What do you find meaningful in the activity or major? What connects with you and what makes it so special to you? What do you do with it? Where did the interest stem from? And then bring it back to the school. How are you going to take your special interest, major, future career plans, or EC and make it meaningful in the environment of their college?

Why College?

u/CatOwlFilms

On "Why this school?" essays, should you talk more about the school or about yourself?

I get that I shouldn't say cliché stuff about the school, so should I just connect my interests with what the school is doing?

> [–] admissionsmom
>
> The most important thing to remember about a "Why College" essay is that it's really a "Why You" Essay. This essay

is just as much about you as it is the college. Why do they need you on their campus? What will you bring? So, in essence, this should be an essay that only you could write about only this school. If any sentence could apply to any other school or applicant, scratch it.

Write a love letter to the college explaining all the reasons you need to be together. Here's a great idea that I borrowed from Ethan Sawyer, College Essay Guy: take a sheet of paper and divide it down the middle. On one side, list all the awesome stuff about you. On the other side, list all the amazing stuff about the college. Where do you see overlaps? Where do you match? Where does the college bump up against you? And where do you bump up against the school? That's the substance of your essay. It's kinda like thinking about any kind of relationship really.

Make sure you include specifics. For specifics about your college, do your research:

- If you've visited, say so. And talk about what you saw and liked and why it was specifically appealing to you.

- Read the student newspaper online. Find events and articles that appeal to you.

- Follow the admissions department on social media. Mention something they've profiled recently and why it's specifically interesting to you.

- Read the website, especially the admissions website, carefully. Most college websites tell you exactly what they're looking for. Are you that person? If so, demonstrate to them why. If not, well, maybe this school isn't a great fit for you.

- Check out classes that look interesting to you. Look at course lists on the website. Tell them why this would be a great class for you. What will you get out of it? What can you contribute?

- Find professors who appeal to you (ratemyprofessor. com can be your friend here).
- Check out clubs and activities on campus. What can you bring to the campus and how do you see yourself being involved?

my thoughts

As you're planning and organizing your college apps, be sure to keep up with the supplemental essays. I think you should create a spreadsheet and make lists of all the supplements you have to do. Make a column for Why Major, Why EC, Why Career, Why School, and Your Background. Then for all of them except for the Why School essay, be a green essay writer, and Reduce, Reuse, and Recycle as much as you can. Just be EXTREMELY careful to tailor each essay to the correct school if you're doing so. Putting the wrong school name in an essay can be the kiss of death.

Also, be sure to take these essays seriously. They are not afterthoughts. In fact, at many colleges, they spend more time considering your supplementary essays than your Personal Essay. They ask those specific questions because that's what they want to get to know about you. Even though these essays can often be short, they are super important and must show that you've taken your time, given thought, highlighted yourself, and done your research. Every word counts.

The Tough Stuff: The Additional Information and Disciplinary Action Sections

u/allurredditsrbelongtous

Would it work for me to write about my mental health issues as my personal statement?

I suffered from anxiety and depression my freshman and most of my sophomore year. I had to be hospitalized part of the year. Now I'm so much better and have reclaimed my place as a top student in my school, but sophomore year tanked. What should I do?

[−] admissionsmom

For mental health issues and any other personal issues that may have affected your transcript and or if there's just something you think that they need to know about to understand you as an applicant better, I recommend that you discuss this in the additional info section of your application. Do this by briefly explaining your issue, then focus on your recovery and how you're handling your problems and then spend the remainder discussing how having gone through your problems will make you a stronger classmate and student on their campus.

anonymous

Is it a bad idea to write about some heavy topics like drinking/drugs/bullying? Or is that taboo?

I actually got an out-of-school suspension last year for smoking weed at school. Idk how to handle this. It was my only time, and I just got reaaallly unlucky. Do I have to even tell the colleges? I have learned my lesson. My parents are mega disappointed in me and even made me go to a rehab group.

[−] admissionsmom

Yes. You'll need to address this in the Disciplinary Action Section of the Common App. You'll approach it in the same way you would any other serious issue. Start by honestly and openly addressing the situation. Don't try to deflect blame; just own up to what you did. Then, after briefly explaining what happened, talk about what you've learned from the experience, how you addressed your issues, and why you are a stronger student because of what you learned.

my thoughts

Generally speaking, the additional info section is perfect for exploring topics you feel are necessary for the admissions office to know about so they can better understand who you are. In fact, I think you should avoid dealing with mental health, learning disability, sexuality, or gender issues in the Personal Essay and leave them to the Additional Info section. This way, you aren't defined by any specific aspect of who you are.

Of course, the Additional Info session is not limited only to those issues. It could be used to explain a death in the family, a severe illness, divorce, or sudden family problem that took a toll on your performance. Or maybe you need to discuss a disciplinary issue that came up while you were in high school in the Disciplinary Action Section. If you were suspended, asked to leave a school, or even expelled, my advice is to treat this issue just as you would the information in the Additional Info section — as an opportunity for a second chance for them to hear your voice and get to know you.

Overall, you should briefly and matter-of-factly discuss the issue, then focus on how you coped or are coping, what positives you have learned from the experience, how you are moving forward and will continue to move forward, how you have learned to handle setbacks, and how having gone through the experience has made you a stronger student. Make sure most of this essay focuses on the now and the positive.

More Additional Info — When You Just Need More Space

Of course, the Additional Info you might want to share isn't just about the bad or hard stuff in your life, you might also want to use it to profile an EC that you didn't have space to fully explain, or talk about some other aspect of yourself that you feel like they should know. Basically, my overall philosophy about the Additional Info section is that if there's info you feel the Admissions Office should know in order to be able to fully and completely evaluate your application, this is where it goes.

For more on writing Additional Info Essays or explaining Disciplinary Infractions, see the relevant chapters.

tl;dr

- Supplementary essays are important. Don't blow them off until the last minute.
- Treat them as a chance for the admissions officers to get to know even more about you.
- A Why College essay is really a Why You essay.
- Make sure they connect back to you and to the college.
- Double- and triple-check to make sure haven't put the wrong name for the wrong college, then feel free to Reduce, Reuse, and Recycle.
- Use the Additional Info section to explain anything you feel they need to know about in order to properly evaluate your application. Briefly address the issues, then focus on the positives of personal growth.
- Own up to any disciplinary issues causing you to be out of school.

CHAPTER 19

Tell Us More –The Additional Info Essay

Personal Essays are supposed to give colleges a window into who you are as a person. But how can the personal essay capture *all* of your hopes, your personality, your dreams, and all you've been through to get to this point? What if you'd like to go into more detail about your experiences and extracurriculars? What about if you've experienced adversity or hardship, and the college really should know about it in order to properly evaluate your application?

Maybe you'd like to expand on one of your activities or ECs, and there isn't room in the provided space? The Additional Info section gives you that space to go into more detail about your activities and their effects on you. Furthermore, there might be aspects of your life that could provide useful context for your application — sexual orientation, gender identity, family income and background, mental health issues, deaths, drug-related incidents, illness, and legal problems. It makes sense to write about these experiences, especially if they've affected your application. Colleges want to know all about you as an applicant, and if you have overcome a difficult challenge in your life or faced a unique obstacle, they want to know about it and how it's reflected in your application.

Keep in mind that I feel like your discussion of these challenges should not be the focus of your Personal Statement. That's because you are much more than your difficulties and issues. You should reserve the Personal Statement for showcasing who you are as a person.

Extenuating Circumstances

anonymous

Low GPA With a Reason

Hi. Due to moderately bad family issues, my 3.8 (uw) dropped to a 3.5 (uw). Issues weren't so bad that life was risked at all, but I was too anxious to do work and was the main psychological dependent for a mentally ill parent for a year. I moved out, which was mentally exhausting and taxing, during junior finals. My school counselor has enough experience with my situation to advocate for me via letter. My extracurriculars are absolutely stellar (since I needed somewhere to go instead of being at home; lots of recognition from regional to international level in relevant subjects to interests).

Will colleges, just in general, understand what happened? I am working hard to achieve a 4.0 (uw) senior year and am retaking the classes that I just couldn't focus on due to the home drama. Are there any schools I should take a special interest in (STEM focus with a mild interest in theater arts minor), or any schools I shouldn't waste my time on?

> [–] admissionsmom
>
> Good for you for working so hard to get your life back in order. It can be very difficult to do under the circumstances you describe.
>
> Have your counselor discuss your situation in the letter. Make sure you and your counselor are on the same page, and your counselor understands the situation.
>
> Then, in your additional information section, write an additional essay (650 words or fewer) about your situation. Be

honest about what happened, but don't spend too much time talking about the issues. Just tell the story as simply as you can. Then spend the rest of the essay discussing how you handled the situation, how you have moved forward from it, and how you have learned and can bring those lessons you've learned into your college experience with you.

what you need to know

Life isn't fair. Bad stuff can hit you hard, adversely affecting your school performance. And that sucks. From family drama to mental illness to substance abuse, you should be proud of yourself for making it through your challenges and moving on to pursue college. And that's the exact attitude to take when explaining these events in your application. One of our parent contributors on A2C, u/Ninotchka, said she heard an AO say they are ok with hearing about your struggle. Just make sure to focus on "the phoenix, not the ashes." To me, that's a perfect metaphor.

In this essay, like in your personal statement, you want to present the very best you on your very best day. When writing about your extenuating circumstances in the Additional Info section, address your issue briefly and straightforwardly without dwelling on it. If you contributed to the situation, whatever it was, own up to it. Take responsibility and don't make excuses.

Next, focus on what you did to take care of yourself and how you handled the situation. Describe how you've moved forward and what you learned from the whole experience. Then write about how you will apply those lessons to your future college career and how you plan to help others with your self-knowledge as you continue to help yourself as you learn more and grow.

Show them that, while you couldn't control the situation before, you've taken steps to regain control over your life and are prepared to be the best college student you can be. Always remember to keep the focus on the positives and what you learned from your experiences. Make sure your essay is at least 90% phoenix, the rest ashes.

If appropriate, you can also consider asking your high school college counselor or a teacher to discuss your situation in a letter to your college. If you go this route, make sure your counselor grasps the reality of the situation so he or she can advocate for you, demonstrating that you have reached out for help and have shown that level of maturity and vulnerability.

Explaining More about your Application

u/chanceme1234321
Can I write about coming out to my parents?

u/allurredditsrbelongtous
Would it work for me to write about my mental health issues as my personal statement?

here's my take

Generally speaking, the Additional Info section is perfect for exploring topics you feel are necessary to understanding who you are. If the other essays, the Personal Statement, or the rest of your application don't give you space to adequately explain everything you want to cover, you can do that in the Additional Info section. I think you should treat this issue as an opportunity for a second chance for them to hear your voice and get to know you.

It doesn't only have to be about a circumstance that undermined your performance in schools or another aspect of your application. You can write about your sexual orientation, gender identity, immigration status, family background, or any other characteristic that has molded you. Do this by briefly explaining the issue, then focus on how you're handling your problems and issues, and then spend the remainder of the discussing how having gone through your problems will make you a stronger classmate and student on their campus.

Make sure most of this essay is on the positive.

Need More Space to Explain Activities?

If you run out of room to explain your activities thoroughly, you can do that here in the Additional Info section, too. You can bullet point some aspects of a certain activity, discuss a few different ones, or write a short essay detailing your involvement in one activity. Basically, this space is available for you to provide whatever context you feel the admissions counselors and readers need in order to understand and evaluate your application.

tl;dr

- If you want to write about challenges you've overcome in your life because that will add important context to your application, I encourage you to write about those situations in the Additional Info Section, not your Personal Statement.
- You can use the Additional Info section to discuss aspects of your life such as sexual orientation, gender identity, immigration status, and family background, to name a few.
- You can also use the Additional Info section to explain specific challenging situations that contributed to a dip in your performance.
- Whatever you choose to write about (and you don't have to), be sure to explain the situation briefly but focus on how you've overcome it and what you've learned from it. Show them that you've grown from the experience and that it will make you a stronger college student.
- Or you might need some space to expand on your Activities. You can do that here, too.

CHAPTER 20

The Yucky Parts — Disciplinary Infractions

Unfortunately, disciplinary infractions happen. They're not good, and it would be easier if you didn't have to deal with them, but by no means is a disciplinary infraction going to derail your college quest completely.

It's easy to get tangled in knots about disciplinary infractions, but you can get past them, learn, and come out stronger no matter how bad you think your offense is.

As James Joyce said, "Mistakes are the portals of discovery." Look, we all f*ck up sometimes, so let's take the focus off the circumstances and instead think about what you learned from your mistake. Where can these discoveries take you? This idea is the key to handling your disciplinary issues on your application. It's also excellent advice to carry with you for the rest of your life.

Minor Infractions

u/chanceme1234321

Oh god someone please tell me I haven't torpedoed my acceptances

So my school has this no-cell-phone rule for classes where you can't even take your cell phone to class. You're supposed to leave it in your locker. Which no one ever does. Basically, I messed up and was checking my phone during class because I was obsessing over finding out if I got a certain scholarship, and of course, my teacher caught me. Now I have an in-school suspension. Because I was trying to see if I got a scholarship for a college, I may get rescinded.

I'm freaking out. How bad is this?

> [–] admissionsmom
>
> When it comes to minor disciplinary infractions, like detention or in-school suspensions, you don't need to worry about it too much. You didn't break the law — you broke a school rule. In-school suspensions probably won't even be reported by your school, and if for some reason they are, you can easily explain it away. If you're worried, you should ask your school counselor about what infractions your school reports.
>
> Seriously, though. Don't give this another thought. Just keep being a good kid.

When It's More Serious

u/stuportrooper

How to talk about MIP?

So I know I've talked about how I was a late-bloomer or whatever, but I haven't really given details on here before. I was going through a tough time because of my parents' divorce during freshman and sophomore year. I didn't handle it well and got into drugs and stuff. And then, sophomore year, I got caught drinking and smoking outside during a basketball game. I got into a lot of trouble. Minor in Possession, suspension, all of it. But it was a wake-up call, the one I needed, and that's why I got myself all the way together.

So now, how do I tell colleges about this? *Do* I tell them about it? My guidance counselor says our school's not gonna report. I don't want to lie, but I don't want to be blocked from good colleges.

here's what you need to know

When it comes to more serious disciplinary infractions, like cheating or fighting or illegal conduct, or something else where you got an out of school suspension, I think it's best to come clean. Be honest. Full stop.

Seriously, I've heard horror stories where, even if the school doesn't report the offense, a "friend" might. And then that non-reporter eventually got rescinded for lying on their application. There is no reason to deal with that stress. So, I suggest you talk to your high school counselor and see if you can come up with a game plan about this.

I know it's embarrassing to talk about, but you can turn the focus away from what you did to what you've learned by baring your soul about how you've grown. If they still can't look past your infraction, then it's not the right place for you.

First, you'll want to address whatever happened in the Disciplinary Section.

Then, briefly tell the story. Step up and take responsibility for your actions. Don't blame anyone else even if someone else provided the alcohol or provoked you or whatever. Spend most of the time talking about what you've learned, what positive impact that lesson had on you, and how you've grown from the experience. End by explaining how the experience will make you a better college student. Here again focus on the positives.

Show them how you took steps toward changing your life. Demonstrate that you won't hide from this event and that you've worked hard to move past it.

tl;dr

- Disciplinary infractions happen. There's no use beating yourself up about something in the past.

- If you have a minor violation on your school records, such as detention or in-school suspension, you most likely don't have to worry about it at all.
- If you have a more serious infraction on your records, such as cheating, fighting, or alcohol/drugs, I think you should come clean and take responsibility. Own up to it, but then instead of focusing on the disciplinary infraction, focus on what you've learned and how you've grown from the experience.

CHAPTER 21

Showing Colleges Some Love — Demonstrated Interest

Let's get one thing straight — I know you think college admissions is fiercely competitive for applicants, but in reality, most colleges are competing against each other for bright students. As many Redditors have pointed out, college is a business, and as such, colleges constantly jockey for position. They want to assemble the best incoming classes they can, and they want to do so while making their yield stats look good ("yield" is the percentage of students offered admission to a school who actually end up enrolling).

Thus, many colleges want to make sure that they only offer acceptances to applicants who are serious about enrolling at their college. This helps the college meet their enrollment goals in a more efficient way. And because so many kids shotgun their college applications and apply to tons of schools, colleges have more incentive than ever to find kids who are more likely to attend if offered acceptance.

That's why, if there's a school you would really like to attend, and they say demonstrated interest is a consideration in admissions, you should definitely show them some love. By the way, you can check what schools consider important for admissions by looking at the *common data set*, which you can find by googling "common data set" + the college's name.

However, keep in mind that while demonstrated interest is critical for more and more schools, the most highly selective schools normally don't measure it. The logic here is that schools like Yale and Harvard already know people are genuinely interested in attending their schools, so they simply don't bother.

Ok, So how do I demonstrate that interest?

u/warrior__princess
How do schools count demonstrated interest?
I am trying to find ways to show demonstrated interest. How do I find schools that want to see my interest in them? I thought about following them on social media. Is that stalker-y? Asking for a friend :)

> [–] admissionsmom
> From my experience, most schools do consider demonstrated interest except for the most highly selective and some really large public schools. You can check on their common data set and see what they say.
>
> And, yes. For some schools that consider demonstrated interest, following them on social media might be one way to show them you're interested if you use your name. Make sure you clean up your social media accounts first though! But mostly, the benefit of following the schools and their admissions offices on social media comes from what you learn about the school and the admissions process. This can be valuable info that can be used in a Why College essay or a Letter of Continued Interest, demonstrating interest that way.

u/roouel
2 Questions on Showing Demonstrated Interest
My ED school doesn't care about demonstrated interest, but I still feel it may be a good thing to show, especially through supplements and other areas.

If I choose to do an off-campus interview in which I learn new things about the school that I want to bring up in the supplement, can I quickly mention in the essay for like one line that "hearing this from an alumni interview made me blah blah blah?" It's only a few words, but it shows my willingness to seek more info about the school (given that interviews are optional).

ALSO, even though my school doesn't care about demonstrated interest, can I still mention all that I did to show my interest in the Additional Info section (going to 2 info meetings, the interview, contacting a former admissions rep, contacting an admissions representative, etc.). I don't have anything else to say under Additional Info, so I thought I could just add this here...is this good?

Thanks in advance!

my two cents

For schools that consider demonstrated interest, it counts. But you don't have to do a ton. To find out if a college values demonstrated interest, all you have to do is check that school's common data set. A simple Google search will tell you if demonstrated interest is important to the school or not by googling the college's name and "common data set."

If it is, here are some ways you demonstrate your interest:

1. Apply Early Decision

The best way is to show demonstrated interest is to apply Early Decision, but you should do that only if the school is absolutely your first choice, and you know your financial needs will be met. (I discuss this more in the Early Decision chapter.) If you can't commit financially or you're not 100% sure it's where you want to be, then strongly consider applying Early Action if that's an option.

2. Submit Your Application Early

Sending in your app early (but not necessarily for Early Decision or Early Action), is also a marker of demonstrated interest for some colleges. They want to know you are a priority for them and submitting early shows that. This doesn't mean that you last-minute procrastinators don't have a chance, especially if you've been demonstrating interest already, but I've heard more than one school say they considered when an applicant submitted their app.

3. Go for a Visit
Colleges like to see that you visited them, so if you can, go for a visit and be sure to go on the official tour and attend the info session. It never hurts to reach out afterward and tell them how much you enjoyed your tour.

If you can visit, but can't go on the official tour or to the info session, you should still be sure to sign in at the admissions office. When you get home that day, send an email with a few details about your unofficial tour and how bummed you were you couldn't be there for an official tour. Ask a follow-up question or two.

If you can't visit, you can let them know that you'd like to visit, but it's financially unfeasible for you.

4. Diversity Fly Ins
Don't forget to sign up and apply for their free diversity fly-ins if you qualify. You can find a list of those on the websites www.getmetocollege.com or collegegreenlight.com. Even if you don't get admitted to them, just applying counts as demonstrated interest.

5. Engage with the Admissions Office
Sign up to have information sent to you on their website — even if you're already receiving mail from them. Open every email they send you and click on the links (if they track interest, then they track this!). Check your spam and trash folders to find emails from them that might've been filtered there. Email your regional admissions officer (you can find out who that is on the admissions website) and ask legitimate questions. Answer emails from them if they email you. Read their website. Click on links. ***Open your portal once you've applied to check on your status.***

6. Attend their local events like Info Sessions and College Fairs
Colleges often attend college fairs and other events around the country, which is great news for those students who can't visit the college itself. If a school you're interested in visits anywhere close to you, go and sign in with your name and email address. Sign in at their tables at college fairs.

7. Get Social
First, clean up all your social media pages and follow the school on Instagram, Twitter, Facebook, and Snapchat. Even if they don't consider your follow as demonstrated interest, they often put out helpful and updated info and links to their admissions blogs. And don't do anything stupid on your social media!

8. "Why College" Supplement
If the college has a Why College supplementary essay, make sure to include details about your visits if you took them, details from reading their website, class and club options, professors who interest you, any contact you had with them at a local event, and also read their student newspapers online to see if you can learn about interesting events or news you might like to mention.

9. Check Your Portal
Once you've applied, be sure to check your portal to see if you are missing documents and to make sure they have everything you need. You don't need to be obsessive about it, but if you are missing something, and they see that you've never checked to find out, that will let them know your level of interest.

tl;dr

- Colleges want to make sure they offer acceptance only to kids that really want to attend. Thus, loads of schools try to measure this factor with the student's demonstrated interest in the school.

- The most highly selective schools don't pay much attention to demonstrated interest (they're pretty confident everyone wants to attend them).
- You can demonstrate interest in a variety of ways — applying Early Decision, applying Early Action, visiting, engaging with schools, getting to know their admissions office, and attending recruitment events and college fairs, if possible.

CHAPTER 22

Up Close and Personal: The Interview

Trust me when I say that a college interview, either on-campus or off-campus, is something to get excited about. This is your chance to have one-on-one, personalized, face-to-face contact with either an admissions officer, current student or an alum. It's the kind of exposure that an application can't capture. In an interview, you can show off your personality, that special spark that makes you—you. You can make it clear to the interviewer what you hope to contribute to the school and what has attracted you to the school.

That being said, an interview may or may not tip the acceptance scale in your favor. Like all the other parts of your application, the interview is merely one factor admissions officers use to put together your student profile and make a decision.

Do the interview. Data for some schools shows a striking difference in acceptance rates for those who interview and those who don't if the opportunity is available to them. So, if the school offers you an interview, it's in your best interest to accept. That's even if they say that the interview is technically "optional" (you do know that there is no such thing as truly "optional" in college admissions language, right?).

Landing an Interview

u/stuportrooper

I still haven't heard from my school about an interview. What should I do?

All my friends in my school are getting emails and calls about interviews. I haven't heard a thing. I'm afraid I'm gonna be skipped over.

> [–] admissionsmom
>
> Please be sure to check your junk/trash emails and make sure your voicemail is cleared out and accepting messages. Also search the word "interview" in your search box in your email. My youngest son missed out on three interviews because he wasn't checking his junk/trash mailboxes!!

a little real talk

Lots of schools have different methods for the way they conduct interviews, so you need to **read their websites carefully.** For some, you are automatically put on an interview list when you apply. For others, you have to sign up and arrange it. Often, this sign-up will have a deadline, and sometimes you have to apply to the school before a certain deadline to eligible for an interview. Some do summer interviews, but most interview in the fall or winter after you've applied.

    Interview time is also an excellent time to start regularly checking your inbox for communications, as well as your spam and junk folders, and make sure you have your voicemail set up and cleared out on your phone. Life Pro Tip: Regularly search your email for the word 'interview" if you aren't seeing interview invites that you're expecting. You don't want to miss any communications from the college (which you should be opening for demonstrated interest reasons), especially not for something like an interview. Note — one of my own children missed three interviews because he wasn't checking.

Most interviews last anywhere from half an hour to an hour, and they usually take place at coffee shops or somewhere nearby if they're not at the college. If you get to pick the place, choose somewhere quiet so you can easily hear each other.

Advice for Nailing the Interview

u/warrior__princess
How to best use the interview to demonstrate interest?
If an interviewer asks me what I like in particular about the school, what should I say? It seems a little silly to talk about the nice weather and the school's ranking...

> [−] admissionsmom
> Campus and weather are ok, but dig much deeper into why the university speaks to you. What kinds of classes, campus traditions, activities, professors, and programs on the campus are interesting to you? What do you see future you doing there? I'd leave out the prestige part.

It's easy to become anxious and stressed about interviews, especially if you're in the midst of the interview swamp right now. It's fun, but it can be a little sticky, and gooey, and uncomfortable. Or dry and desert-like maybe. Or maybe even moist and dessert-like.

Regardless, you can do this! You've made it this far, having surmounted obstacles like grades, extracurriculars, and organizing and preparing your application. So instead of stressing, focus all that nervous energy into what you can do right now: prepare.

Top Ten Potential Questions They Might Ask You

You shouldn't memorize your answers to these questions, but it won't hurt to think a little about your answers. Focus on how these questions can help you authentically present yourself, not how you can make yourself seem like the most impressive, perfect candidate of all time (the interviewer will see right through that).

1. "Tell me about yourself."

2. "What do you like to do in your free time?" Follow-ups: Be prepared to talk about some of your extracurriculars and why you enjoy them, how you got interested in them, etc.

3. "Why X College?" Follow-ups: Here you should have specific details — amazing classes or professors or programs you've heard about. Do not mention the school's ranking in your conversation. Do describe what first drew you to this college and why you think you're a good fit. What will you contribute to the college community?

4. "Why do you want to study X?"

5. "What are your strengths and weaknesses?" As a follow up: What do you do to remedy those weaknesses?

6. "Describe yourself in 1-3 words." Some say one. Some say three. Make them varied, addressing different aspects of you (not just academic, athletic, social)

7. Be prepared to talk about "supplemental essay" questions:

    a. Your favorite X (author, mentor, person, etc.)

    b. An obstacle in your life you've overcome

    c. What has influenced you the most in your life

d. Talk about a time when you had to resolve a conflict

e. Talk about a time you've demonstrated leadership, etc.

8. What are your plans after college? You don't have to be super specific — maybe say what field you're generally interested in, and perhaps offer one or two ideas you have in mind and why.

9. "What would you do differently about high school if you had to do it again?"

10. "If an alien offered to take you on an epic space journey, but you could never see your friends and family on Earth again, would you go?" (In my experience, many interviewers like to throw weird or unexpected questions at you just to see how you react in the moment. Here's another one: "If you were a kitchen utensil, what would you be?")

Preparing for Your Interview

In the days leading up to your interview, instead of preparing and memorizing whole paragraphs to lob at the interviewer, think about why you love the school so much. What is it that you love? Because what you love is the version of "you" that you see there. And "you" will be wherever you go. Figure out how you fit that school (it all comes back to fit!).

I suggest bringing a one-page resume. There are others who disagree with me, so go with your gut, but if the college or the interviewer doesn't explicitly tell you not to bring a resume or anything, I recommend bringing a one-page highlights resume. This way the recommender has something to refer to as they talk to you and as they later write their notes. Simply hand it to them when you meet them. If they toss it to the side or say they don't need it, no biggie. Check the Resume Chapter for tips on how to draft a resume.

Also, bring a notepad and pen so you can take notes if you like.

The night before the interview, do the basic but essential preparation stuff — make sure your outfit is clean, pressed, and ready to go. Check out the route to the interview location to anticipate transportation challenges and make sure you make it on time. Go over the next day's schedule and make sure you've given yourself enough time to get to the interview location and get into the right frame of mind. Get a good night's sleep.

Making a Good First Impression

Appearance

Contrary to what some students believe, you do not need to wear a suit to your interview. But you must have a tidy, neat appearance.

For example, you could wear a clean shirt with a collar, tucked in, and a clean pair of pants or jeans with a belt (if you have pants other than jeans, wear them). You could also wear a clean skirt or pants with a blouse or shirt, tucked in if appropriate. Or you could wear a nice dress (but nothing too fancy). Wash and brush or comb your hair. No need for anything too elaborate, clean and neat hair is fine. Shave or trim your beard, if you have one, so it looks controlled. If your hair looks a little messy and you think you need a haircut, well, maybe get a haircut.

Wear something you are comfortable in, and that makes you feel confident. However, DO NOT WEAR inappropriate t-shirts or dirty, stained, or torn clothes. Avoid t-shirts, hoodies, and ripped jeans if you can — even if they tell you it's casual. Probably don't wear gear from that college—trying too hard. If you wear tennis shoes, make sure you clean them up. Also, I personally feel like you should take out any piercings beyond ear piercings, but maybe that's just me being old-fashioned and frumpy *[AdmissionsSon's note: yes, that is definitely you being old-fashioned and frumpy, though unfortunately many interviewers are also old-fashioned and frumpy. Students, try to gauge your audience a bit with this one. I'd be totally cool with whatever piercings.]*

Arrival

Arrive early, so you don't stress yourself out rushing to the interview. Figure out how early you need to leave to arrive 15 minutes early, and then leave 15 minutes before that time. So yes, you might be 30 minutes early. That's ok. When you get there, go to the bathroom. After you take care of your business, look at yourself in the mirror and put your hands on your hips and stand up nice and tall. Do the Superman Pose and take some deep breaths. It's a thing. Google it.

Introductions

Smile! Don't force a big fake smile, but you're not at a funeral, right? Again, the interview is going to be like a little chat between you and the interviewer. You might as well relax and try to enjoy it a little bit.

Make eye contact. This is very important. Make sure you look the interviewer in the eye, so they know you're engaged and paying attention. But like, not too much. It's not a staring contest. Just be confident but natural.

Introduce yourself. The easiest and most casual, confident way to do this is to simply state your name during the handshake.

Shake hands. Think of a good handshake as about the degree of firmness you would need for a doorknob.

During the Interview

Put your phone away. Silence it and tuck it away. Don't take it out again until after the interview. The only exceptions would be something like they ask to see a picture of an art project you did and you happen to have one on your phone. If you do show them a picture, make sure there's nothing potentially embarrassing to scroll past!

Remember to breathe.

Being nervous is ok. Own it. Many of you are shy and introverted. Lean into your nerves. You can tell the interviewer. They might be introverted too, and this will help them know to help you along. Your interviewer's not looking to catch you in an awkward moment or waiting for a mistake to pounce on. They don't want you to fail. As you respond, think about stories about you that can sum up your responses. I've heard it explained like this before: Imagine you're the parent and they are your baby, and all you have to do is tell them some bedtime stories about your life.

Listen to your interviewer. The one piece of advice that the admissions counselors for colleges ask us to share with you is for you just to come and listen to the questions and respond. Don't come with an agenda of what you want to say or come off as overly practiced. They could end up noting that in their write-up. You don't want to come off as over prepared, but you could consider asking about their experience at the college, what the students do for fun, and if they know anything about the program or major you're interested in.

After the Interview

Ask for a business card so you can write a thank you note to your interviewer! When you get home after the interview, jot down a quick thank you note and send it in. Here's a good rule of thumb — if your interviewer is your parents' age or older, a hand-written thank you note will be great if you have his or her home address (without creepy internet snooping); otherwise, an email is fine. Be gracious, be grateful for their time, and be sure to bring up something they talked about in the email. Don't worry if you don't hear back from them. It doesn't mean anything at all.

Interview Nopes

Don't treat the interview as the magical ritual that will automatically get you admitted to the school of your choice. As stressed above, this should be a conversation, not an audition, not a monologue. You need to treat your interviewer with respect. Above all else, you need to let your best self shine through.

To achieve that goal, avoid these common interview mistakes:

- Arriving late
- Wearing dirty, torn clothes
- Having your phone out/Looking at your phone
- Offering a limp handshake
- Being over-prepped
- Spewing canned answers that sound like you've tried to memorize them
- Coming with an agenda of what you want to or think you should talk about
- Not listening to the interviewer! The number one thing admissions officers and alums tell me to tell students is to LISTEN in interviews. They say far too many students come with rehearsed responses and you are not actually listening and responding to the questions presented to you. Listen. Be present. Smile. Engage. Breathe.

Canceling Interviews

u/CatOwlFilms

Canceling Interview?

I signed up for an alumni interview at Oberlin because I thought I would apply RD, but later on, I decided not to (once EA decisions came out, better options opened for me). Does anyone have any experience in respectfully canceling an interview? It's in a week (if that makes a difference).

> [−] admissionsmom
>
> Just send a short, polite email saying that you've decided not to apply, so you need to cancel your interview.

tl;dr

- There are different ways to get an interview — you might be invited, or you might have to sign up. Keep an eye on your email inbox (check spam and voicemail too).
- Read the admissions page website for more information!
- Don't be upset if you don't get a ton of interview requests, or if you don't get any at all. Lots of kids get into amazing colleges without an interview.
- Don't overthink your interview performance. That means you should not memorize answers ahead of time.
- Before, during, and after the interview, put your best foot forward. Look clean and neat, be attentive and polite, and send a thank you note afterward.

CHAPTER 23

Taming the Admissions Stress Monster

Anytime you put yourself out there, stress can creep up on you, and this applies hundredfold when you're applying to college. Sometimes stress can be good for you, like when you're taking a test or playing a sport, but too much stress can hurt you. And if you don't take steps to limit your stress, it can get ugly.

I call it the Admissions Stress Monster. It's natural, and it's coming your way, but you don't have to be afraid of this monster. Instead, look for ways to calm that beast down and find your Zen in the admissions journey.

Finding your Zen

u/amonaroll

Does anybody else sleep 3 hours at night
Then 5 hours during the day

> [−] admissionsmom
> That's really unhealthy. You should put away all your electronics about 20 minutes before your bedtime and then go to sleep. Your school work will benefit from sleep. You can process and learn better.

u/TheDuke127

The college admissions process is making me sick

In the past 24 hours, I've barfed 10 times and had diarrhea twice. Please just accept me, college.

> [-] admissionsmom
>
> Well, you might have a stomach virus! Maybe see a doctor? But if it is stress, try taking your mind off college. Take some deep breaths, go for a walk, or do something like drawing, cooking, or exercising!

u/Spherical_Melon

Anybody else feel they overestimated themselves?

I sure did. Why did I aim so high? It's been like a wrecking ball to my motivation and self-esteem.

> [-] admissionsmom
>
> First, you have to recognize that it's ok and normal to have these feelings. This is a stressful time, and sometimes you just have to lean into the feelings to get past them. So, go through the frustration, sadness, and worry. That's normal. And right now, this is what it is for you. Give yourself permission to feel stressed out for a few days.

u/NoHopeOnlyRope

Any of y'all feeling a persistent sense of doom?

Like no matter what you do it will always be pointless and you'll fail, so it's not even worth attempting?

"Why bother trying to get a summer job when you know that it will make you even more unhappy?"

"Why try to get an internship when you know that there are so many more qualified candidates?"

"Why go to community college when you know it'll be high school 2.0?"

"Why transfer to a UC when you know you'll be at the bottom of the pack?"

"Why get a master's when it only adds stress and debt while not significantly improving employment chances?"

"Why study what you love when no one cares about what you love?"

"Why try to find a career in your field when it's essentially a dead end anyway?"

"Why bother?"

> [−] admissionsmom
> Dear NHOR,
> I know we've talked many times over the last few months.
> Please try some of the following:
> Go outside and go for a walk.
> Listen to books and music.
> Take care.
> Go see a therapist.
> Please please explore Mindfulness and Mindful Meditation. (How many times have I asked you about that?)
>
>> [−] NoHopeOnlyRope
>> As for the walking thing, I know I should totally do that, it's scientifically proven to make you feel better. Instead, I've been doubling down on TV, junk food, and video games. I consciously know that's a dumb thing to do, but it makes me feel better. The former two provide distractions from my stressors and allow me to forget about my problems momentarily. In a similar vein, video games make me feel like a winner even when I know I'm not. The underlying issue is just me being a weak-willed person. Seriously, go look at my post history, and you'll see that it's 100% annoying insufferable whining.
>>
>> I am trying to be more cope, I know there's literally no upside to rope, I just can't stay on track for longer than a few days-weeks. Forcing positivity and thinking about what I do right does make me feel

well, but then I'm reminded of all the things I don't do well and all the things that could go wrong. I know I'm my worst enemy. I am the "Stupid piece of shit" monologue from Bojack Horseman.

I don't have a therapist anymore. I know that I'm an 18-year-old, which automatically puts me in one of the dumbest and most arrogant subsections of society but holy shit after repeatedly interacting with those people I cannot for the life of me continue to give them any form of respect.

I know I sound hostile. It's because I kinda am. I do not like being lied to or mislead. I'm spicier than Indonesian food, and I've got so much salt in my system that there are actually tiny Mormon settlements in my brain.

> [-] admissionsmom
>
> You know, you won't get anything from therapy or mindfulness or meditation if you don't open yourself to it.
>
> I have two people who are very close to me who were having a difficult time last year. They connected to mindfulness and fought for ways to feel better. I saw it change them. I hope it does the same for you. That's why I push it.
>
> Mindfulness was recommended to me on another subreddit when I went looking for a way to help these important people in my life, and I felt at a loss. Just trying to pay it forward. I'll stop bugging you about it when you tell me you want me to stop.
>
> And keep writing. You got some killer metaphors there:)

let me break it down for you

Everyone has to go on their own journey and find their own way. The college admissions process is no different. What's sad is that a lot of kids beat themselves up for getting "bad" scores and grades, for not doing the perfect extracurriculars, for not being impossible geniuses. They feel like they're letting their families down if they don't get into a "highly prestigious" college. The pressure placed on these kids at young ages is insane. How can you be expected to handle all of that stress before you've even learned the right skills for coping with it? In my opinion, parents and kids across the country, and really all over the world now, are in serious need of some chill pills.

Know this: your mental, emotional, and physical well-being are not worth acceptance to any college. No matter how prestigious. No matter what job you think you'll get when you graduate. Your well-being isn't something to ignore or neglect.

Jon Kabat Zinn says, "Wherever you go, there you are." Don't sacrifice your happiness today because you think it'll make you happier a year from now. Because, guess what? In a year from now, you and your stressed-out self are gonna be right there with you.

As a wise philosopher once said, "YOLO." It's truly freeing when you realize all that matters is the moment you're living in. Instead of worrying about the future and regretting the past, focus on the now. Because that's what's up. You can only control what is happening to you right now.

If you start feeling overwhelmed by that damned admissions stress monster, take a break and step away for a moment. Your feelings are completely normal. I know it's hard to own up to those kinds of feelings, but admitting you're stressed and you need a break doesn't mean you're giving up or that you've failed in any way. Judging yourself isn't healthy, and it won't get you anywhere. Instead, acknowledge and accept how you're feeling. Maybe you'll find some of these suggestions helpful:

1. Recognize that you can only do what you can do.

2. You can't control what the colleges decide and how they evaluate your application. All you can control is your response to their decisions.

3. Understand that you'll have these moments of stress, but that they will pass because they're only feelings. And feelings pass.

4. Work on letting go of the idea of a dream school. Instead focus on the schools that you feel are a good fit for you. At a college admissions conference, I heard one speaker who put it this way: be a sock, not a shoe. While a shoe is rigid and firm, a sock can fit on a whole array of schools.

5. Make sure you have lots of options on your list that you are excited about and that might reasonably accept you, including a Sure-Fire Safety School.

6. Breathe.

7. Be mindful enough to not ignore the admissions stress monster. Simply acknowledging your stress is a challenging and essential step that can help relieve anxiety on its own.

8. Breathe again.

Or to help tame that admissions stress monster, try some of the stuff on this smorgasbord of a stress-zapping list:

- Talk to a counselor or a therapist and tell them how you're feeling.

- Read a book about mindful meditation. One that I love is *10% Happier* by Dan Harris. It's not really for kids, but you might enjoy it. Another book I found helpful is *The*

Happiness Equation by Neil Pasricha. I have lots more books about meditation and mindfulness in the Resources Section.

- Make a list of five gratitudes every day. Studies show that if we can train our brains to focus on three to five things we are thankful for every day, we'll be happier. Taking a minute to recognize the simple stuff, like air conditioning or the texture of peanut butter on your tongue, can actually relieve your stress. You can check out the Gratitude Chapter for more info.
- Do five nice things for other people every day. Even just small things. Help someone at the grocery store get an item off the top shelf. Do the dishes before your parents even ask. Pick up trash off the street. Read a book to someone in a retirement home.
- Get outside. In nature, if you can. It's called green-bathing and is good for the soul.
- Do 3-minute meditations. Sit and focus on your breathing. Don't worry if you have other thoughts that are bothering you. Acknowledge them and go back to your breathing.
- Practice yoga.
- Eat all the healthy food. Veggies and fruit are your friends.
- Take breaks. Let those brain batteries recharge. Your brain requires resets to do its best work.
- Implement no-college-talk zones and times with your friends and family.
- When you start having self-doubts or thoughts that make you feel bad, tell that asshole brain of yours to shut the f*ck up.
- Sing. Dance. Play music. I walk every day outside along the bayou listening to my favorite music and singing at the top of my lungs. Sure, I get a few strange looks, but I

don't care because I've got Freddy and Bob and Bruno and Beyoncé and Taylor and all my other legendary friends to sing with.

"A flower does not think of competing with the flower next to it. It just blooms." ~ Zen Shin

Stop worrying about others. You're not in a "living your life" competition with them. You are just "living your life." Bloom on your schedule. Bloom well. Let other people worry about how and when they will bloom.

Furthermore, don't spend all your time on college applications. Living is about finding a balance that works for you. Keep your hobbies. Get your rest. Don't completely sacrifice your social life or your vacations or summers. If you feel like you're sacrificing, then you haven't found that balance. There will be times when you can't go out, for sure, because you've got a difficult test to study for or a paper to write, but there are other times when you'll have to recognize that socializing is more important than rewriting that paper for the twentieth time. As my mom always said, "Don't let the perfect get in the way of the good." I think Voltaire probably said that before her, but I like to give Mom credit.

Prioritize your school work. Do the stuff you need to do to get into college and do it well. Make the best grades and get the highest test scores you can while staying physically, mentally, and emotionally healthy, and, most importantly, learn. But don't let school work totally consume you. It's all about the balance. Give yourself time to explore and discover your interests. If you find that balance, your college admissions journey will be a much more positive experience. You'll have a better attitude, write better essays, and have a better shot at getting those acceptances.

I just can't deal anymore.

u/Stuportrooper
Freaking out
I think I'm really screwed on college. I'm not the best student in the world, but I've worked my ass off since junior year, and I've done so much better, but I just know it won't be enough. I can't stop thinking about all the time I wasted and how I've shot myself in both feet. I feel lost. Exhausted. I don't want to deal with this anymore. I don't want to deal with anything anymore.

> [–] admissionsmom
> I'm so sorry you're going through this. If you're experiencing suicidal ideation at all, it's essential that you get help and fast. Please do these things right away:
>
> • Talk to your parents, your school counselor, or a trusted adult and tell them what you're feeling.
>
> • Ask your parents to find you a therapist and tell them why.
>
> • Call the suicide hotline and talk to them. http://suicide-hotlines.com/national.html
>
> It feels terrible now, and you should acknowledge that. Try to breathe. Take five minutes and just sit still and focus on your breathing. These feelings are not who you are. You're so much more than this. They're just really shitty feelings. And feelings are ephemeral — they'll go away.

If you are feeling at all suicidal, please get help. Right now. Today. Don't wait.

I want you to call a suicide hotline right now. Here's a number for one of them: 1-800-273-8255, and I have more resources at the bottom of this post. Talk to your parents. Today. Tell them what you're going through. And, if necessary, ask your parents or a friend or a neighbor to take you to the closest emergency room. Tell your parents you need a counselor or therapist. See your school counselor. It's essential that you get help and fast.

I'm not a therapist, psychologist, or psychiatrist. I'm just a mom, a teacher, and an educational consultant, and I've never gone through the specific pain you are going through. But, I've learned that when you feel like life is beating you down, your brain actually makes physical changes and isn't working properly. You can't trust it to make wise decisions. It was described to me as if someone was putting heavy weight after weight on your brain - eventually, it's going to collapse.

I want you to promise that you will seek help before you do anything to hurt yourself.

And get outside and go for a walk. But that's not instead of calling the suicide hotline, talking to your parents, and getting a therapist. Those are imperative. Take care. People care about you. I know it seems random and strange that people you've never met before are here for you. But we are. Call the hotline now.

More resources:

National Suicide Prevention Lifeline: 1-800-273-8255 (TALK)

National Hope Network: 1-800-SUICIDE (1-800-784-2433)

National Hope Network: https://www.imalive.org/

www.crisischat.org

Online Chat: http://chat.suicidepreventionlifeline.org/ GetHelp/LifelineChat.aspx

Crisis Text Line: Text "START" to 741-741

https://www.reddit.com/r/SuicideWatch/wiki/hotlines

my thoughts

Your lives are about so much more than college acceptances. I know for some of you that's hard to understand right now, but please know that you'll find your way and will become the person you want to be wherever you end up.

I've had my share of f*cked up, shitty experiences when I didn't know where to turn. It really hurts. What I discovered was that I had to go through the pain. I had to experience it to move forward and beyond it. I call it "going on a bear hunt," like the children's book. My therapist calls it going through the train tunnel. I walked through that swishy-swashy grass and thick gooey mud. I didn't go over it. I didn't go under it. I went through it. I went through that tunnel of shittiness and pain and came out the other side stronger and more of a badass. You will, too.

tl;dr

- It's completely normal to be stressed out about one of the most important milestones of your life.
- Sometimes you simply have to lean into your stress and anxiety and let it be.
- Investigate your feelings.
- Learn about Mindfulness and Meditation. You can read more about it in the Mindfulness Chapter
- Try yoga.
- Go outside.
- Eat healthy food.
- Explore gratitude.
- Take breaks so your mental and emotional batteries can recharge.
- Breathe.

CHAPTER 24

Grow Your Attitude of Gratitude

Throughout this book and all over my Reddit posts, I aim to actively cultivate an environment of gratitude.

Every once in a while, especially around stressful dates like application deadlines and decision days, I like to encourage students to take a break from college admissions and focus on the good things in life. It's vital to keep sight of what's important in life because college is just one piece. Yes, college has the potential to be a life-changing experience, and there's a lot of pressure to do well, but college isn't worth forgetting about your family, your friends, and all the beautiful parts of life that make you feel content and special.

That's why, in November, I like to encourage students to share what they're thankful for. It can be anything, but they have to share at least one thing. This helps them break out of the college application stress cycle, where it's so easy to think nothing will ever go right and focus on all the good things in life.

Plus, in all honesty, being mindful and feeling gratitude will make you a stronger person more in touch with who you are, and guess what? That leads to your being a stronger applicant! So, it's really just a big win/win all around.

Thankful Thursdays

u/admissionsmom
Thankful Thursdays

This month, I'm inviting you to pause from the frenzy and think about what you are thankful for in your life and, if you like, share one thing here. Research shows that people who stop and take a minute every day to have gratitude are happier in general. Also, pausing for a minute to focus on the positive helps you reset and become a happier healthier person leading to becoming a stronger applicant — so I'm really not veering away from the admissions journey here.

I'll start: this morning I'm grateful that I have my new rescue kitten, Harvey, in my life. She is so much fun to watch as she chases balls all over our house like a puppy, and she's so happy to be with us and shows that with lots of kitty cuddles!

> [–] TwinPurpleEagle
> I'm extremely thankful for my school administration and teachers who helped me get out of an abusive home life last month. Yeah CPS had to be called, and I was angry about it at first, but now I'm thankful someone did something.
>
> > [–] admissionsmom
> > I'm super grateful to them, too. I hope you are safe and happy and moving forward in your life now. They are brave people to make that call for you, and you are a brave person for allowing yourself to be helped eventually. Please let them know how much you appreciate their efforts. A note or email would mean the world to them.
>
> [–] stiffspaghetti
> I'm grateful for Reddit
>
> > [–] admissionsmom
> > Me 2!!!

[-] nc4228
I'm thankful that I found a new game osu! To play in my free time between psets, piano lessons, midterms, labs, and the rest of the shitstorm.

[-] crowbarmlgjenkins
I'm thankful I finally submitted my EA and ED applications!!

u/admissionsmom
I'm grateful for my mom.
She was an amazing force in my life. She always saw the best in others and had high expectations for them at the same time. She helped many, many people turn their lives around, and she was an amazing example for me. She was dedicated to helping low-income, first-gen college kids get an education. She taught me that I am in control of my future and that life sucks sometimes, but that doesn't mean I am a sucky person. My mom had some bad shit happen to her; her life wasn't perfect. She was a college drop-out and a single mom, but she graduated from college at age 44 and then went on to get her masters. After that, she developed and was the head of the Early Childhood Department at her local college until she died a few years ago. I help out here on A2C partly in homage to her, so I'm grateful to her for leading me here to you, too! I miss her every day, but I'm thankful I had her in my life and that I had a mom who supported me no matter what decisions I made or whether she agreed with them or not

[-] heymylittlefishies
Honestly, I'm just thankful that this sub and people like you exist. It gives me hope and encouragement and makes me realize I'm not alone in this. So yeah, thank you for existing. I'm sure your mom would be so proud of you, /u/admissionsmom!

[-] FeatofClay
I am thankful that we have such a diverse set of colleges available. I know it can be confusing for students because

there is so much variety, but ultimately, it's a great thing that so many options are on the table for students, and that they nearly all have something special and desirable to offer.

u/admissionsmom

Today, I'm taking a moment to be thankful for my friends.
I'm not a hugely social person, but I do have a few very close friends who I know I can go to if I ever need support or an ear, but mostly I have fun with them. We laugh and walk together and listen to music and watch movies and just hang out and enjoy being together. When I was younger, I was even more of an introvert and didn't really realize the value of my friends because I spent most of my time reading. Now, I'm so happy that I have created these bonds with some very special people.

> [–] iphsyko
> I'm thankful for my friends too, and I love how you put it - sometimes it's just nice to "hang out and enjoy being together." I can't really find the words to describe the relationships with my best friends right now. I think the best way I can say it is that they are people I don't see leaving my life anytime soon. And it's like we're living life together - sharing, learning, and growing together.

> [–] carmy00
> I'm thankful for my guidance counselor. She has allowed me to challenge myself and create the schedule I want. Also, thankful for the opportunity to even go to and afford college, especially with options! I've gotten into 3 schools with merit $$$ from each, and it's amazing to know that these schools are all affordable! I thought that I'd only have one school offering significant FA, so now I'm really looking forward to visiting these schools and hearing back from my other ones. I never would have imagined it working out this well!

This is it: Decision Day Gratitudes

u/admissionsmom

Dear Beautiful Seniors

This is THE Day you've been waiting for. For many of you you've been waiting for this day – not since Dec. 31 or the fall sometime when you hit submit on your apps, but for years. And as I think many of you recognize, some of you are going to be extremely disappointed today, and others will be over-the-moon excited. I want to tell you how proud I am of each and every one of you. In all the months that I've been on this subreddit nagging at you to remember to breathe and to keep life in perspective and to open your mind about colleges, I've seen such growth in many of you. I've seen you mature from kids, who seemingly only care about prestige and where you get in and writing obnoxious braggy essays, to young adults, who are giving each other truly awesome advice and pieces of wisdom. It has been an amazing process to watch. Your support for each other is real. I'd never been part of an online community before or spent any time online actually, and I had no idea what to expect, but I certainly wasn't expecting this level of bonding and care for each other. You all are incredible kids. You really need to remember that today. And tomorrow. And next week. And next year.

So, I want you to do me a favor today. Going to take the focus off college acceptances for just a few minutes. I want each one of you to write to me today and for the next few days or the next week or hell, forever, and tell me three things in your life you are grateful for. You come from around the world and so many different circumstances, and I know many of you have struggled with parts of your lives. I've heard your stories, but today I want to focus on the good stuff. Big or small.

I'm thankful for my own kids. They are a little wacky. All very different and from them I've learned that there is no one certain way to live life. I have my oldest son, who's going the path-following route and becoming a doctor. And I have my middle, who turned down Columbia and NYU law schools to become a sculptor and part-time improv artist. And then there's my baby, a happy recent college grad, who just landed an internship with a documentary company and is looking for a job in the creative industries, but really who knows? They are all smart, yes, but I'm most thankful for the fact that they are nice.

> [–] GammaHuman
> Alright. I'll try to do my 3.
>
> 1. I am thankful to know where I am attending university and having a University to attend in the first place. Months ago, I would have said that I wouldn't be going to Texas A&M, but now I'm so excited to go. I get to be there with my brother. I'll be in the business program, and I'm gonna live on campus. The rec shouldn't go under construction anytime soon. I'll get to yell at anyone wearing a hat in the MSC. I won't be in the corps, but I sure as hell won't be a 2 percenter! [*admissionsmom note*: As a proud Longhorn myself, it kills me to have to explain that a 2 percenter is a disparaging term used to describe someone who attends Texas A&M University but has no school spirit and doesn't participate in Aggie traditions. HOOK 'EM!]
>
> 2. I'm thankful for my parents, for letting me decide what I wanted to do and where I wanted to attend. In conjunction with that, I'm thankful for being in a financial situation where I don't have to worry too much about the cost of attending school.
>
> 3. I'm thankful for all the music that has ever existed. While I don't listen to a majority of it, the songs I have been listening to have helped me get through this crazy process. Whether it was Taylor Swift's *Safe and Sound* on repeat after I got denied from UT, or Noname's *Telefone* being played on the commute to and from school, music has helped me understand that I'm not alone in whatever I've been feeling.

4. An extra one! I'm thankful for this sub and all its contributors. Especially you admissionsmom. Thank you! I may not have gotten the responses I hoped for, but I've become a better person since this process started and I have to credit all the contributors here for that. My mentality wouldn't have been the same without the folks here. Thank you for this post admissionsmom, and thank you to your sons for introducing you to the sub. :)

[–] USS-Enterprise

10 things I'm thankful for [yes, I know you only asked for three:')]

1. I'm thankful for my best friend. She's the sweetest person alive, and I love her so much. She's supported me since middle school, puts up with my weird quirks, and gives the best hugs. We're not going to the same college, and I'm going to miss her a lot... She gives A+ advice, is so generous with her time, is willing to chat about anything from literature to ice cream flavors, and lets me draw her. :') There's a reason I call her ma princess. <3

2. I'm so thankful for this subreddit. I've made so many friends on here; it really feels like we're a community. We make fun of CC [*AdmissionsMom's note:* "College Confidential"] for a wide variety of reasons, but what makes /r/A2C really special is the love and support. Thanks for both the shitposts and the camaraderie for the past few months, A2C. <3 <3 <3

3. I'm thankful for my dad. I won't say he's an über-supportive parent because he's mostly left me alone throughout this whole process. But I'm thankful that he loves me and is proud of me regardless of what happens. <3 He always makes me laugh and feel better, whether I need it or not. I'm thankful for the connection we have; he understands me, and we don't need that

many words to converse. I'm especially thankful that he's driven me whenever necessary for most of the past 16 years:')

4. I'm thankful for music. I don't know where I would be if I didn't have my favorite two songs to listen to. Both genuinely feel like magic; they make me feel like I can do anything, but more importantly that we can do anything together. They're one of many reminders I have that there's so much to explore in this world.

5. I'm thankful for literature and poetry and words, too. They're escapes into a new universe, into lives that I will never know, but I'm grateful because they remind me of the possibilities of life. I'm grateful that they remind me that happy endings are possible, love is possible, joy is possible.

6. I'm thankful for paper and paint and pencils and pens. Partly because of the alliteration ;) but mostly because of what is possible in their combination. I've been contemplating the work Nighthawks [by Edward Hopper] lately, and it makes me think of college admissions. We're all trapped, in our own ways, by this process. But this sub contradicts that. A2C has allowed me to turn to my side and chat with the person next to me at the counter. But I digress: I'm grateful to art for the representations it gives, for the truth it reveals. I'm also grateful for the distractions it has given me from countless lectures. :)

7. I'm pretty thankful for cameras, too...I love capturing the world around me. However, even more than that, photography taught me that noticing the beauty in the world is a choice. I try to make the choice to see beauty as much as possible. :')

8. I'm thankful that I'm not allergic to milk. I love milk and cheese and chocolate and ice cream, and I'm thankful

I can eat them. They make me happy, and I'm going to eat way too much ice cream today. :)

9. This one is a weird one, but I'm thankful that I'm able-bodied because working out has been my most intense stress relief lately.

10. I'm thankful for the existence of caffeine. Actually, I don't care much for caffeine [it actually makes me sleepy], but I love the taste of both coffee and tea, and I wanted to combine both into my 10th point. They relax me when I need to be relaxed. :)

Finally, I'm thankful for YOU, admissionsmom, for allowing me the opportunity to write this all out and reading it, and for the reminder to appreciate all of the wonderful things I have. <3 :)

[−] szi8890

My brother (and family). I appreciate my parents a ton: for raising me, for taking care of me, and for supporting me. But my brother has been extremely great throughout this entire process. He constantly checks up on me, and even though stuff doesn't always go the way I want it to (quite a bit because I have taken numerous rejections whoops), I appreciate the dog videos he sends me and the reality checks he gives me.

This is kind of an awkward thanks, but I really appreciate my freshman year AP World Teacher and my AP Lit teacher... This is weird, but I had a really rocky freshman and sopho-more year where my dad physically and verbally abused (idk if that's a strong word but). I had low self-esteem, and honestly, sometimes I think of him (my teacher) as a father figure in my life who's been there to talk about literally any-thing from life to art to throwing books out windows...

I'm thankful to be alive in this generation and thriving in my existence. I'm so blessed to be able to have the opportunities to try new things. I've started rock climbing, started cooking and baking a lot more, and just talking to more people. Also, I really freaking love math and having THE INTERNET at my disposal is honestly one of the greatest gifts of life. And just talking with other humans. Experiencing emotion. Laughter, kindness, caring, and joy. Having the friends to get me through to the end, no matter what. EVEN WHEN I CAME OUT LMAO OH GOD THIS STORY's REALLY AWKWARD BUT IF YOU'RE READING THIS I WROTE THE DUKE OPTIONAL ESSAY ABOUT ME STRUGGLING WITH BEING BI, AND THEN I SENT IT TO A FRIEND WHO DIDN'T KNOW THAT AND WAS LIKE WOAHHHH DUDE AND I ACTUALLY SCREAMED A LITTLE INSIDE. Ok yeah. But friends are great, and I love having them.

Also, I'm thankful that people here are supportive and, as cliché as it sounds, people like you admissionsmom, who enjoy and support other people's successes and existence :)

Also books.

Ok, I'm done.

my thoughts

Try to take some time every day, even if it is literally just one minute, to be grateful for the things you have and the incredible parts of your life. Everyone has something to be grateful for, whether it is family or friends or food, or even the simple fact that you are alive today, or healthy, or that you have a pet or a piano recital or someone in your life who wants you to be happy.

When I asked A2C for their gratitude lists on College Decision Day, their lists were interesting — and so cool. Yes, they were grateful for their parents, along with family, friends, teachers, and pets, but they also included responses like:

*all the music that has ever existed

*air conditioning

*chocolate – of all kinds

Each of them mentioned that taking time out from that stressful day to appreciate the goodness of their lives — no matter how difficult their lives seemed — lightened their mood and made them take a minute to reflect on what was important in life.

Have gratitude for the little things, because a compilation of the world's little things is what makes the best big things possible. The insignificance of not having traffic on your way to school or work can brighten your whole morning. The insignificance of your mom buying your favorite cereal can mean the world to you. The insignificance of your pet coming to smile at you is what makes your day. The seemingly insignificant is beautiful — be grateful for it.

Why not take a minute today or this weekend to write some thank you notes to your teachers, counselors, friends, and family who have helped you along on your journey? This will be a good way to help you focus on the positives, even if it feels like life might not be so positive.

tl;dr

- I encourage you to notice new things you're thankful for every day.
- Be specific about what you're thankful for, and think about the details.
- It's ok to focus on something you might think is insignificant or normally take for granted.
- Take time to write thank you notes and acknowledge those who are helpful along your life's journey.
- A gratitude journal can be a great way to help you focus on the positives in your life.

CHAPTER 25

Mindfulness – An Admissions Journey with Intention

College is supposed to be one of the most exciting times of your life. However, for many students, the college admissions process causes a huge amount of stress and unhappiness that can get carried away by our thoughts. Some people call these rampant, racing thoughts your "monkey mind" or your "puppy mind," or even your "asshole brain." But by learning to focus inward and practicing the techniques of mindfulness, you can become aware of your thoughts and feelings to understand them better and start actually enjoying the college admissions journey.

Focus on the opportunity, not the obstacles.

Here's the truth: there are a bunch of well-qualified students your age who are all fighting to get into the same schools you want to get into. And not all of you can go. That's simple math. Instead of focusing on where you might NOT get in, focus on what lies ahead for the places you DO get in. This is the first time you really get to take the reins of your life. This is what freedom feels like. And you should enjoy that.

Remember that the key to your college admissions journey is YOU. You're the one who'll be going to school there, living there, and putting in the hours, no one else.

We all have stress in our lives; the difference is how we respond to it. Maybe some of these suggestions can help you out a little with taming that admissions anxiety. I cover many of these ideas throughout the book, but I wanted to bring a little collection of them in one place.

Honesty is everything.

One of the biggest keys to mindfulness is being honest with yourself. If you feel the need to lie on your college application, either by inflating your extracurriculars, misrepresenting your background (yes, this really does happen), or even fabricating why you want to go to that school, then it's time to take a step back and ask why you're not being honest.

My opinion is that you shouldn't go to a school that the real you can't get into. After all, do you really want to spend your entire college experience pretending to be someone else? Four years is a long time to keep up that charade. There's also this feeling of relief that will wash over you once you decide just to be you. I'm not saying all your stress will be gone, but accepting what you can and can't do about your admissions journey is a huge step forward.

Just breathe.

No matter how much mindfulness you attain, there will, of course, be some stress along the way. And some stress can be good, even necessary, to achieve goals. It's all about finding balance.

But, when you do feel overwhelmed, whether it's by test prep, personal essays, or deciding where to go, make sure to take time to drop everything and recharge your batteries. I always tell students to remember to breathe, and while that may sound simple, I promise it helps. Just give it a try.

Take time to exercise or go for a long walk. Read a book that you actually want to read, not one that counts for credit. Let yourself get bored for a bit. Maybe even play some video games to unwind — in moderation of course.

Meditation helps too. Short, five to ten-minute meditations can open up whole new pockets of your brain that you didn't even know were there. It can be like giving that puppy brain a bone or getting the tetris shapes in sync.

Get thankful.

Many students find the college admissions process to be extremely negative. It can start to feel that it's all about what everyone else has and what you don't.

Make it a point to list five things you're thankful for every day. Studies show that if you focus on gratitude, you'll start to feel more content. It's just how our brains work. And they don't have to be big, sweeping declarations. Simple stuff like the cool side of your pillow on a hot night or the softness of your kitten's fur is totally valid.

Focus on what you do have and not what you don't. Self-doubt gets you nowhere. You're in control of your thoughts a lot more than you think.

Live in the now.

Look, being a teenager sucks sometimes. Everyone knows that. But it's also this narrow, little window in our lives that we can literally never get back to again. So, don't spend your remaining teen years stressing about adulthood. Trust me when I tell you there will be AMPLE time for that later. You also can't waste time worrying about the mistakes you've already made. NO ONE gets through this time without making them; it's how you grow.

Today is the day you can make changes. You can't go back and change anything from your yesterdays, and it's impossible to control your tomorrows. What you have is what you can do today.

Live in the now. Do nice stuff for others. Sit outside. Sing. Dance. Even if you feel silly doing so.

Take life in. Be a teenager, as lame as that sounds.

Right now, this is what it is: dealing with feelings.

And when your feelings and doubts start to get the better of you, take a step back and remember RAIN, a way of understanding that it's important to pay attention to and accept our feelings, but also to be aware that they are separate from us, and they are fleeting.

RAIN is all about:

Recognizing your feeling.

Accepting that feeling instead of pushing it away.

Investigating why you feel that way.

Naturalize your awareness of the feeling, but don't identify with it. It's a feeling. It's not you.

Talk to someone.

When things start feeling like too much, talk to someone about how you're feeling. Find a person you're comfortable sharing your thoughts and fears with. Simply venting can take a considerable weight off your shoulders. Keeping everything inside definitely doesn't help anything. Some studies say that happier people are actually the ones who recognize their unhappiness. They don't sweep it under the rug. They confront it and ask why.

Go on a Bear Hunt.

Going on a Bear Hunt is a British children's story and chant; it's also a metaphor for overcoming challenges while keeping a mindful outlook on life and understanding that, in order to reach our goals, there is no avoiding the challenges, struggles, and pain that we might meet as we go on our journey through life. We can't go over them. We can't go under them. We can't go around them. We have to go through them. A simple story, nevertheless, the book holds an important and valuable lesson about overcoming adversity.

On a bear hunt, to be successful and find that bear (or calm your asshole monkey mind), you have to go through all sorts of stuff to get there, like swimming through deep mud and walking through the tall swishy grass. You can't go over it. You can't go under it. You can't go around it. You have to go through it.

Make your way through the train tunnel.

Related to going on a bear hunt. If you are feeling stressed and in that stress tunnel, you have to make your way through to the other side. If you try to put your stress aside and hope it goes away, you are going to be stuck in that tunnel for a loooong time.

First, visualize a train tunnel. Let's say right now your asshole mind has caused a breakdown and you are stuck in the middle of the tunnel. If you don't deal with your feelings, you're going to be stuck there. So, let them in and move through them to the end of the tunnel.

Meditate mindfully.

I started meditating a couple of years ago after I went through some pretty hard times in my life. Like many of you, I thought I could never meditate. I don't like to sit still. My mind is always racing. And I just knew there was no way I could "clear my mind." But, I decided to give it a try anyway because I needed something to help me deal with the feelings I was having. What I learned was life changing! You don't have to clear your mind. You do have to sit still for the most part, but I can actually do that for a few minutes or even more.

Mindful meditation, even for five minutes or ten minutes a day, is very helpful. You can try it for even two or three minutes. Set your timer on your phone. Sit in a comfortable but upright position and close your eyes or let them rest on the floor. Breathe normally and focus on your breath. If you find that your mind has wandered, that's success! Simply bring it back to focusing on your breath. The more you notice your mind wandering, the more mindful you are being. And when you can notice where your mind is and what it's doing, you can, with practice, learn to have more control over it. The whole point is to get comfortable with being with yourself — not to relax or clear your mind.

Think of your thoughts as a flowing river carrying you along. Being mindful can give you a chance to get out of that river and climb up on the bank and watch the river of thoughts flow by. Or you can imagine your thoughts as clouds floating by, just moving right along. Imagine your mind is like a snow globe that you shake up. When you allow it to settle down, then all the "snow" settles, and the view becomes clear. Or if snow globes don't float your boat, you can imagine your mind as a pond after you've thrown some rocks into it. Meditation helps you to calm the surface of the pond, allowing your brain to settle and letting the view become clearer.

You are the fire.

Sometimes it will feel like you've been thrown into the fire when you're feeling overwhelmed by all the deadlines, essays, and forms to fill out, but the real fire burns within you. When you practice meditation, and focus on your breathing, you're giving oxygen to your fire. Keep that fire burning with your practice. In fact, as you continue your practice, you'll learn that you're not thrown into the fire — "You are the fire," as Mama Indigo would say.

> Check out Meditation Apps. My favorites are *10% Happier* (Jeff Warren is my go to Mindfulness Teacher on the app, but there are a kajillion others who are equally amazing) and *Koru Mindfulness*. I've also heard good stuff about *Calm*, *Headspace*, *Waking Up with Sam Harris*, and *Smiling Mind*.

tl;dr

- Stress happens.
- Anxiety is inevitable.
- The only thing you can control about any situation is your response.
- Be honest with yourself and others — especially on your college applications.
- Try meditation.
- Talk to someone.
- Go through your feelings. Experience them — don't suppress them.

CHAPTER 26

Dealing with Your Parents

One of the reasons I call myself "AdmissionsMom" on r/ApplyingToCollege is because I wanted to emulate that parental vibe for kids. I wanted to make it clear that I would be a warm and affirming but honest and straightforward presence on the subreddit. I wanted them to feel like they could trust me even when we disagree and that, at the very least, I had their best interests at heart.

I recognize that not all of you have that kind of relationship with your parents, and college admissions can make it even worse. Unfortunately, many parents feel immense amounts of pressure about your college decision (even though they're not the ones going to college). They could feel pressure about the financial burden of college, the perception of prestige, or your chances of being able to lead fulfilling, independent lives.

More times than not, parents can turn that pressure on you (as if you don't have enough to deal with). They shouldn't do that, but they do.

Look, most parents want what they think is best for their kids. But sometimes they don't know enough about the process to be helpful. I mean they probably know this on some level, which only makes them feel more helpless and less capable of protecting you.

So, whether you like it or not, you are going to be the one who has to open your parents' minds to the realities of modern college admissions (in the United States, at least). It is truly a different world than the one they went through back in their day, assuming they even experienced American college.

How to Handle Parents

u/allurredditsrbelongtous

Too much

I can't deal with my parents right now. They have really high expectations of me that aren't even about me. They're convinced I should not only do engineering but that I have to go to either Georgia Tech or Carnegie Mellon. They refuse to admit that even if my grades were good enough to go to either school (they're not) that it's tough to be accepted. I want to go to my state school, but that's not good enough for them, and they say I can't even apply there. They won't shut up about it. What should I do? I'm worried that because of my parents' anxieties I won't get in anywhere since they don't even want me to apply to my safety.

[–] stiffspaghetti

Make the argument that you should apply just in case and that you can always transfer to a better school later on

[–] admissionsmom

I think you should consider making a PowerPoint or some other visual slideshow to explain your points to your parents. I've had other kids do it, and it seems to have been successful. Present your arguments about your chosen schools. Show them how they fit you. Show them what you love about the school, professors, classes, and potential activities, and be sure to include stats about graduation rates, research, job placement, opportunities, and the career center.

u/USS-Enterprise

This is a vent, with bad formatting and possibly [probably] TMI

Hey, fam, my parents are being really crappy, and it's getting to the point where I can't keep brushing it off. My mom has been guilt-tripping me with how she did "so much" for me to get into MIT when she's literally only driven me to a few activities, and not in the past year and a half. I was explaining to her then that the two colleges I'm considering are actually pretty good, and I'll be fine, she thinks I'm trying to justify my failure. She keeps telling me that I should've applied to CS, which I hate, or I should go into medicine because she needs to live through me, or pharmaceutical shit. I told her I didn't want to do pharmaceutical stuff because of the ethics, and she told me I shouldn't care about that, and I need to focus more on the money. I explained to her that I also have no possibility of top colleges because of shit ECs, and she pretty much said that I should have done ECs then.

my take

First of all, if your parents are putting added stress on you, I'm so sorry you're going through this. I'm sure you're feeling super frustrated like you're at your wit's end. It's hard to understand this, but most of the time, your parents are coming from a position of love — and fear.

They are terrified of putting you out into the wild, unprepared and defenseless. They are fearful of and for your future. They are also afraid of losing control over you. Sadly, some parents don't know exactly how to show their love, and instead, allow themselves to become wrapped up in their fears.

Consequently, that means you have the opportunity to help them turn it around by understanding that their nagging and prodding and hurtful words are fear-driven. Now, understanding that fear does not mean giving into it. It's more about internalizing and accepting who you are and who they are instead of resisting. If you have the inner strength to understand yourself (and that takes time and is a struggle for anyone, much less a teenager), then when the battles come up, you can hold onto yourself a little tighter. That doesn't mean you fight more or even disobey them. That means that you live your life in a way that is respectful to both your parents and yourself. Don't lose sight of who you are.

The fact is that many of you are just going have to find ways to communicate your needs with your parents and recognize their fears. In the end, all you can do is control your own behavior. One day I hope to have a revolution of super chill polar bear parents, but until then, you will simply need to work things out on their terms while keeping a tight hold of who you are.

Here are some ways to go about doing that:

1. Get outside and go for a walk to clear your head.

2. Try talking to your parents and explaining to them the impact their words are having on you. Try writing out what you want them to hear from you. If you're feeling really down, tell your parents you need a counselor or therapist. Or, if things are bad, find a trusted adult to talk to, fast.

3. If your parents don't approve of your top-choice school, create a presentation. Break down your choice based on the factors that are important to you, like school culture, cost, freshman retention rate, graduation rates, weather, professors, job placement, career center, advising, etc. Show your parents that you are serious about this and you have made a serious effort to ease their apprehensions. Cover all their arguments and let them know that you have been listening and understand their point of view. Show them the benefits of the school where you want to go and why other schools aren't as good a fit for you.

4. I think it's imperative for your parents to know and understand that their point of view is being heard and considered. When they're talking, repeat their words back to them — this is a technique called Active Listening. Let them know you're listening. Be patient with them. This, your burgeoning independence, is scary for us parents, too. Make sure they know that you are still going be their child, but that you are coming into your own.

5. Also, compliment their parenting. Let them know that they've done such a fantastic job of parenting you and teaching you that you are ready for the next step, and you are so grateful that they've provided such a fantastic foundation for you. I mean, don't force yourself to lie — I know some parents are...well...the worst. But most parents at least did something good for you, and many did lots of good things.

6. I also suggest — for all rising seniors and even juniors, too — that you make a No-College Talk Zone or time period in your house. In my house, it was our kitchen table. That way my kids knew that they weren't going to be interrogated by their somewhat college-admissions-obsessed mom (but in a totally good way) while having dinner or eating a snack. It helped keep some balance in our lives.

I know it's intimidating to sit your parents down like this, but it's worth a shot. You may be surprised at how much you can assuage their fears and anxieties by showing them the smart and competent person you are. I speak from personal experience after all. If my kids had wanted to go to some college I was not excited about, then I would have been worried and anxious. However, I would have much, much, much rathered that they explain their plan and be honest with me about how they planned to approach the college process. If my kids had had a great plan they believed in, I would have tried my damnedest to respect it, understand it, and appreciate their reasons.

tl;dr

- When parents give you a hard time about college admissions, they're usually acting from a place of fear that they won't be able to protect you.
- Many parents don't understand today's college admissions process, which contributes to their fears.
- You have the power to educate them on the process and on your reasons for selecting your top choice schools.
- Sit your parents down. Make a presentation with your reasoned, detailed argument for your college choices. Answer their questions. Make them feel heard. Thank them for molding you into the independent, confident person you are today.
- Just because you listen to them and are respectful of them doesn't mean that you have to let go of who you are. Hold on tight to that. You have that no matter what.

CHAPTER 27

Hello, Parents. This is just for you.

Parents, we have a problem. I'm going to be real and upfront with you from the beginning here. Some of you are stressing your kids out. A lot. I understand that this is a stressful time for you, too (I've been there — three times), and I get that there's a lot at stake here. But let's keep in mind that there's more at stake here than college admissions — you have to worry about your child's health and wellbeing, emotionally, physically, and mentally. This is the time when you need to really dig into your reserves and start modeling behavior for handling life's stressful times, because we all know that this won't be the last time they encounter stress, right?

Delve into your own personal quest for mindfulness, yoga, meditation, and better physical health if that interests you, but no matter what you do or how you go about it, please model to your kids that their lives are about more than college acceptances. Take a break to talk to them about other aspects of your life and theirs. Recognize that their odds of getting into the most highly selective colleges are slim, no matter how "perfectly" you've raised them and how exquisite their application is.

For those of you who went to US colleges and universities, I'm guessing the current college admissions scene is a whole new ballgame from when you applied to college. I'm also guessing that, for many of you, whether you attended university here in the

US or not, my philosophies and suggestions might not mesh with yours. That's ok. If nothing else, you might want to take a minute and listen to the things your kids are talking about and worrying about. The number one thing the kids on A2C say about their parents is that they don't listen. So, take a few minutes every day or even once a week if you're strapped for time and actively listen to them when they are trying to talk to you about whatever it is that's bothering them. More than likely they won't talk when you ask questions, so you have to wait until they're ready, and that won't always be at a great time for you, unfortunately.

But you know what? Sometimes we just need to put down our cell phones, close our laptops, turn off the television, and pay attention to the most important things in our lives — our children. Of course, if it's impossible to stop what you are doing, then explain that and make sure they know you aren't just blowing them off. Say, "Hey, I really want to hear what you have to say. Can we circle back to this a little later?" When my kids were juniors and seniors in high school, if they started talking, if I could manage it at all, I'd put down what I was doing or set it aside and just listen. Odds are, they won't talk for long, so it will probably be for only a few minutes :)

What They Want You to Know

I asked the kids on Reddit what they wished their parents knew and understood about the college admissions process. Spoiler alert: there was a whole lot of financial aid stuff and wishing that you understood that sometimes you're putting too much pressure on them and that they are overloaded by stress. Here's some of what they had to say:

- Be proactive and get involved. Research and learn how it all works, so you understand the process. Read websites of the schools your kids are interested in. Help them make spreadsheets with deadlines and required materials. It can be overwhelming. And they'd like you to do this *without* having to discuss admissions every night at dinner.

- On the other hand, be balanced. Know that this is their process and back off when they need you to back off. Be supportive, but not overly involved. You can be engaged with the process, silently.

- Understand the difficulties and the ins and outs of financial aid:

  o A lot of the financial aid aspect requires your participation. You can't just say "I'm not paying that" or "I'm not gonna fill out that form." To get any financial aid, your participation is mandatory. You will have to open up about your finances, whether you want to or not.

  o It's crucial to turn the CSS Profile and the FAFSA in on time. Please don't get lazy with that stuff, because then your kid won't get all the aid for which they're eligible.

  o Learn how to run the NPCs (net price calculators) on each college's website so you can see what your expected family contribution (EFC) is. If this is your first child going to college, it could likely cost far more than you'd ever expect. Get real with figuring out the costs before your child invests their heart and soul into an application to a school that is financially unrealistic.

  o Often scholarships reduce grant aid, so filling out all those scholarship forms gets you nowhere if you're already getting financial aid.

  o It's highly unlikely that private/merit scholarships will cover the cost of tuition and room and board. And even institutional merit scholarships are super competitive. This is likely a lot different from when you were applying to schools. Don't bank on your child getting merit money.

o Perfect grades and perfect SAT and ACT scores don't automatically mean you get a full ride. And even if you do get a "full ride," you'll still likely have room and board to pay for.

o Financial aid isn't dependent on what you will pay, or you think you can pay, but what the colleges determine you can pay. It's pretty much impossible for kids to be considered independent for financial purposes. If the parent is alive, the college is going to assume they're helping with the financial responsibilities of paying for college costs.

o If you're low income, don't think you won't be able to afford college for your kids. There are more financial aid opportunities available than you might think — especially if you open your mind to the wide expanse of colleges out there.

• Your kids wish you understood the importance of the Personal Essay and how personal it needs to be. They know you think you know more about writing than they do, but this essay needs to showcase their voice. No, it doesn't need to be more formal. No, it doesn't need to be focused on impressing the admissions officer. It needs to be honest, open, and vulnerable. Only your kid can decide what to write about. Otherwise, it's simply not a personal essay.

• Don't be insulted if they don't want you to read their essay. Sometimes, your kids may have things they want to write about that they just aren't comfortable sharing with you yet. They are entering adulthood, and this means they deserve some privacy. Trust that they do care about their futures (even if they don't always show it). Trust that they often

know a lot more about this process than you do. Trust that
they are doing the best they can.

- Recognize that they're working their asses off, and sometimes the college applications alone can feel like a full-time
job on top of everything else they're balancing.

- They want you to look at the realities of admissions. The
admissions process isn't just about an individual's merit;
it's about shaping a class.

- Be accepting of how competitive admissions is nowadays.
For everyone. Your kids want you to understand these stats
so you can be realistic: about 17,000 kids will score in the
top 1% of the SAT, and around the same number for the
ACT. Then there are the more than 30,000 valedictorians
and 30,000 salutatorians in the US alone. There are lots of
exceptional kids out there (although none quite as amazing
as yours I'm sure :))

- They want you to know that there is no magic formula for
their ECs. Every college has their own needs.

  ○ Eight years of violin or doubling up on lacrosse and vol-
  leyball for four years is not the silver bullet that will get
  them into college.

  ○ Being a member of the Resume Booster Club or doing
  random community service they're not interested in
  won't necessarily boost their application.

  ○ Give your kids a chance to figure out what might be
  meaningful for them. (Note from me: Of course, sometimes they need to be pushed off their screens to explore
  what might interest them, but allow them to have input.
  Don't just push them into ECs that you've heard colleges like. That often backfires.)

- They want you to recognize that the college admissions
process is NOT the same as it was thirty years ago. It's

much more competitive and expensive than you could have imagined.

- Any college in the top 200 in the US is pretty darn good and can give your kid a fantastic education. Prestige isn't everything.
- Community college can be a great way to save money and get started on the college path.
- They want you to be aware of just how stressful and anxiety-inducing it can be, and that not going to a highly selective school doesn't affect their chances at a successful, happy life.
  - Also, please note that going to a top 20 school doesn't ensure success or happiness either.
  - They want you to be aware of the stress culture surrounding applications and admissions and recognize that you might be contributing to it by pushing your kid too hard.
  - Until your kids have been accepted to all their schools, they will be super stressed out and nervous; you might even call it irrational sometimes.
  - If you see them crying because they're stressed, saying "stop crying" won't help. Neither will ridiculing them or pressuring them to talk more about college admissions, essays, and their future. They consider this to be a hellish journey at times, and sometimes they're just looking for a little empathy — or a little space.
  - If things don't go their way with acceptances, they will likely be crushed. You might be too, but focus on your child. Expect tears and anger. Nothing you say will make them happy. This is a great time for hugs and ice cream.
  - They want to make sure you know they'll get over it eventually, they promise.

- They really, really, really want you to stop comparing them to other people's kids.
- They think you should go on a separate tour when you visit colleges. That way you can ask as many questions as you like without mortifying them. (OK, actually it's my suggestion for you to go on a different tour from them so you can interrogate the tour guide without embarrassing your child. They just want you to be quiet and respectful on tours.)
- Encourage early applications, rolling applications, and safety schools. Getting those acceptances in early can help with the stress throughout the journey. Make sure you have a financial backup safety school too.
- Learn about the Standardized Testing Process. Learn what the SAT and ACT are and recognize the importance of prepping for the tests, maybe even buying a book or two to study.
- Don't destroy your relationship with your child by keeping them away from their friends or by smothering them with tutors. Don't threaten to take away the money you've saved for them just as a threat to get them to do what you want.
- Curating a child to perform a certain way creates failures in many ways. Instead, inspire your kid to enjoy learning.
- Emailing a professor who teaches in the department they want to major in doesn't double their chances. No, they're not just being lazy.
- The best colleges for your child could very likely be ones you've never heard of. Don't get obsessed with name recognition or rankings. Learn about the merits of small colleges and Liberal Arts Colleges.
- You had your turn. Allow them the space to grow and learn about themselves. They're eager and excited about it.

And just in case you need more convincing, here it is straight from the Reddit kids in their own words:

u/admissionsmom
Hi Kiddoes. What do you wish your parents knew about the college process?
I would like to let your parents know what you think they should know about your college journey. This is your opportunity to get your voice out there to them.

> [−] conceptalbums
> Financial aid and the importance of having a merit aid backup. My mom made me apply to NYU and was devastated when I got in and couldn't afford it, even though I knew this from the beginning just by simple research and using their cost calculator.
>
> Also, I think most parents just don't understand how insanely competitive admissions are to top universities. My mom also thought I was a shoo-in to Ivy League schools, and I got rejected from all of them. I wasn't even that disappointed, but I felt so bad telling her and then she still proceeds to remind me that I can always transfer, and she is in disbelief about the rejections. So I guess the key advice here is to be supportive of wherever your kids go and accepting of how competitive admissions are nowadays.
>
> > [−] admissionsmom
> > So, you would recommend that I talk about the financial aid process and also merit scholarships.
> >
> > In addition, you think showing them some realities about how incredibly selective some of the schools can be could be helpful? Like there are 38,000 valedictorians in the US alone. Would you also recommend that I talk about opening their minds to the hundreds of other amazing schools?

[−] conceptalbums

Yeah, I think also discussing how competitive merit scholarships can be. I often see a general attitude from parents of "well, my kid can probably get a full ride at a local state school, he/she is valedictorian has 4.0 yadda yadda," and the reality is that nothing is guaranteed and competition is fierce.

So yeah, definitely emphasize that there's a lot of good schools out there, and anything in the top 200 in the US is pretty darn good for the most part.

[−] A2cthrowaway27416

I wish they knew to fill out financial aid even if they don't think you'll qualify for it! During the application process, they told me not to bother applying for aid because "there's no way we'll get any." Fast-forward to April when we found out how much tuition will cost for next year, and suddenly we need to find $3k. So, I applied for a few scholarships in the hopes that it'll help... we'll see how that goes.

[−] PhAnToM444

Sooooo true. I go to an upper-class high school, and you'd be shocked how many kids, who are taking out huge loans, didn't bother with the FAFSA. I got grants from roughly half of the schools I applied to plus one work-study offer, and my parents have 6-figure incomes, a relatively large 529 saved for me, and rental real-estate assets. Some colleges, especially private schools, have higher bars than people think.

[−] d6410

Don't let your parents edit your essay so much it sounds like they wrote it.

[−] PhAnToM444

I would suggest, to be honest, to not have them edit it at all if that's an option. They are too partial and involved in you to make anything productive happen. The best people in my experience to edit it were my college counselor, English teacher, and some of my co-editors on my school newspaper. But parents don't bring all that much credential-wise to the editing process and can easily take over and mess it up because they are so invested in getting their child into college. I didn't let my parents read it until I submitted everything.

> [−] admissionsmom
> You're probably very right. Most parents who hire me don't even see the essays, and they are cool about it. But they are hiring me so they can take themselves out of the process and land their helicopter just a tiny bit.

[−] carmy00

Financial Aid!!! They don't understand this at all. My parents really don't understand the application process, so it's difficult to talk to them about it.

> [−] admissionsmom
> What do you think could have helped them and you to understand it better?

> > [−] carmy00
> > I think they should understand how to run NPCs, and that most schools don't even meet that full need. Also, how competitive merit scholarships are, and why you shouldn't be banking on your child getting merit.

[-] TwinPurpleEagle

So, I'm a junior starting to think about colleges now, and my parents and I disagree on where I should go. Let me explain a bit about me and my parents and how it pertains to our conflict.

My parents immigrated from southeast Asia, and I was born here in the US. They did not attend college in the US and don't know much about the American education system. What they do know, however, is that I must go to a prestigious university because that is what all their friends' children are doing. We live in California, so that means my parents want me to go to Stanford and the UC schools.

However, I feel a smaller university would be better for me because I am visually impaired: I am completely blind in my left eye and have 20/100 vision in my right. I feel that going to a smaller university would enable me to receive the support I need. Good disability services are a must. I want small class sizes and individual attention from professors, the more, the better. I want to know everyone in my classes and see them around campus. I want to be seen as a unique person.

I don't want to be a small fish in a big pond. I don't want to be in a lecture hall with hundreds of students taught by TAs. I don't want to be just a name on a roster. I feel like I would drown in an environment with tens of thousands of students.

The other day I suggested to my parents that I want to attend the Claremont Colleges for the reasons listed above. Their reply was, "What? I've never heard of them. Why would you go to a college? Go to a university, a UC school like UCLA or Berkeley." I tried to explain why a smaller university would be better for my needs, and my mom replied "But you'll easily get a job if people see you went to UCLA. Why does it matter? You'll be in your room all the time anyway." WHAT? I am not an antisocial hermit. Obviously, my parents only care about prestige, not what would be best for me as an individual.

That's not all, though.

My parents have told me they are not going to pay for tuition because they don't approve of my major. I plan to double major in marine biology and environmental science. We have an annual income of 250k+, so financial aid is not an option.

So basically, the main message I want my parents to try and understand is that PRESTIGE DOES NOT MATTER AND LARGER MAY NOT BE BETTER.

> [–] admissionsmom
>
> I think both of your lessons for parents are on point. My advice for you would be to ask your parents to take you to visit the Claremont schools and maybe another LAC or two. The Claremont schools are actually prestigious and highly selective.
>
> Also, please encourage your parents to read these two books: *Where You Go Is Not Who You'll Be* by Frank Bruni and *Colleges That Change Lives* by Loren Pope. It really is just a matter of educating them.
>
> Perhaps even make a presentation emphasizing your points and your seriousness about them.

Helpful Hint: NO COLLEGE TALK ZONE or TIME

Give them (and you) a little space. Create a No College Talk zone or time in your home. At my house, it was our dining room table. This way my kids could eat breakfast, dinner, or an after-school snack without an interrogation from me or my husband (or their siblings!). We all need space to be able to grow and develop, and you want your child to show growth and development for college apps – and life.

a little parent to parent real talk

Reading some of the stories on A2C can be immensely gratifying, and many kids, it seems, are on even ground with you, their parents. But there are just as many stories that will rip your heart out. There are kids who are depressed, riddled with anxiety, and suicidal. Either they feel like their parents are putting far too much pressure on them or they feel that their parents don't care. They want to please you. This is not a rebellious generation; they want your praise. They want to bring you honor and prestige, but they're worn out.

The reason I became a college admissions consultant was that I saw the friction and the stress levels rising in so many families in my community. I saw families struggling through the college admissions process, and it was eating away at the parent-child relationship. I knew that harming family relationships over college admissions just wasn't worth it.

Curating your child to fit into your idea (or your friend's or aunt's or neighbor's idea) of what an admissions officer at a specific school on a specific day in a specific year might want is going to create a dissatisfying experience for everyone. What I think colleges want is just reality — they want to know who your kid really is. Most kids who get into even the most highly selective schools aren't published or nationally-ranked or cancer-curing.

Maybe your kid wants to be Mr. High School and enjoy those teenage years. Great! Or maybe your kid wants most of her time and energy to be spent outside the high school walls focused on a sport, community service, research, or a job. Maybe your kid wants to master the art of making artisanal peanut butter or something else that might seem silly to you, but that could actually catch the eye of an admissions officer or maybe even turn into a career someday (as an aside, did you know professional League of Legends players have an average starting salary of $320,000?).

Allow your child to develop according to their personal developmental timeline. Then see which colleges will serve them best. Encourage your child to read, explore their interests, and develop their intellectual curiosity, and that will show up in their applications through their essays and teacher recommendations. A kid with authentic curiosity and a desire to learn for learning's sake can't be created by a parent, but they can be encouraged.

Join the Polar Bear Parent Revolution

Join me in landing your helicopter just a little and in putting those tiger-parent stripes away and becoming a Polar Bear Parent. A super chill Polar Bear Parent, that is. It's a thing. Well, not really. Not Yet. But together we can make it a thing :)

---

tl;dr

- For some families, especially low-income families, the cheapest schools are the handful of highly selective private schools that give a lot of need-based financial aid.
- Unfortunately, it is a heck of a lot harder to get into those highly selective schools than it used to be back in the day.
- In many cases, merit aid has little to do with the actual merit of the student. Often, it is a small discount on tuition to get otherwise full-pay students to choose this school over another school.
- Work on modeling how you handle your stress.
- Listen to your kids — especially if you want them to listen to you.
- Make NO COLLEGE TALK zones or times in your house. Stick to it. Your kids need a breather from the pressure now and then.

- Look beyond rankings and college names. The best colleges for your child could be ones you haven't heard of.

- You are responsible for the financial aid aspects of the application. Even if you have no money to pay or you don't intend to pay for college, you have to be involved. Your kids can't fill out the financial aid forms like the FAFSA and CSS Profile without your cooperation.

- Get educated about college admissions these days. Read these books:
  - *Colleges that Change Lives* by Loren Pope,
  - *Where You Go Is Not Who You'll Be* by Frank Bruni, and
  - Check out the Resources Chapter for a longer list of books that might interest you.

CHAPTER 28

When It Doesn't Go Your Way: The Pain of Rejection

No one wants to be rejected. After all the time, sweat, and tears you put into your applications, getting a denial can feel like the end of the world.

You might feel stupid. You're not.

You might feel worthless. You're not.

You might feel like you wasted months only to have missed your goals with nothing to show for it. You didn't. All that work you did for college acceptance won't be wasted. You learned something every single step of the way. You are learning more and more about yourself right now as you go through the pain.

So, if you get one of those dreaded thin envelopes in the mail, the email or portal doesn't light up with a big "Congrats!" or "You're Accepted!" with confetti and flashing lights, or if something else doesn't go your way like the financial offer isn't satisfactory, be pissed off. Experience that anger, disappointment, and resentment. Then refocus on the good things in your life and what you can do about your situation.

Preparing for Decision Day and the Possibility of Rejection: Emotional Planning

anonymous

I know I can't get in, but I'm still so scared.

I applied early to Princeton. Yeah, like I know rationally that there's no real way I can get in. I get it. Buuuuut, when I read over my application, I realize it's beautiful af. My essays rock. My activities are awesome. My recs are solid. My stats, while not perfect, are also in a reasonable-ish range.

A2C, I need your help. Convince me that I'm not getting in! I want rock bottom expectations. I'll be excited beyond belief, of course, if I do get in, but just totally chill if I don't. Please help!

> [−] admissionsmom
>
> I like to call this Emotional Planning. You know that you've done everything you can. You feel great, like you do, about the app you've put out there. And now, it's out of your hands, so you have to hope for the best, but prepare for the "worst" — and I say that somewhat ironically because I know far too well that things often work out the best even if it's not the outcome we thought we wanted.
>
> Georgia Tech admissions often kills it with their blogs, and they've done it once again by announcing Preparation Day a couple of weeks before Decision Day. It has a nifty little pledge and all to make it official: "National Preparation Day! By or on this day, henceforth, any high school senior applying Early Action or Early Decision to a college with an admit rate of less than 50 percent must put their hand on a large, preferably leather-bound book of some kind and take this pledge: 'I, (state your name), being of sound (though overly caffeinated) mind and (sleep-deprived) body, do hereby swear that I will not presume anything in the admission process. Upon advice [sic] of my wizened counselor sages, I acknowledge that I will not look at middle

50 percent ranges and expect that my scores, though in the top quartile, guarantee my admittance.

I will not look at middle 50 percent ranges of hitherto admitted classes and expect my scores, though in the bottom quartile, will be overlooked based on my amazing essay, parents' connections, pictures of me in a onesie from that college, or the 12 letters of recommendation that have been sent on my behalf. I understand the heretofore explicated concept of holistic admission is neither fair nor perfect, wherein I will likely not agree with, nor be capable of predicting all results, despite the complex algorithms I employ or the kingdom fortune tellers I visit. Furthermore, I agree that I will not view an admission decision as an indictment of my character, a judgment on my hitherto demonstrated preparation, nor a prediction of my future success.'

Note: Slightly misused Olde English conjunctions does not negate the spirit nor effectiveness of this pledge."

here's the deal

Waiting for decisions can be godawful, super stressful. But the groovy thing is that if your decisions don't work out, you're still gonna have lots of great options. I promise. (spoiler alert: even if you didn't have a surefire safety that you love and every college rejects you, you'll still have lots of options. Crazy, right?)

I'm a big believer in doing everything you can to be who you want, get what you want, or position yourself in the best place for it. I'm all for putting everything into it while being reasonably balanced. I want you to try your hardest, knowing that you couldn't have done any more, so you have no regrets, but then you just gotta let the universe take control. I'm old, so I've seen it time and again, life works out the way it's supposed to more often than not. And I hear you when you tell me you hate hearing this shit, but it's just so true, I have to say it.

It's real important that you do some EP right now. Emotional Planning. Your mental and emotional health is far more important than where you go to college. So, hope for the best, of course. You've worked your asses off to get to a position to even be able to apply to the schools you applied to. You wrote killer essays and presented yourself as your best you on your very best day. It's only natural to be hopeful and you should be, but come on, you gotta be real too. The realities of admissions are that there are just too many of all these beautiful yous to be funneled into that tiny little teacup full of colleges you're applying to, and some of you (many of you -- I'll be honest) won't get in. So hope for the best, but please prepare yourself for the "worst." I put "worst" in quotation marks because I know that often what seems like the "worst thing that could possibly happen" can turn out to be something really quite wondrous in the end.

The fact of the matter is that we have to live our lives in the moment, and some of these moments suck and some of them blow us away with their amazingness, and some are just ho-hum. So buckle up, and prepare for some sucky moments to head your way in the next few weeks if you are still waiting for decisions, but don't forget to take a look around you right now, this minute, and see your friends, the beautiful blue sky (well, it's kinda cloudy and hazy here in Houston today but you get my point), the snow on the ground, your pets, your teachers, your warm bed, and whatever it is in your moment right now that you can appreciate.

So, here's the real deal, the honest to goodness truth: you are an incredible person (Hard to believe I know that without knowing you isn't it? But it's true), and you're gonna kick ass wherever you go. You don't need any certain school to do that. You don't need a school to light your fire to get you going to be the person you want to be in the world. You don't need any certain name-brand school or schools to light your way. That fire? It's in you.

Rejection Sucks Big Time

u/saada100
Does anyone have tips on handling rejection
I'm really anxious about potential rejections from colleges.

u/thehalima
3 rejections in four hrs., can someone plz make me feel better?

> **[-]** VA_Network_Nerd
> You wait for your other admissions responses to come back. If (when!) you get accepted, you enroll in classes and you go in there, and you kick some ass. Study harder than you have ever studied. Discuss coursework with class-mates more deeply than you have ever discussed anything. Engage your Professors and TAs directly and meaningfully. Ask tough questions.
>
> LEARN ALL THE THINGS
>
> Then get your final grades for the year and do one of two things:
>
> 1. Apply to your "dream" school as a transfer applicant.
> 2. Take your amazing grades and apply for more scholar-ships so you can keep on kicking ass @ "safety" University and graduate from that mutha' with academic honors as a massive, personalized EFF-YOU to "Rejected You University."
>
> Then go out into the world and rip your own personal suc-cess out of the chest of the world.
>
> Silly story aside, the reality is that your personal success is inside YOU. It's not locked away in the walls of any spe-cific institution of learning. It's already in you. Any good university can teach you how to find it. How to access it. How to wield it.

YOU are going to make YOURSELF successful — not "Rejected You" University.

Come on. Get up off the floor. Life kicked you in the nuts today. But it's not about how hard you can hit life. It's about how hard you can get hit by life, and keep moving forward. Now brush yourself off and get back in the game. We need you out there. Show this fecking world exactly how great you are.

u/Ultimatun

Just got rejected from another college and instantly made jokes about it. It's a good sign.
I think I'm going to be fine.

u/ USS-Enterprise

rejection, again
Hey guys, I got rejected from Olin :(I actually thought I was going to get in – they have evaluative interviews, and I thought mine went amazing. Guess not. :(I'm not that sad, but it was a cool school. :/ Ah well, on to the next one.

u/voltroom

The feeling of acceptance
Counter-intuitive to the title of the post...it's not about actual college acceptance. I have this feeling of acceptance about all the rejections that I've been receiving so far. My first ever rejection was Caltech. And then MIT. And then UChicago. And then Williams. So forth...

Well, 4 rejections so far ain't that bad, some of you might think. The first ever rejection hit me real hard. The second, real hard too, but not that bad. Third, meh. Fourth, haha. I think like I have this sense of immunity to rejection and I really don't feel anxious waiting for the rest of my college decisions.

> [–] admissionsmom
>
> Two things: 1. It's ok to be disappointed about not getting into your top choices but really open your mind. I hope

you have lots of top choices. Be disappointed; it's natural. You have 3 days to be sad. Then, you have to move on. 2. It's ok (and actually quite good) to be pessimistic right now about your remaining chances. It's not going to affect your admissions. That's out of your hands. And honestly, your odds (anyone's odds) are ridiculous. So be pessimistic, for sure. That's called "Emotional Planning," and it is the healthiest way to approach what's happening in your life now. If you get in, you can be pleasantly surprised. BUT, be optimistic about the fact that you will get in and attend a college that will be great for you. And if not, you can transfer if you are really unhappy.

u/NoHopeOnlyRope

It's official: I was rejected by all of the schools I applied to. This past November I did what was quite possibly the stupidest f*cking thing I ever did, even surpassing the time I stapled my own palm: I applied to only the UCs. No CSUs, no liberal arts schools, none of that. I was wholly convinced that I was so guaranteed to get in where I wanted that I completely wrote off everything else. I had a grand total of five schools on my list, which works out because years of shitty math scores meant that's as high as I can count. But jokes aside, plans A-E have all failed, and now I don't know what to do.

I know that ultimately it is entirely my fault. It's my fault for not applying to more schools. It's my fault for writing such drab essays, it's my fault for doing so awful both in school and on the SAT. I was snobby and cocky, traits I despise in other people, so now it's only fair that I suffer for my own wrongdoing. I would not accept me.

It really does feel like my entire high school career was a complete waste. Not once did I get a GPA higher than 3.5 and not once did I feel accomplished or happy in any way. I could have dreamt everything since 2014, and the end result would've been the same. I get genuinely angry when I see people be with their friends or talk about where they got in, and I know that's just pure, unadulterated jealousy. In that sense, I am truly a pathetic excuse for a human being.

I currently see no reason to give a shit anymore. The only reason people even go to school during the second semester of their senior year is to avoid getting rescinded, but you can't get rescinded if you didn't get in anywhere.

i'll be straight with you

Can I just say that rejection really, really hurts? For all of you dealing with rejection right now, I'm pissed off and hurt for you. And, here's the deal — sometimes colleges make f*cked-up-poopy-headed-stupid decisions. This is not a reflection on you at all; this is getting caught in the ridiculousness of the college admissions numbers game, and I am so sorry. Another Redditor explained it like this: every college has an ice cream cone to fill with students, and they have many favorite flavors. Sometimes you just can't fit all your favorite flavors on your cone, so you have to make a decision. That decision is not a reflection on the mint chocolate chip or rocky road or cookies and cream you didn't choose. You'd probably choose them next time. It is what it is. There simply wasn't enough space.

But disappointment and heartache make us stronger, and one day — and I promise this, even though it doesn't seem like it right now — you are going to look back and see how much stronger you've become.

Right now, there is a lot of disappointment and pain you will need to go through. You can go through this pain because it's temporary. It won't last forever. Disappointment is merely a feeling. But it's not who you are. You are still the same person, and you are going be that much stronger because of this experience. You are the same amazing person who did their extracurriculars because they had meaning, who worked their ass off to get amazing grades and test scores, who tried to please their parents. That's all still you. That hasn't gone away. And you are going to take those skills and experiences and characteristics with you for the rest of your life.

If you're staring down at that rejection letter, **do these seven things**:

1. Know that it's ok to be disappointed about not getting into your top choice, but open your mind. There are lots of schools where you can get a wonderful education and be very happy. So be disappointed; it's natural. Take a day or two to be sad. Then you have to move on.

2. Remember that this isn't about you; it's about numbers and how another person interpreted some words you wrote down when they read your application for 15 minutes.

3. Recognize that holistic admissions is an art. Not a science. There's not one or two things they can list that turn the tides in your application. Don't forget they are looking for fit, just like you were (I hope). If you focus on fit in your applications, you are going to receive far more acceptances than rejections. If you don't think about fit and just apply to "top" programs, the admissions offices will have to figure out the fit for you. It would be nice if we could see their institutional needs on this side, but all we have to go on is their admissions information and common data set and what you can deliver.

4. Get some physical exercise. Go on a long walk or run, preferably outside. Have a dance party in your room. Practice yoga. Lift weights at the gym. Move that body. When I'm upset about something, I walk. For miles.

5. Sing. There are all kinds of studies that show singing makes positive brain changes. So, open up Spotify, line up your favorite sing-along playlist, and let those melodic notes soar out of your soul. Here's my go-to "I need to sing out

loud" playlist: Bob Marley, REM, Eminem, Bruno Mars, Rihanna, and Beyoncé.

6. Go on a Bear Hunt. Do you remember the children's book and chant, "Going on a Bear Hunt"? In order to find that bear (your inner peace), you have to go through it. You've got to let yourself experience that tall swishy grass, that thick oozy mud, and the swiftly flowing river. You can't go over it; you can't go under it, you can't go around it — you gotta go through it. Your feelings are like this. Allow yourself time and space to experience them. You have to go through them to be able to let them go.

7. If decisions don't go your way, it's their loss. You're gonna get your shit together, "Thank you, Next" them, and move on. You are a badass. You don't need them. You have YOU.

RAIN is a technique borrowed from Mindful Meditation that can help you go through the feelings and thoughts that accompany the disappointment of rejection. When you get overwhelmed, remember these feelings and thoughts are temporary, and they will pass.

R ecognize that you are having those thoughts and feelings
A llow the experience to be there, just as it is.
I nvestigate your thoughts and feelings with kindness.
N on-Identify. These are thoughts and feelings, but they are not YOU.

And DON'T do these things:

1. Don't try to figure out why you were rejected. There is no way to compare your application with others. You have no idea how their application reads. Admissions is a very human process. Computers don't read applications, so it's

impossible to know exactly what clicked in an application with one human to the next. Here's what u/PeteyMIT says about trying to figure out why you were admitted or denied: "Almost no one knows why they were admitted or denied from a given school. This is because any applicant only has partial information about their own application. Searching for proximate causes is something we do to give us comfort. Let us not confuse that for making us think it is correct."

2. Don't refuse help if you need it. If rejection has made you feel bad about yourself, such that you're worried about how to get up in the morning, don't try to power through it. Talk to your parents. See your school counselor. Reach out to others for support.

Let it go.

Letting go will be hard, maybe one of the hardest things you've ever done — but you'll need to channel your inner Elsa and let it go so that you can enjoy your summer. I promise you that in six months, you're going to look back on this time and remember the pain and disappointment, but it won't be consuming you. It will be making you stronger. Also, you'll become a more empathetic person and be more sensitive to others' painful experiences. Then you'll be able to reach out and try to comfort them.

If channeling Elsa and Disney Cartoons isn't your style, maybe this story about hunters and monkeys will resonate more with you: Some hunters attach a coconut to a tree, cut a hole in it, and place a banana inside. A curious, innocent little monkey comes along, smells that banana deliciousness, and puts his hand through the hole and grabs the banana. The unfortunate thing is the hole is too small for his fist to get back through, so he is stuck sitting in that tree holding on to that damn banana. To be free, all he has to do is *let go* of the banana.

Rescinded

u/warrior__princess
could I be rescinded for a C in Calc?
So, I found out today that I'm going to get a C+ in Calc. I'm really upset. It's the only C I have in high school. I worked so hard in Calc, but the teacher's style is not my learning style (no excuse), and I just couldn't seem to pull it together. All my other grades are good, so I think it's obvious I'm not slacking. But my mom is freaking out and making me feel so bad. Will I get rescinded for this?

my thoughts

You can't slack off your last semester. Try to keep up your grades as much as you can. You don't want to put all your hard work in jeopardy only to mess up right before you cross the finish line. I had a Redditor contact me last fall because their admission to a UC school was rescinded over three Cs. So, it happens. Be careful. Rule of thumb: don't go down over one letter grade per class and don't do that in more than a class or two.

However, know that one bad grade isn't the end of the world. If you earn a low grade the last semester despite your best efforts, you'll probably be ok, especially if your other grades remain steady. It happens. Colleges know you have a whole other semester left when they accept you. If your college becomes concerned, they'll ask you what's going on, which gives you and your guidance counselor the opportunity to offer a valid and reasonable explanation.

Should you have to answer that nerve-wracking question, talk about how you learned your lesson and have learned to manage your time more wisely. You can say that you got in over your head, and you have learned how to deal with that situation now. Explain that if you catch yourself in a bind in college, you will immediately go to the tutoring center and meet with your professor and TA. Talk about how your experience will make you a better college student now. Reiterate that you made mistakes and you have learned from them and you are ready to steer your academic ship in the right direction.

Something else to be aware of beyond your grades is being a good person, especially on social media. On the Tulane Admissions Blog, Jeff Schiffman says "the most frequent reason I rescind admissions is dumb stuff you do on social media." He goes on to explain that they aren't looking for it, but someone will send them a screenshot of something offensive, and as he explains it, "being a jerk on social media to your peers or your community" is something he has no patience for.

For whatever reason (and I hope this never applies to you), if your application is rescinded, reflect on what happened, learn from the experience, grow from what you learned, and move on to the next experience.

Appeal Letters

u/senatorswank

I got into UCI today from my appeal letter – I graduate from HS in 1 day.
Never lose hope guys. I was rejected by every UC, and I even though I knew it was a long shot, I sent my appeal to UCI and waited. In the meantime, I made plans to attend my local community college and then I saw the email today. It's so crazy, especially considering that I graduate from high school in just a day's time. It just goes to show you can never tell. It was a humbling experience, and I wouldn't have had it any other way.

[–] admissionsmom
Wow! Wow! Wow! So cool.

here's the truth

Unlike a letter of continued interest, which I'll discuss in the Deferred/Waitlist chapter, an appeal letter is a formal request you send to the college asking them to reconsider the decision to reject your application. An appeal letter can work, but more times than not the college will not reverse the rejection. And that's if they even accept appeal letters at all, since many schools don't accept them.

You should write an appeal letter only if you have a very solid reason why you feel that you should not have been rejected. Being sad, upset, or disappointed won't cut it. Schools know rejection is upsetting, so explain why they didn't have all the facts in making their decision. Provide any additional new, relevant information about your academics, activities, leadership or awards. If it is true explain, for example, how well you did your fall semester senior year when you had so much on your plate. If schools have a specific format for your appeal letter, follow that. If they don't, write the love letter of your life. Bare your soul even more than in the Waitlist Love Letter.

If you feel like your application should be reconsidered, write a formal and polite letter clearly laying out your argument. Do not come across as angry or emotional. Do not blame the school. Proofread and proofread and then get your English teacher to proofread it. Then send it, bring back your inner Elsa, and let it go. You've done all you can.

So now what? What if you are rejected to all your schools ("safety" included, since you clearly didn't apply to a Surefire Safety School)?

What if your appeal doesn't work or the college doesn't accept appeals?

Amazingly enough, you still have some great options:

1. You can take a gap year. You can travel, do community service, or work to make some money for your college years

— or do a combo of all three. Read more about that in the Gap Year chapter.

2. You can enroll in community college for a year or two and get some of your basic credits out of the way while you save a shit ton of money.

3. You can check out schools that are still accepting for rolling admissions or the National Association for College Admission Counseling ("NACAC") Colleges Opening Update. It's a list of colleges with space available that comes out every year with colleges who are still accepting applications even into May and the summer. You'd be surprised to see just how many excellent schools are accepting apps into the early summer — some of them will still even offer decent money.

tl;dr

- Practice Emotional Planning as you prepare for your admissions decisions. Hope for the best, but expect the worst. Once you've sent in your application, those positive vibes aren't going to make a difference — so be real.

- Rejection sucks, but it's not the end of the world, nor is it an accurate reflection of who you are.

- It's ok to be upset about rejection. It's natural and expected. Take a few days to process your feelings, and then focus on the schools that have accepted you.

- Avoid a school rescinding your application by keeping your grades up as best you can. I know the siren call of senioritis is strong, but you don't want to sacrifice all your hard work. And, don't be an idiot on social media — or in life.

- Appeal letters are to be used only in those rare circumstances where you feel there is a genuinely good reason that a school should not have rejected you and when the school will accept them. Provide any new information. Pour your heart and soul into it. At this point, you have nothing to lose.

- You have options: A gap year is never a bad thing, especially if it allows you to find a better college experience or work on preparing yourself for college. Community college can save you lots of money. Or you can check out that NACAC list of colleges still accepting applicants.

Wise Words from Rocky Balboa:
(reintroduced to me by u/VA_Network_Nerd)

Let me tell you something you already know. The world ain't all sunshine and rainbows. It's a very mean and nasty place, and I don't care how tough you are it will beat you to your knees and keep you there permanently if you let it. You, me, or nobody is gonna hit as hard as life. But it ain't about how hard ya hit. It's about how hard you can get hit and keep moving forward. How much you can take and keep moving forward. That's how winning is done! Now if you know what you're worth then go out and get what you're worth. But ya gotta be willing to take the hits, and not pointing fingers saying you ain't where you wanna be because of him, or her, or anybody! Cowards do that and that ain't you! You're better than that!

CHAPTER 29

Hanging in Limbo — The Uncomfortable World of Being Waitlisted and Deferred

You know what sucks? The *Last Airbender* live action movie. Do you know what else sucks? Making sure everything is ready to go so you can meet the early decision deadline only to have the school tell you that you've been deferred. Or working really hard on your application to your top choice only to find out that you've been waitlisted.

Of course, being deferred means you have to wait until the regular decision cycle for any kind of answer. And getting waitlisted means that the school hasn't told you no, but it also means they haven't told you yes. In both cases, that's a difficult place to be.

So, if you find yourself in the waitlist/deferred limbo, take a deep breath, exhale, and do a few things: write your LOCI (Letter of Continued Interest), send them any updates they request or that you feel like will help them make their decision, and then let that one go and move on to your acceptances. Whatever you do, don't watch *The Last Airbender*!

Waitlist — so they kinda like me?

u/life_heymikey

waitlisted as transfer

I'm waitlisted for one of my top choices — anyone want to tell me how this works and if I can do anything to help me move to the accepted list?

> [−] NoHopeOnlyRope
>
> Alternatively, you could realize that schools that already deal with literal tens of thousands of more qualified applicants probably don't want to read yet another plea from some stranger whose app they only had to glance over before making their decision.
>
> You can't always win, that's just a fact of life. Sometimes you must accept that you lost and that there's nothing more you can do. I'm reminded of Chief Joseph and his "Fight no more forever" speech. Rather than eternally claw and beg, you must learn to concede defeat with at least some dignity occasionally.
>
> > [−] admissionsmom
> >
> > Hi Hope, I'm so glad to hear from you, and you def bring up a valid point. At some point, you have to let it go. But what I learned from this sub last year is that a lot of people aren't willing to give up until they've done everything they can for what they want. Otherwise, they are left feeling unsatisfied.
> >
> > Also, just a note to add for anyone else reading this, many schools are now using the waitlist to complete their class. So, writing to them is a good move if they don't say not to send anything. Still, for the most highly selective schools, it is better to write your best WLLOCI (Waitlist Love Letter of

Continued Interest), send anything else they ask for or that you think will be beneficial, and move on in your mind. You can look at their waitlist histories for the last few years and see how dismal the prospects are (but certainly not impossible!).

u/gooonster

waitlist question

If I am waitlisted, how important is it to go and visit the college before May 1? I've heard of other students visiting to talk to admissions? Or is this very extra and I should just save my money? Thanks!

> [–] admissionsmom
>
> Hi. Most colleges will tell you whether they will even accept visitors or not. I do have to add, though, that I personally know a kid or two who get off the waitlist at schools by going and respectfully waiting outside in the hallway for an appointment for a few days. I don't recommend this. I do recommend writing a great love letter LOCI and then bonding with the colleges who've accepted you.
>
>> [–] gooonster
>> what do you mean by bonding?
>
> [–] admissionsmom
> Emotionally bonding. Connecting. Once you've sent your WLLOCI with the waitlist college and sent any updates you think might help your cause, you need to move on and connect with your schools who have accepted you.

u/chanceme1234321

Do I have any hope for getting into Yale off the waitlist?

I got waitlisted at Yale and Stanford. I know I should focus on other schools, but I don't want to give up on Yale. What are my chances of getting in?

here's my take

If you meet the admission requirements, but a college has already filled its incoming class, you might be put on the waitlist. If spots open up, then the admissions office turns to the waitlist to offer applicants acceptance and fill the spots back up.

The waitlist can be torturous, which is why you can't take it personally. You'll drive yourself crazy trying to figure out why a school waitlisted you. Colleges don't rank waitlisted applicants, nor do they accept waitlisted applicants randomly. They fill spots as they arise to create what they think is a balanced class. And that looks different at every college.

That's why you need to balance doing what you can to get off the waitlist with focusing on a different school, especially if you're waitlisted at a highly selective school. Do your heart and mind a favor by committing to another school — mentally, emotionally, and financially. Then, if you're still interested in that waitlist school, write the love letter of your life, tell them all the reasons they need you, and you need them. Bare your soul. Send it. And move on and focus on the school you've committed to.

This whole process can feel intensely personal and frustrating, which isn't surprising given how much work you've put into your application, but try not to let it get you down. You can take steps to put yourself at ease.

1. First, you need to decide if you want to stay on a school's waitlist. Usually, when the school notifies you that you've been put on the waitlist, they will ask you to confirm your spot. If that's the right decision for you, do it.

2. Write what I call the WLLOCI – *Waitlist Love Letter of Continued Interest*. I'll talk about that below.

3. Keep your grades up. You want to remain a competitive applicant, and continued devotion to your studies will show that.

4. Bond emotionally with your acceptances. Once you've done your WLLOCI with the waitlist college, you need to move on and connect with your schools who have accepted you. Be excited about what you've accomplished so far.

Deferred

u/Skrapman2
Deferred from Rice
I got deferred from Rice and read their FAQs, but what does this really mean? Do I have a decent chance since I didn't get rejected or is it basically getting rejected?

> [−] admissionsmom
> I mean you kind of have to look at it as a rejection because you have to be able to move on in your head. But if you still want to go there, follow through with your next steps. Send any updates about your application and send a LOCI if they don't specifically say they don't want one. Do all that with positivity and put your best self out there again, so you'll have no regrets, but recognize that often a deferral doesn't turn into acceptance. Then go full on with your regular apps, making sure you have colleges you'd be happy to attend with varying levels of selectivity.

u/Aerophage1771
Deferred...
Why did I even waste my time applying? RIP

> [−] admissionsmom
> I hope that you're going to be able to go through your disappointment and allow yourself to feel these shitty feelings at first - for a couple of days, but then you'll be able to reflect back on everything you've learned about yourself in the process. But first, be mad. It's ok. Then, get busy writing your LOCI if you still want to be considered for regular decision.

u/elkakey

Deferred from Barnard. What now?

Hey y'all!

I'm trying to make this a non-somber post, so I might be using exclamation points excessively to cope with the news.

So, I was deferred from Barnard College, my top pick and ED school. But hey! At least I still have a fighting chance. Right?

I know my first quarter grades were weak (in the B-/B range, whereas I am usually in the A-/A range), and I definitely want to work on that. I've dealt with some health issues over the past few months, so I missed a lot of school, which in turn affected my grades... Other than raising my grades, do any of y'all have ideas to show my committed interest and developments in my life?

My individual service project for National Honors Society is coming up, and I think I'll be doing something with Girls Who Code. I feel like this will be worth mentioning in a couple months' time.

Also, I'm trying to figure out who my additional recommender should be (this was advised in my deferral letter). I need someone who brings something new to the conversation, who would that be?

I need honesty here. How often do deferrals lead to acceptances in the RD pool? I'm applying to many other schools – Sarah Lawrence, Yale, Vassar, Swarthmore, Columbia, NYU, McGill, Drexel – but I am in love with Barnard. It is my place. I want to be realistic here though, so how do we feel about all of this?

Also, to anyone else in a similar situation as me, as said in *Groundhog Day: The Musical*, "NEVER GIVE UP HOPE!" We still have skin in the game. Let's make the most of it.

Thank you to anyone who read this ridiculously long post, and much love for my fellow deferrees (is that a term? If not, it is now!).

let me break it down for you

This might hurt to hear, but you need to look at deferrals or wait-lists as a kind of rejection because you have to be able to move on in your head. But if you still want to go there, follow through with your next steps: send any updates about your application along with a LOCI (if they don't say they don't want one).

Do all that with positivity and put your best self out there again, so you'll have no regrets. However, you must keep in mind that, unfortunately, a deferral or waitlist doesn't necessarily become an acceptance.

LOCI

u/CatOwlFilms
LOCI Subject line?
I'm about to write my LOCI for UChicago. What should I put in the subject line of the email? Should I put in my applicant ID?

> [-] admissionsmom
> I think it won't hurt to put your applicant ID in, but for sure, put your full name and let them know that you accept your spot on the waitlist in the subject line.

u/USS-Enterprise
Cornell LOCI
See title. I get the feeling that sending a LOCI to Cornell probably wouldn't change much anyway, so I was considering writing mine in the format of a short story. Is this a fun idea or just stupid? The alternative would be just enclosing a short story with the letter.

what you need to know

A letter of continued interest (LOCI) is the best way to show a school that you are interested in attending, despite your being deferred or placed on the waitlist. You can also use the letter of continued interest as a way to update the school on what you've been doing since you applied, which might be enough to tip the scales in your favor (though that's no guarantee).

The letter of continued interest is where you go for it! Swing for the fences. Pour out your soul. You won't know until you've tried, and you have nothing to lose. And you won't want to look back on this opportunity with regret. Write the college the love letter of your life. Convince them that they need to be with you just as much as you need to be with them. I don't call it the Waitlist Love Letter of Continued Interest ("WLLOCI") for nothing.

Also, have fun with it!

Here's how:

The Waitlist Love Letter — The Nitty Gritty Lowdown

1. First, fall in love (or strong like) with at least one of your acceptances. Go visit them. Accept a place in their class. Mentally move on from your waitlisted or deferred school.

2. If you're still hung up on a school that waitlisted you, this WLLOCI is your chance to prove to them that you are the perfect match for them, but be sure to read the letter from your college and see if it is open to a letter of continued interest.

3. Make sure you include full name and any ID numbers they have given you.

4. Be nice. Be positive. Thank them for the continued opportunity to be considered. Don't complain or whine about being waitlisted in your WLLOCI.

5. Be yourself. As in your personal essay, use your normal word choices and voice. It's ok to throw your personality into the LOCI, but be sure it doesn't come off as trying too hard. While you need to show your voice, be yourself, and be friendly and warm, it is a bit more formal. Be polite, but friendly.

6. If they don't give other specific directions in your waitlist or deferral letter, address the email to the admissions officer who signed your waitlist/deferral letter and to your

regional admissions officer if you have one. Additionally, copy the email to the general admissions office.

7. Include any updates to your application. You can bullet point these, so they are easier to identify. If you've improved any test scores or grades, tell them. If you've won awards or competitions since your application or last update, tell them. But updates can be more personal, too; maybe you reached a personal goal of walking 3200 miles, benching 200 pounds, writing one poem a day for six months, winning a game in Fortnite, winning the March Madness bracket pool, or building a castle out of toothpicks. You can start this paragraph with something like, "Since my application or my last update...."

8. Don't make it too long or wordy. Keep it short and sweet at about 250-500 words. You want them to get right to what you have to say. Consider bullet-pointing your updates. They are not going to glance at this for more than a minute. Make sure they learn what they need to know.

9. If you will attend if you are admitted, tell them so.

10. If you can visit, do. Then either describe the visit or tell them about your plans. If you can't, and you've already visited, describe something specific from the visit. If you haven't had a chance to visit, explain why and how bummed it makes you.

11. This is it. There is no holding back now. This is your time to let it all out. Show them why they need you. As I said, bare your soul.

12. Write your letter, thank them again, and send it. Then be like Elsa and let it go. Life is too short to wait around on college acceptances.

And to help you out even more, here's a list of Don'ts for your WLLLOCI:

1. Don't send one if they ask you not to.
2. Don't express anger or frustration. It's ok to be disappointed, but don't be whiny or pouty.
3. Don't make any assumptions about your acceptance.
4. Don't make your letter too long.

tl;dr

- Being waitlisted or deferred sucks, but it's not the end of the world.
- Focus on the acceptances you do have if you're waitlisted and on your other applications if you are deferred.
- If you want to stay on the waitlist, check to make sure your school is open to letters of continued interest, and then write one. It's the love letter of your life.
- If you are deferred, treat it like being waitlisted. Decide if you are still interested in the school, write a letter of continued interest, and then move on mentally and emotionally.
- Keep it friendly, short, to the point, and polite. Inform the school of any updates, either academic or personal.
- If you will definitely attend if accepted, tell them.
- Once you submit your LOCI or your WLLOCI, let it go and move on emotionally and mentally, for your own good.

CHAPTER 30

Taking a Gap Year

u/stuportrooper

Should I even go to college now?

I don't know if this is the sleep deprivation talking but I'm starting to think maybe college isn't right for me right now. I haven't gotten into any of the schools that "fit" me and the one school I've gotten into I only applied there because my parents made me. Even they know how much I don't like it. Would it be bad to take a gap year, work, and then reapply when I get my shit more together?

anonymous

Telling colleges about a planned gap year?

I'm an incoming senior, but I'm already planning on a gap year – I want to apply this year and then defer enrollment. This is because one of my immediate family members has a terminal disease, and I'd rather spend the last couple rides with them rather than on the other side of the country feeling guilty. I also plan to do a lot of internships, service, hackathons, online certifications, the like. (This is also because we might want to get our finances sorted out straight too.) Should this be a thing that colleges would consider positively and would want to see, or should I not mention this and just defer my enrollment when I get in?

I think your plan sounds like a great idea, but make sure to read the policies about gap years on each college's webpage. Some are way more in favor than others.

here's my take

Many students take a gap year or years. It's more than ok to decide that college isn't right for you at this point and maybe you (or your family) need just a little time. A gap year is never a bad or shameful thing. If anything, it might be the smartest choice to give yourself some time, depending on your situation. You might not like any of the colleges you've gotten into, or maybe you're not in a good place financially, mentally, emotionally, or physically to handle college. If it helps you get your head on straight and appreciate college and take advantage of all the resources, then take that gap year.

If you decide early on that you want to take a gap year between high school and college, great! You have a lot of options for what to do with that gap year. There are amazing gap year programs, but they can be costly, or you can work for a year and raise money for college. I would also apply to one or two schools that you have a good chance of being accepted to. It will be good for you to go through the process and you will be prepared in case you change your mind.

This way, you can take the time you need to be ready for college. You will make tons of friends and potentially even be a leader among your peers because you might be a bit older. There's not much difference between an 18-year-old or a 20-year-old, so don't let those concerns stop you.

tl;dr

- Feel like you need more time to figure out what you want to do, recharge your batteries, or make a little money? A gap year might be a good idea for you. Even so, I encourage you to apply to colleges and then defer a year.

- Your admissions journey didn't quite work out the way you wanted it to, and you want some time to catch your breath and reassess? Consider a gap year. I suggest you accept a space at one of your acceptances and ask for a deferral.

CHAPTER 31

You Did It! Acceptances

This is it.

You've spent a lot of time and effort and dealt with loads of stress to get to this point. Once you receive that fat envelope of acceptance or confetti filled decision letter on your portal, you'll feel so accomplished. You'll realize that you've done something amazing.

But you're not quite done. There are a couple other things to consider once you receive your acceptances. You might have to choose between schools. There might be people who want to weigh in on your decision. Just remember **this is your choice.**

This part of the process shouldn't be as stressful though. While it's normal to feel worried about one of the biggest decisions you've ever made, I've found that life usually works out the way it's supposed to. It might not seem that way at first, but I promise you'll learn more from the challenges you overcome even in making this decision than the straightforward paths you follow.

So, take your acceptances, look at yourself, and take a deep breath.

A Word about "Likely Letters"

u/GeneriksGiraffe
Other than stats, what do you need realistically to get a likely letter from Ivies?

anonymous
How likely is a likely letter?
I haven't gotten one yet, and I'm lowkey freaking out.

> [−] penguinoloopo
> Likely letters are very uncommon, and only the top applicants get them. Not all colleges send them, and nobody should really be expecting one. It's more of just an extremely pleasant surprise that colleges use to help increase the odds of your accepting their offer. No need to panic, my guy!

let me break it down for you

A likely letter is a good thing. A very good thing. Essentially the college or university is saying they're really into you and want you to come to their school, and they're trying to beat other schools to the punch by being the first to tell you just how bad they want you. It's not an official acceptance (that happens when you get the acceptance letter), but a likely letter is a damn strong sign that you'll be accepted.

So, if you're one of the lucky few to get one of these letters, own it. Be proud of yourself. It means that something about your application connected with the school.

If you don't receive a likely letter, that doesn't mean you won't get in. Likely letters are extremely rare, and tons of kids at every school don't get them but still earn acceptances.

Accepted — Let the Party Begin!

u/musicman0910

I cried for the first time in about 7 years today...

So today I ditched a thespian meeting to go build guitars at my apprenticeship, and I was feeling pretty good because last night I was notified that I was one of the two people from my state traveling to Charlottesville for the final interview for the Jefferson scholarship at UVA. As my best friend and I are walking out to the parking lot, I get a call from New Haven. The next few minutes are an absolute blur, and it was a complete sensory overload. All I know is that my friends were screaming and carrying me around the parking lot, and I was shaking and screaming.

On the way to my apprenticeship, I called my mom to tell her, and I cried for the first time since middle school, but these were tears of joy.

I ran into this subreddit on the same day that I got rejected from Stanford, so I didn't really have time to utilize any of the resources, but I lurk daily. I have loved the process of seeing people achieving their dreams and driving forward with the ambition to change the world around them, and I wish the best of luck to everyone as we approach these final months of waiting.

> [–] admissionsmom
> Mazel Tov! So happy for you!

u/warrior__princess

I can't believe I did it

I'm holding my first acceptance packet in my hands...and I still don't believe it. Even if I don't get in anywhere else, I can go to my flagship state school! I feel overwhelmed. I feel so grateful. I never thought this process would end. Thank you, fam. I really don't know if I could have done this without y'all.

> [-] VA_Network_Nerd
> Write a letter to yourself. Describe this excitement. Tell yourself all the things you can't wait to do and

experience. Make yourself a list of experiences or adventures you can't wait to take on. Remind yourself about that one cool part of the school's promotional video or the campus tour that sealed the deal for you about this particular school.

There will be periods of darkness ahead. They seldom last terribly long, but they can be powerfully oppressive while they last. You might have a glorious asshole for a professor who will do everything you can imagine to crush your spirit. It might feel as if the very light is being sucked out of your world.

1200 words from yourself to your future-self describing the light, the future brightness, the wonder and glory of life-experiences may be the very beacon of hope and renewal of determination you need to find a path out of temporary darkness. This level of motivation & excitement is uncommon, and a very powerful emotion. Put a little of it in a bottle for a rainy day.

If nothing else, call it a practical exercise in descriptive writing or self-reflection.

here's what you need to know

When someone comes on A2C with an exciting post about their acceptances, I usually respond with a "Mazel Tov!" or "Congrats!" with some balloons or smiley emojis that blend right in with the mountain of congratulatory responses. I love how supportive everyone on our subreddit is of each other's successes.

Be mindful of this feeling you have right now. The feeling of knowing that your hard work paid off. The feeling that your long journey into discovering who you are was worth the while. It was hard, no doubt, but it was worth it. Hold on to your feelings of self-worth, excitement, joy, and pride. You made those feelings happen. You'll encounter more challenges in college, and it can help to remember those good feelings and thoughts you earned during this process. Keep on being your awesome self no matter how amazing your feelings are or how shitty they are at some point later in your life. You're still the same badass person who got these acceptances.

Making a Decision

u/chanceme1234321
Can't decide!
Dartmouth vs. Brown. Advice? I'm just so glad I got in that I'm having a hard time choosing.

u/23dagreatest
Purdue or Indiana U?
Title. I want to stay in state. And public.

my thoughts

Congrats on your acceptances! Now comes the fun part — deciding which school to commit to. This is something no one can decide for you. You have to go with what feels right for you.

If you're having a hard time, here are a few tricks you can use to help you decide:

1. **Visit.** Visit the campuses and talk to kids. Maybe sit in on a philosophy class. Or meet a biology professor. Definitely, do the **Bench Test.** Sit in the space. Put your phone away and simply sit on a bench in the middle of campus, like on the quad or at the student center, and absorb the vibe for about half an hour. Eavesdrop. Maybe get a book out on your lap, so you don't look weird. Can you see yourself walking around and going to class there? Do you like the conversations you're hearing and want to be a part of them?

2. **Pros and Cons.** Make an oversized list of pros and cons on paper for each school. Like make it poster sized. Put the name of the school at the top and then list all the pros and cons that you can think of for each school. Consider aspects like culture, vibe, departments, finances, honors, social, academics, geography, weather, surrounding area, and distance from home. Put it on your wall and leave it there for a few days so you can look it over and add and subtract from it as you absorb the thoughts. Hang out with this lists for a few days and add to them as you think of something. When one has more cons than pros take it down.

3. **Do the 10/10/10 test**. Ask yourself: "How will I feel about my decision in 10 hours? 10 weeks? 10 years?"

4. **Tell a Few.** Make a choice. Tell your parents and maybe a few friends, and sleep on it. What's your gut feeling? Does it feel right? If so, go for it. If not, rethink.

5. **Coin Toss.** Try the coin toss trick. Assign a side of the coin to a school and toss it. That's your school. Tell your parents and a couple of friends. Then sleep on it. How do you feel?

Don't let anyone make you feel bad about your choice.

u/stuportrooper
dealing with judgment
I've talked about how I didn't have the best grades in high school. I know I turned it around too late to have a shot at more of the highly selective schools, but I'm proud of what I did do. And I'm proud that I'm going to my local state university, which I'm genuinely excited for.

But I can't handle these people telling me I'm settling for a shit school. No one has said those exact words, but I have family members that are being snooty af about it. Even some of my teachers are being buzzkills about this. They keep saying that they know I can do better and that I can transfer later, but I like my school. What can I say to get them to back off?

let me be straight with you

All you need to worry about is that you're going to a school that best serves you. Wear that college t-shirt proudly! Slap those stickers on your laptop. Be proud of your achievements, because believe me, going to college is a huge achievement. Be excited for the future and this new path you've found for yourself.

Most of all, don't accept the words of anyone who tries to denigrate your college choice. It's rude and, frankly, none of their business. As in most things, my advice is **"You do you."**

Here's a story I love from Neil Pasricha's *The Happiness Equation* adapted by my son, Joseph. It's all about Buddha's philosophy concerning the value we give to other people's words.

Buddha spent a lot of his time wandering around and teaching folks about how to live a good life. One day he was going about his business, sitting under the Bodhi tree, spreading his ideas when another Brahman, let's call him Fred, got all up in Buddha's face and said, "Hey, man, who said your ideas are right? You're not as smart as you think you are."

Buddha sat silently and smiled at Fred, only making Fred's cheeks grow red with rage. Fred spoke up again, "Hey! I'm talking to you! Stop smiling at me, freak."

Buddha kept smiling and then replied, "Do you ever have guests at your house?"

"Yeah, of course," Fred answered.

Buddha then asked, "And when you have guests, do you give them snacks, maybe some chips and dip?"

Fred replied, "Of course! I'm not about being a bad host."

Then Buddha chuckled wisely, "Well, if your guest says they don't want some chips, like they're not hungry or something, then to whom do those chips belong?"

"Uhhhh, weird question," Fred retorted. "But I guess me."

"Well," Buddha said, still smiling, "just as your guest didn't accept those chips, I'm not accepting your hateful words, and so those words are yours and not mine."

"Whoa," Fred said, "Mind. Blown."

You deserve it – A Look at Imposter Syndrome

Sometimes kids will come onto our subreddit who've had great success with their applications. They've been accepted to the schools they'd always imagined they attend and that they've worked so hard to be accepted to. Yet, to them, it still doesn't feel right. They wonder why they were accepted over others.

anonymous

Since I was a freshman in high school, and I first heard about the Ivies, I "knew" they were my destiny. I worked my butt off in high school: great grades (#4 in my class), pretty high scores on my SAT (1490), captain of two sports, and I worked 20 hours a week to help out my single mom. When it came time to apply, I was confident that I'd be a strong applicant to HYPSM, so that's where I focused my applications. Well, last week I got my acceptances: Harvard - yes, Stanford - yes. OMG. Now, I recognize that there is no way I should have been accepted to those schools — I mean, I probably shouldn't have even applied. Wtf was I thinking? I look at the average SAT scores and see all the kids with college-level research and Carnegie Hall performances, and I know that there's no way I can compete with those kids. Why would they even accept me? I think Harvard and Stanford probably made a big mistake, and Princeton, Yale, and MIT were right. I deserve a big rejection.

I'm so confused. Wondering if I should just go to my state school or community college now.

> [-] admissionsmom
> Oh my. I'm so sorry you're feeling this way. This is called Imposter Syndrome, and it can really f*ck with your brain if you let it. Remember though: it's just a feeling. Here's the deal: You are good enough. You are worthy of getting into a ton of schools. I can tell that by reading what you just wrote in a few words. Harvard and Stanford spend a lot of time and resources evaluating applications. They don't screw up. If they feel like you can handle the work — you can. Look, there will always be people who have stronger this and better that. That's never going away. Harvard and Stanford took you because you are you. That's what they wanted. Congrats on your amazing acceptances! You are gonna kill it in college.

tl;dr

- A likely letter is a message from a school telling you that you're probably going to be accepted. They are very rare and it doesn't mean you're rejected if you didn't receive one.

- Acceptance is a stellar accomplishment. Be proud of yourself!

- If you're struggling to decide between a few schools, visit them all if you can. Make a pros and cons list. Tell a very select few people which school you've chosen, and then sleep on it to see how you feel.

- Don't accept the words of those busybodies who think they have the right to be rude about your college choice. Be like the Buddha, and let those words roll off you.

- Imposter syndrome is when you feel like you don't deserve the successes you've earned. It is a feeling, and it can be hard to shake. Don't let it mess with you. You are worthy.

CHAPTER 32

International Students – Coming to America

There are a ton of international students on r/ApplyingtoCollege, and they're some of the kids who need the most help navigating the complex US college admissions process. They log in to Reddit from all over the world. There are little pieces of A2C advice in Nepal, China, Iran, Tajikistan, Singapore, India, Pakistan, Bangladesh, Vietnam, Chile, Peru, Burma, Thailand, Ghana, Indonesia, Uzbekistan, Scotland, Brazil, and more — really all over the globe.

We do our best to help them with what we can, but the fact of the matter is that applying to colleges in the US from abroad is a challenge, especially when it comes to financing their education.

u/ RouJoo

How can I, a citizen from Canada, become competitive enough to get in one of the Ivy League or top 10 US schools? I'm currently in grade 11, and at this point, I'm getting really desperate and frustrated. First of all, there isn't much opportunity here in British Columbia. AP classes only start during grade 11 (this honestly pisses me off), and I was only able to take one this year and will take 3 next year. I've done the SAT once (1320) and will definitely rewrite again since I only had 2 weeks to prep. I have about a 95 avg and a 4 GPA (they don't weight GPA here). I do a decent amount of extracurricular compared to most students here, but it's still nothing compared to US students since there aren't as many clubs here. I need help on what else I can do. I am just so desperate to not end up in UBC when I know I have the capability to do so much more. Any help will be appreciated, thanks.

> [–] admissionsmom
>
> It's extremely competitive for international students at highly selective schools. I do know international students who've gotten in, but they demonstrated a great level of not only amazing grades and test scores, but intellectual curiosity and a desire to create change — either in their community or school. They also usually had some very strong interests that they were pursuing. We can't do that for you here. You're going to have to do some self-reflection and figure out who you are and who you want to be first. Good luck! I'm sure you're going to have all sorts of amazing choices in the end.

u/RouJoo

Applying to US schools as a Canadian citizen

If I would apply, am I compared against US applicants or international applicants like me? If it's US applicants, I would lose by a landslide since there aren't as many opportunities here for me and seems quite unfair. I think I MIGHT still have a chance if I'm compared against other international students. Also, if both my parents got a college degree outside of Canada (Philippines) do I still count as a first-generation immigrant since they technically do not have a degree from Canada?

here's my take

One of the major concerns for students coming to the US from abroad is how they will stack up compared to US students. Well, colleges don't evaluate your application in the same pool as American applicants. Instead, you will be evaluated in the international pool, and often against students from your own country. Colleges know that you may not be able to take APs or that your opportunities for extracurriculars may be different in other countries.

However, colleges still adhere to their standards for admittance. If your grades are low, even when taking into account your circumstances, you may not get into your college of choice.

If you feel like your grades might be too low, you can always go the community college route. Community college involves two years of study at a smaller institution before transferring to a four-year university to complete a degree. This arrangement allows international students to adjust to the US in a more intimate environment at a much lower cost than the traditional four-year university. As a former community college professor, I've taught students from China, Portugal, Brazil, Vietnam, El Salvador, Nigeria, Congo, Iraq, Iran, Syria, Argentina, and Angola, among many other nationalities.

Financial Aid for International Students

u/DADA_always_DADA
Financial aid for International students?
I'm coming from India, hopeful to study at an Ivy. While my parents are well-off here, the cost of college is a lot for them. Does anyone know of any good scholarships or other opportunities for international students?

let me break it down

I won't sugarcoat it: some schools have limited financial aid for international students, and applying as an international who needs full aid is super tough. Many of the financial aid resources I mention in this book are for US students only.

The financial reality is another reason why I recommend community college for many international students. You'll find the coursework rigorous, the environment supportive, and the cost much easier to handle. And then you can save money for the two years at a four-year university to complete your degree.

tl;dr

- International students are evaluated in the international pool, not in the US students pool.
- Financial aid for international students can be very difficult to come by.
- Community college for two years before transferring to a four-year university might be the best course of action. You'll save money, adjust to the US in a smaller environment, and be challenged by the coursework.

There are lots of other issues for international students that haven't been covered here that you'll need to research:

- TOEFL and other language tests for English proficiency
- International interview process
- Transcript translating
- Grade comparison
- Lack of multiple testing opportunities and locations
- The costs of travel and lack of ability to visit colleges before applying and even before you enroll

CHAPTER 33

Transfers

Transferring colleges is not as uncommon as you might think. Things happen that make what was once your excellent college fit no longer the right choice, such as a change in financial position or a family emergency. Or, you could decide that you don't like the college you've selected after all. Or, you could be finishing up your time at community college and planning your next steps toward a four-year institution.

Whatever your reasons for transferring, you should approach college applications in largely the same way as a high school kid going straight into a four-year institution. Yes, you have some extra considerations to plan for and hurdles to overcome, but it's nothing you can't handle.

Do your research.

u/life_heymikey

Anyone know how many transfers T20s take?
Title. I'm trying to ascertain my chances of getting into one of these schools from my community college.

u/soft_kittywarm_kitty

Have to change schools
I finished my freshman year at a small private college, and it isn't for me. Anyone here who's been in the same boat and has advice for a possible transfer?

i'll tell you the truth

Before you get your hopes up about any particular school, please research how many transfers that school accepts each year. Not that you can't get in, but you should be aware that some highly selective schools will be a reach for each and every single transfer applicant — just as they are reaches for every single freshman applicant. Some of the most highly selective schools, like Harvard or Stanford, accept only one or two transfer students a year, if that. It's tough. I've had transfer clients with 4.0 GPAs, and hella cool extracurriculars get rejected because, despite their stellar applications, schools like Harvard took one transfer out of 1000 transfer applications. Just as with freshman college admissions, you shouldn't put all your eggs in one basket.

But that doesn't mean you can't transfer to a quality school that excites you. When you're creating your college spreadsheet and evaluating college fit (as every applicant should), add the transfer acceptance percentage to your list, so it becomes another piece of the puzzle that you can easily see and track.

Another critical part of your research into transferring includes reassessing your test scores and grades. One thing to consider is the timing of your transfer. If you choose to transfer after your freshman year, your SAT or ACT scores still carry a good amount of weight for the admissions process. However, if you wait to transfer until after your sophomore year, your scores become a lot less important for many schools. Again, it all comes back to properly researching the schools where you want to transfer.

Regarding grades, if you feel like they might be a weak part of your application, reach out to the college you're interested in and ask them. This is especially true for transfer applicants who have struggled at their previous college or who had some other situation that impacted their grades. You might need to rehabilitate your record in community college for a semester or two to demonstrate to them that you are ready to be a serious student.

Furthermore, you need to make sure you check each school's transfer requirements. Some schools require certain classes, so make sure that you have taken those or will have completed them by the time you transfer.

Additionally, you need to do your research to make sure that your new college will give you the positive college experience you want and deserve. Be very specific about what each school you consider can provide for you over your current school. Will a new private college provide you with research experience that you'll be more excited and less apathetic about? Will the big state school provide you with the college feel you want after a few years of community college?

The only right answers are the ones that help you become more engaged with your studies, make better connections with your professors, and enjoy your time as a student. Don't be afraid of the answers you come up with. You have to do what's right for you, what will nurture you as a student. Depending on your situation, you might find that you should seriously consider taking a gap year or taking another year at community college before you move on.

Applying as a Transfer

u/softkitty_warmkitty
Transfer deadlines
When do transfer applications go live? I've seen different dates all over the place.

u/life_heymikey
Advice for transfer hopeful
I know it can be hard to transfer, especially to T20. Anyone know how many schools I should apply to?

here's what to do

Because you are applying to college, which can be complicated, transfer students need to be aware of the practical considerations. Here are some of the major pieces of advice to keep in mind as you embark on your journey:

1. **Be mindful of application dates.** Usually, applications open August 1. Some applications open on July 1, but spring transfers will usually have different deadlines. Those can be found on a school's website. Sometimes transfer applications show up a little later on the Common App.

2. **Apply to lots of schools.** Because it is so crazy selective for transfers, I encourage you to apply to as many schools as you can afford, provided they are a good fit, and you can afford the fees.

3. **Tailor your essays.** For my transfer clients, I usually suggest that they tailor their personal statement essays based on school if they can. I don't suggest that for freshmen. Colleges want to know why you need to transfer to their school. What is it specifically about their school that will provide what you need versus the school you currently attend?

4. **Be aware of additional application requirements.** You can use the Common App or Coalition App, depending on the application platform the schools have chosen, but keep an eye out for some additional requirements that can vary by school. For example, you might need to write an additional essay about your reasons for transferring. Such essays are usually a little more specific and direct than the ones for freshmen. While the essay remains focused on you, and admissions officers are eager to see your authenticity,

you also need to address why you are transferring and what you're looking for in the school.

5. **Don't forget to tell them your story!** If you need to explain certain aspects of your application, explain your situation in the additional information section of the application.

tl;dr

- Transferring colleges, for whatever reason, isn't as rare as you might believe.

- If you want to transfer, you need to do a lot of research to make sure you set yourself up for success. That includes transfer requirements, how your grades and test scores will stack up, and how many transfer students the schools accept in a given year.

- Make sure you can clearly express why your potential transfer school would provide for your needs better than your current college.

- Stack the odds in your favor by tracking application dates, applying to a lot of schools, tailoring your essays to schools, being mindful of application requirements, and sharing your story with admissions officers.

CHAPTER 34

Veterans — Thank You for Your Service

First of all, for all of you active, reserve, or former service members, let me say thank you for your service, and good for you for looking to keep moving your life forward!

The college admissions process is not an easy journey for anyone, but it can be particularly intimidating for veterans. I know it can be easier said than done, but put aside the past and focus on who you are right now — a capable, dependable, skilled service member. You've given up years of your life to serve your country and gained tons of valuable experience along the way. Tons of colleges would love to have you and the unique perspective you offer. If all these kids can do it, you can too.

You might just need a little help finding your way.

It's never too late for college.

u/gulfcoast_babe
Vet trying to get back in the school game
I wasn't a good student the first time around. But I joined the army, got my sh!t together, and I'm ready to give this another shot. I want to go to college, maybe even grad school (I'd love to get an MBA). What can I do to get myself back on track?

[-] admissionsmom
Many thanks for your service.

Here is an amazing program I have heard about. Please look into it. http://www.warrior-scholar.org/ Also, I think you should consider enrolling in community college and getting into the habit of being a student. Maybe you can take just one class to get back into the swing of things or go full-time if you're feeling ready to go. You should consider beginning to study for either the ACT or SAT. Take some practice tests and see how you do to decide which one to focus on. Then prepare for the one that feels the best to you and that you have the chance of being most successful. Many colleges are happy to have vets on their campus. Talk to the veterans' affairs or admissions offices at the colleges you are interested in.

my thoughts and some helpful info

Before you start on your college admissions journey, I encourage you to look at the Warrior-Scholar Project mentioned above. It's a really impressive and helpful program helping bright former service personnel find their way into selective schools. In the program's own words, it was "Designed to provide mentoring and other forms of guidance for enlisted service members wishing to attend four-year universities." The program also, "seeks to teach the skills required for effective and successful learning in the college environment."

The Warrior-Scholar Project offers free college transition courses for enlisted military service members currently on active duty, on reserve duty, or who have already separated. As long as you haven't completed a four-year bachelor's degree, you can apply for this program. During the immersive course, you will brush up on everything from analytic reading to writing skills. You will also learn about the challenges you will probably face in your transition from life in the military to college. The program includes two models: a one-week Liberal Arts Model and a two-week Liberal Arts + STEM curriculum model.

The course includes room and board, and all the books and course materials are provided to you. On their website, http://www.warrior-scholar.org, you can find a long list of dates and locations for their courses, all of which are held on college campuses around the country. You can even attend the course at a school where you don't plan on applying.

Applications for the Warrior-Scholar Project open in January and continue on a rolling basis. Admission is first-come, first-serve, and admitted service members will start their courses beginning the following summer.

You should also check out Service to School (https://service2school.org/), a non-profit that provides free college application counseling to service members. It comes highly recommended by veterans, especially those on r/ApplyingtoCollege. The primary goal of Service to School is to provide mentoring and assistance to service members and veterans through a list of awesome resources and their impressive Ambassador network.

Founded and run by veterans, Service to School pairs each veteran with an "Ambassador" who will guide you through the application process and offer helpful advice and information. Each Ambassador used to be in your shoes, so they know how to answer your questions and point you in the right direction. Ambassadors help you with everything from test prep, resumes and transcripts, to applications, essay review, interviews, and networking. In fact, the Service to School Ambassador network includes over 200 veterans all over the nation, which will help you make real connections with schools from UT Austin to Smith College to Yale.

Applications for the Undergrad Admission Support program are available online and can be filled out in less than ten minutes.

Also, be sure to check out the Student Veterans of American (SVA) Chapters. Most schools have them and they can help answer questions you might have about individual schools.

Assess your current position.

u/sofresh__and_soclean
Need some advice on where to start with applications
I have several questions for my application. For the record, I'm a Marine vet, and it's been a while since I've thought about college stuff.

- What's the difference between the ACT and the SAT?
- Will colleges look down at my not-great high school grades, or will they be more impressed with my service?
- Any tips for colleges that have good sports medicine programs for vets? Is that a thing?
- I'm sure I'm not thinking of something.

> [–] admissionsmom
> After you check out the Warrior-Scholar Project and Service to School, evaluate your student profile. You know you'll need to submit test scores for college, so consider beginning to study for either the ACT or the SAT. To decide which one to focus on, take some practice tests and see how you do. Then focus on the one that feels the best to you, and you'll have the chance of being most successful. This also goes for those of you who may have taken the SAT or ACT in high school before you began your service. Depending on your scores, how long ago you took the test, and your college goals, you may not have to take the SAT or ACT again, or you may be able to raise your scores.
>
> Take this opportunity to evaluate any portions of your application that could use a little work. Community college is a great option for veterans returning to school, as you can

always enroll in your local community college to get into the habit of being a student — even just trying one class to get back into the study groove. For example, if you really want to study STEM at a four-year college, but your high school math grades aren't the strongest, consider enrolling in math classes at your community college. Get a tutor ASAP. Put your best foot forward.

Above all else, don't be afraid to take the initiative and talk directly to admissions officers. It never hurts to make an appointment with a college's admissions office. There, you can talk to them and see what suggestions they have for your situation. Admissions officers are generally friendly and approachable. They will probably have an admissions officer who helps with vets. I'm sure they will be more than happy to guide you through the process or at least lead you to someone who can help.

Tons of veterans have successfully transitioned from the military to college and beyond. You are more than able to do the same and forge your own path.

tl;dr

- Check out the Warrior Scholar Project (http://www.warrior-scholar.org) and Service to School (https://service2school.org/)
- If you haven't taken the SAT or ACT, start looking into the tests and considering which might work better for you.
- Check out your local community college to see whether this would be a good place for you to get your feet wet and get started.
- Check in with the Veterans Affairs and Yellow Ribbon programs at your local universities.
- Don't hesitate to ask for help.

Some words from one of our most popular "Adults" and a fellow parent on A2C:

u/VA_Network_Nerd

$100K+ Scholarship for every US Citizen & Permanent Resident Available Immediately

I'm talking about a Scholarship award that is available to essentially every citizen or green-card holding permanent resident with no requirement of exceptional performance.

You'll need a full High School diploma. Any GPA score will qualify. No AP or SAT tests. No IB scores. You will not have to maintain stellar academic performance for years and years. You will not have to help carry your Varsity Sports Team to State, Regional, or Nationals to win this Scholarship award.

Applying to schools using this Scholarship program can improve your chance of acceptance.

This Scholarship is guaranteed to pay all Tuition and most Meals & Housing at any PUBLIC University in the US. If you can get accepted into UVA or UC Berkeley, all your bills are covered.

This Scholarship will pay up to $100K, and in some cases even more, towards your attendance at a PRIVATE institution of your choosing. If you can get accepted into Princeton or Georgetown or MIT, this Scholarship can help cover a whole lot of your expenses.

This Scholarship award is available right now if you want it. This Scholarship will require four years of service, but you will be paid and provided housing & meals during your service. This Scholarship will provide complete healthcare for the duration of your service. After four simple years of service, you are eligible for your award.

I'm talking about the GI Bill, offered through the US Armed Services. I am not a recruiter, but I am a veteran (USMC 1990-94).

CHAPTER 35

There's a Place for You: LGBTQ and First-Gen/Low-Income (including foster kids and homeless students)

LGBTQ

anonymous
Should I come out in my essay or not?
My parents have no idea I'm gay, and they'll kick me out of my house if they find out, but I really feel like it's important to let the colleges know—because reasons. Would it be hella stupid for me to just come right out and write about it in my essay? I mean I lowkey just wanna write my entire personal statement about it. Would that be too much? And how do I keep my parents from reading?

u/USS-Enterprise
This is a vent, with bad formatting and possibly [probably] TMI
Guys, help. I hate my life as it is. The real reason my applications are sh!t is that I really couldn't handle ECs with my crippling anxiety sophomore year, so I quit them all and also depression means I've had mediocre grades all high school. I'm trans & gay, and my parents wouldn't approve, and I'm honestly scared if I could afford college at all if they kicked me out. I don't want to be kicked out. :(but I also want to leave...but I don't want to be completely f*cked for life. I guess I just wanna die or something sorry for this, guys.

anonymous
So, I'm trans and looking to [trans]fer :)

I might wanna transfer in the future, but there are a few things I'm confused about. Like, do I have to apply with my deadname, or can I apply with my name, and what about my transcript? Do you think they'll change my name on my record? No one really knows that I'm trans around here, and I'd like to apply to my new school without my deadname. Also, do you think T20 schools will care if I'm trans or not, or should I just keep it to myself and not tell them when I'm applying?

> [−] admissionsmom
> I'm not sure how that works with your transcript. Do you have a legal name change? If so, maybe they can officially change your transcript at your current school, so that when you apply to the new school, your name will match your identity. And I don't think you should worry about whether being trans will affect your acceptances or not. It is what it is. Focus on finding schools that will welcome you for who you are.

here are my thoughts

LGBTQ applicants have their own set of special issues to consider when applying. I think, first and foremost, it's essential that you find schools that are safe and who openly accept LBGTQ students. I think you should consider being open about it in your application — especially if you're trans and planning to transition while in college, using the additional information section to explain your situation, whether you've already transitioned for the most part or you are planning to. Trans students have to be aware of some practical concerns that could have an effect on your college experience, like the dorm and bathroom situation. Are you applying with the transcript of one gender, but know you plan to transition while in college? In that case, you might want to look for schools that have mixed gender floors and bathrooms. Also, investigate the state laws and look into how accommodating the school is for trans and other LGBTQ students.

Many liberal arts colleges are particularly safe and welcoming to the LGBTQ community. You can find out by snooping around their website, going on a visit and asking students or the admissions office, or checking out their LGBTQ clubs and groups online and seeing how active they are. If you can visit, definitely stop by and check any services or centers they may have for you. Or reach out to them online or by phone. Ask if there is one; if there's not, that might be a sign that the school wouldn't be particularly welcoming.

As far as writing about it, that will be up to you. It certainly won't hurt to address any concerns and issues you've had in the past and overcome in the additional info section. To me, if a college didn't want to accept me for an essential part of who I am, then I wouldn't want to go there. So, I ask you why would you want to go to a college who wouldn't accept you simply because you're trans, gender non-conforming, gay, or another gender or sexual minority? As far as your parents go, you don't have to let them see all of your application, but if they have total access and you worry they'll see it, then you can always submit a paragraph later by email or in the upload section if necessary. Of course, I think it's good to be open and honest with your parents, but I know that's unfortunately not always the best option.

First-Generation or Low-Income Students

As if college applications weren't hard enough, being a first-gen or low-income college student (or both!) comes with its own set of challenges on top of everything else. In addition to being the first in your family to blaze this trail, you might feel a lot of pressure to make your parents proud by going to an Ivy or studying something that doesn't interest you. Or maybe your family and friends see no value in a college education and ridicule your desire to go.

Going through the process can be very isolating — as if no one understands what you're going through.

But you know what? You can do this. Every year, thousands of first-gen and low-income kids apply to and get accepted to amazing schools. Each winter and spring, numerous first-gen/low-income kids get into schools and make their families extremely proud. Sometimes those schools have famous names like Harvard or Columbia, and sometimes they don't. More importantly, countless first-gen/low-income kids prove to themselves that they could not only hack it with college admissions, but they could bring home awesome acceptances.

If you're reading this book as a first-gen or low-income student, you have already shown that you're ambitious and driven. You've taken a huge first step to fulfill your college plan. Congrats. That's a big deal.

How might being a low-income student affect you?

As you are looking for colleges for your list, keep your financial needs front and center. You're often going to get much more financial aid from private schools, and your in-state schools will probably be your next financially viable bet. Look for colleges that have large endowments and who give lots of aid. Check out the "Colleges that Change Lives" website (www.ctcl.org) for many more options. Lots of colleges are eager for students like you. Help them find you!

Here are some issues that have come up in our subreddit that you might encounter and should be ready for as a low-income college applicant or student:

- Make sure you have a working credit or debit card to pay for when submitting test scores, financial aid forms (I get the irony…), and applications. I've seen far too many kids having to run from family member to friends to find a card that will work. Be prepared before admissions deadlines.

- Once you're attending college, make sure you are prepared for not having access to the cafeteria if you stay in the dorms during school breaks. You may need to stockpile beforehand and take advantage of food pantries and food banks during that time.
- Be careful when taking out loans. Lots of kids get in over their heads with loans and then drop out, therefore being stuck with loans to pay and no degree.
- I've seen Redditors talk about feeling guilty for leaving their families behind and having experiences and lifestyles their families have only dreamed of. Remember that once you graduate, you are going to be able to make not only your life better, but you will bring more value to your family as well.

Recognize that being in college will expose you to all sorts of different people and many of them may have had more privileged upbringings than yours. Sometimes, you might feel self-conscious or out of place at college because their experiences and your experience might feel so different. Keep in mind everyone there is feeling a little of that insecurity. Just know that if anyone is judging you on your lack of finances, then they really don't deserve your time and attention. Move on and get to know the kids who are gonna fall in love with you for who you are, not what you have.

Who qualifies as First-Gen?

u/CatOwlFilms
Scholarships for first-generation Americans?
While I was born here, my parents are immigrants from Eastern Europe, where they graduated medical school (meaning, I think, I'm not a first-gen college student or a URM). Does anyone know of any scholarships for people whose parents are immigrants? I'm already aware of scholarships for my ethnicity.

u/4m_33s
Looking for help in identifying red flags and safety schools.
Hooks: I might be a first gen since my father only has an associate degree, and my mother a high school degree. Honestly not sure if I'm first-gen and would like some clarification.

> [–] admissionsmom
> The rule of thumb is that, if your parents have college degrees, then you're not a first-gen college student. If your parents received their degrees in another country, you simply include that information when you fill out the section about your parents. Schools will determine how they want to categorize you from that information.

Foster Kids and Homeless Students

Out of all the stories I read on A2C, I have to say that some of the most inspirational and heartbreaking come from our homeless students and foster kids. These are kids who have truly risen above what for many would be insurmountable obstacles, and yet, here they are — applying to and being admitted to colleges, and often to colleges many would only dream of applying to. You are examples for us all.

There are some basics that need to be addressed here for you. I know that many of you are working on apps through your phone because you don't have access to a computer, and many of you are making do without some of the necessities of life to pay for your applications. Make sure you talk about your circumstances in the additional information section of your application. Colleges want to know where you're coming from and what you've had to overcome to get that application to them. Also, I want you to think about where you will go on school breaks. This is something you can address with the admissions officers of the schools you are applying to and see if they leave dorms open or if you will have to fend for yourselves. It's better to know that upfront. You should be aware that some states offer full tuition for wards of the state, homeless, and foster students, so talk to your school counselor and see if there are any special circumstances that could apply to you.

here's what you need to know

Contrary to what a lot of misinformed people think, being first-gen, low-income, or even homeless isn't an automatic ticket into your top choice school with a full ride. Of course, colleges will consider your first-gen or your financial status as they evaluate your applications, but it's not an excuse for anything. It's just a factor for understanding your circumstances.

Consequently, first-gen and low-income students need to be educated about all their options. Be sure to look through the Resources Chapter to learn more about helpful organizations, resources, and guides specifically for first gen or low-income kids.

Find a Community

u/ secretgeek69

Where are the low-income, first-generation, students of color at?

If you are a pre-frosh/college student, let's use this place as a hub to voice the struggles we have had to overcome and lend advice to those who were once in our position!

> [–] admissionsmom
> I love this idea and want you to keep coming back with your message and offers of community. There are a lot of you here, and the rising seniors are looking for as much help as you'll be willing to give.

tl;dr

- LGBTQ kids: you are just as worthy of having an awe-some college experience as anyone. That being said, you will probably have various concerns to consider, including acceptance and safety. Make sure you find an environment that supports you for you.

- First-gen/low-income kids: you are just as smart, capable, and awesome as non-first-gen, more privileged kids. Remember that. You can do this.
- You're a first-generation college student if neither of your parents has a college degree.
- There are a lot of resources first-gen/low-income students should check out: The Coalition Application, QuestBridge, the Jack Kent Cooke Foundation, Dell Scholars, Bezos Scholars, and the Posse Foundation, just to name a few.
- The challenges you face are unique. Find a community to gain the support and reassurance you need.

CHAPTER 36

Prepping for College Admissions — Freshmen and Sophomores

To some kids, it feels like once they step foot into high school, college suddenly appears on the horizon, a big black cloud they will spend four years watching come closer and closer. I understand where they're coming from — after all, there's so much pressure these days to perform well and craft yourself into a particular kind of student.

But what ends up happening is that too many freshman and sophomores end up creating a lot of stress and anxiety for themselves way too early. They miss out on enjoying high school and getting to know themselves as teenagers. There's a ton of stuff to do for college, yes, but a lot of that stuff can't be done meaningfully until your junior and senior years.

So, while there are some steps you can take as a freshman or sophomore to make your college admissions journey a little easier, I want you to remember that your job during those two years of high school is to focus on being a high school student. There will be plenty of time for college admissions.

The Freshman/Sophomore Game Plan

u/Checksallovame

Getting started on college admissions

I'm a freshman who is set on attending an Ivy or another really good school. UCLA is a dream of mine. I want to start honing my skill set and polishing my activities/grades/etc., now. Any advice?

> anonymous
>
> Oof you really should not be on these types of forums this early. It really screws with your mindset. Prepping early does indeed help, but you need to come at it with a firm understanding that you are in high school to explore and broaden your horizons and do cool stuff without worrying about consequences, not gunning for college.
>
> That said, I really applaud your ambition! You have plenty of time to smooth it forward. I'd suggest looking at more options by getting involved with school clubs – it sounds like throwaway advice, but honestly, clubs are a cheap, friendly way to get to know majors from across the expanse. I would have never gotten into the major I'm planning on entering if I hadn't literally randomly walked into the club one day attracted by the free food. Get into random clubs, maybe even ones you think sound boring, and really try to get involved. Clubs are only fun if you put in the effort.
>
> Another piece of advice is, don't be afraid to start small. Smart people know when to aim high and, sometimes, when to not. You never know the connections you'll build from the stupid engineering program you're in right now that you find boring. Try hard in everything you're in – your efforts will not be overlooked, and you'll find out that it is always opportunities that lead to better opportunities.

u/and_illwriteyourname
Sophomore college prep?
Hey all, what can I do to start my college prep as a sophomore? I'm in clubs and do my sports and all, plus I'm working on improving my grades as needed. Anything else?

here's my take

Let's get down to basics — you should be spending a huge chunk of your time in high school enjoying your educational experience (as much as possible) and learning about the world, history, science, math, literature, and of course, more about you and who you are. You have four years, and you should not spend all four years writing college essays.

You don't actually need to do much during freshman and sophomore years other than take a few SAT Subject Tests, taking the most rigorous course load you can handle while living a well-balanced, healthy life, doing the best you can academically, finding extracurriculars that speak to you, and exploring yourself as a person and a student. Believe me; there's plenty to do during junior and senior years.

Be aware that my philosophy in this area differs from a lot of other sources. The best way to manage this advice (and all the other advice you may or may not be getting) is to listen with an open mind and then decide what works best for you.

Freshman Year

I know many of you freshman reading this are probably freaking out right now because either you are overwhelmed by the idea of applying to college, or you have no clue if you should be doing anything. Add to that the challenge of starting high school, and you could really be stressing out.

But you don't have to do a whole lot right now. My biggest suggestion to freshman is to consider taking a Subject Test this summer. For example, if you're in biology right now, study for the Subject Test and take it in June.

Take the hardest course load you can comfortably manage. Also, be mindful of the courses you are taking. For example, lots of highly selective schools prefer to see applicants with four years of a foreign language, as well as biology, chemistry, and physics. They also like to see that you will take Calculus by your senior year at the latest.

Aside from course load, be yourself, which means finding out who that is. Explore your interests. Get involved in school clubs or activities. Volunteer in your community. Do something interesting and meaningful to you this summer. Most of all, take care of yourself, physically, mentally, and emotionally.

Sophomore Year

Again, there's not a whole lot of college stuff you can or should be focusing on in your sophomore year. But there are a few things to do now that you will be applying to college easier down the road.

Like you did freshman year, take a Subject Test or two in May or June after your sophomore year. Many schools want to see them, and lots of seniors have to scramble to take them because they didn't know about them. Study for and take one or two for subjects you are taking this year. I suggest taking at least one from math or science and one from humanities by the summer before your senior year. Some engineering programs like to see Math II and Physics. Taking these Subject Tests now will make it easier to apply to schools in all ranges of selectivity.

This year, work to keep your grades up. Take the most rigorous course load you can comfortably manage while keeping your grades up and being involved in activities outside schoolwork.

Consider prepping for the PSAT the summer after sophomore year. You can win a lot of scholarship money and some auto admits with National Merit money, so it's worth spending some time prepping for the test. You'll take it junior year in October.

Do something meaningful this summer. A job. A project. Community service. Be involved. And don't forget to make yourself a priority. Learn about your budding interests. Find out what's interesting about you. And take care of your body, mind, and heart.

tl;dr

- During your freshman and sophomore years, college admissions should not be your main focus. However, there are a few things you can do to make your college admissions journey a little smoother.
- What you can do: take the most rigorous course load you can comfortably manage. And plan to take four years of foreign language and three years of science.
- Take Subject Tests in the summer after you've completed the class.
- Take time to get involved in your school and community, not to pad your resume but to find out more about yourself. Nourish the person you are becoming. Cultivate your interests. Take care of yourself.

CHAPTER 37

Advice and Updates from our Community

When I first came to A2C, you could feel the anxiety dripping out of the computer screen, but I'm proud to report that our little (but growing!) community is evolving into a much more supportive and informative place — not that the anxiety doesn't creep in. It does, of course. But so much of the time now I don't even have to give my normal speeches on breathing, forgetting about rankings, or self-care. There is often a more positive attitude toward college admissions that spreads to new students who come to r/ApplyingtoCollege looking for help.

I see this attitude all over r/ApplyingtoCollege, but I see it a lot in two significant kinds of posts — when older students give advice, and when graduating seniors and college students return to the subreddit to update everyone on their college adventure.

(For the most part, in the following posts, the bolding is mine.)

Advice from Other Students

u/Seemeina_crown
Need help!
Can someone give me a to-do list for college apps? I'm starting to obsess, and I do much better when I have something to focus on and do.

[–] Atvelonis

I drafted the Common App essay near the end of my Junior year and periodically tweaked it over the next few months. This is an important part of the application: **you need to choose a topic that reflects who you are, not necessarily what you assume is the flashiest or whatever.**

You'll want to start early on your supplements, too, of course. These can be very difficult, particularly the "Why us?" prompts for each college. I would strongly suggest touring and interviewing at the colleges you're considering: for me, this was surprisingly helpful in gauging the atmosphere of the schools. Talk to students, admissions officers, everyone — you learn more about the culture of these colleges that way than you would ever be able to on this subreddit.

Anyway, remember that all of these essays should act as channels for your thought processes, so be genuine and be creative. Write about things that are unique and interest you deeply (I can't stress this one enough). Your essays don't need to be about how you cured cancer; they just have to emphasize your personal qualities in a way that stats cannot.

Be authentic.

u/(tau) ivsamhth5

my thoughts on applying to college and life in general
TL;DR: **Do what you love and pursue it hard, because it will make your life more fulfilling and interesting, regardless of whether or not you get into XXXXX College**. And, it has the nice side effect of being what colleges like to see.

Confession: I didn't give a serious thought as to where I wanted to go to college or what I wanted to do until the end of sophomore year.

Side note: I'm Asian. My entire life, I've been pressured constantly and always do my best (meaning: get an A in everything), to get high scores on standardized tests, and even to pursue a career in medicine because that's what all the successful Asian kids do. This wasn't the kind of mindset I wanted. Yes, I realized grades and test scores were important, but I didn't want to spend my life checking off things on a list to be "successful." I wanted to do things that I found interesting, that mattered to me.

I started doing more math-y things, like joining a local math club, and that led to the start of my teaching career. Now, I'm teaching at math summer camp. For econ, I started doing research, working on models and reading papers and helping write one. Now I might be published in a journal before I even start college. For physics, I found some friends who loved science and started a science bowl team. We've since been to nationals, twice.

Basically, if you find areas that you enjoy, you're naturally more motivated to delve into them at a deeper level, and you never have to force yourself to do anything. You might not know where you'll end up in life, but you've got a direction. **Let's take a step back and ignore everything about admissions right now — regardless of whether or not you get into (insert name of selective college). You're a better person than you started out as — you're smarter, have more experience.** Above all, you hopefully now have something that you're interested in, something you enjoy for the rest of your life.

But now, let's go back to admissions. **Authentic — they want to see that you're a person. A real, live person with genuine interests, not someone that's just doing things so that they can get into college.**

Find what you love and do it. Maybe it's a sport. Maybe it's an instrument. Maybe it's research. Maybe it's being a leader in your community. Math. Baking. Napping. Hopscotch. Whatever it is, spend time on it. Immerse yourself in it. Enjoy it.

It's not all about getting into _____. **In the end, what matters is if you are happy. So actively try to make your life**

better, happier. Then, your college acceptances won't matter as much — but I think you'll do better with them too :)

I'll try always to be here to help you all through this process. Lots of love to all of y'all <3

> anonymous
>
> Yeah, ok. This is extra wholesome and all about being authentic, but dude, real talk, we gotta get this bread, and in order to do that, we gotta go ham. That means I gotta be better than thousands of people, bruh. How do I get better than all those other people so I can get into the college of my dreams? It's impossible, right? fml smh.
>
>> [–] (tau)ivsamhth5
>>
>> Think about this first — what makes you different from those thousands of other people that are going to be applying? What makes you better than them?
>>
>> As a truthful answer to that last question, you're probably not going to be — there will always, no matter who you are, be someone smarter, with higher scores/GPA, "better" ECs, whatever. No matter who you are, in every way you can think, someone is always better than you.
>>
>> "F*ck," you mutter. So, then what? Well, here's where it gets good. Every single school ends up accepting people that aren't the best. Every year. Hell, I mean they have to, right, since not everyone is the best? But, then how do you make one of those accepted students you?
>>
>> By being the most interesting person you can be. Have you ever seen someone and be like "Wow, they're so cool, I wish I could get to know them to be their friend"? Well, imagine that, but for admissions.
>>
>> K this is nice and all, but what does this mean for you?

ECs — **do INTERESTING things. Don't just do them because people tell you that you should.** Find something that you actually enjoy doing and do something cool with it! (This is what I usually call a "fantastic" EC — one that someone truly, truly loves doing and you can see it when they talk about it.)

Essays — don't just write a cookie-cutter essay about how getting injured in sports made you grow, or how making new friends after moving was difficult. Talk about something that is truly you. My counselor always talked about the "name" test. If you dropped a (college) essay in the hallway in your school, and one of your friends picked it up and could know that it was actually you that wrote it, then BOOM, that's the kind of essay you want to have.

Trust yourself.

u/doubutsuai

A Test of Trust

Lots of people will give you advice, but it's important not to mess with your voice. People who read your essays and offer advice are amazing people with good intentions, but your own sense of trust should trump the words of others. Nobody knows you more than yourself, and no one can get you into your favorite college except yourself.

Whether I'm accepted or rejected or deferred, I know that I will have had control over this entire process. It seems silly to say, but that fact gives me some comfort about everything around me. If I get in, I'll celebrate my individuality. If I don't, I know I'll have tried my absolute hardest and made my application as strong as humanly possible. I'm comfortable in my own skin, triumphs and flaws alike. So, seniors, please: trust yourself. Take a risk, do something weird, surprise (or terrify) your relatives with your unique voice. It might not get you into your dream school, but it'll definitely pay off in some form in the end:)

You are loved.

u/elkakey

No matter what happens tomorrow, know that you are loved.

I know the title might sound super sappy, but it's true. I have taken some of my rejections very hard, and it's made me question my self-worth. I know it's easy to say that the Ivies don't matter, or that you'll be just as happy at your second pick school, or whatever the adage may be. I've heard all of them, and I still have sleepless nights over my Barnard rejection (which was almost a week ago!).

But I have found a phenomenal group of people in Sarah Lawrence's admitted student pages and group chats. While that's specific to my experience, I think the general concept rings true for many of us.

We may not end up in the places we imagined tomorrow. But know that you are loved by those around you and by whatever community that you become a part of next year.

I wish you all the best of luck.

Updates and Reflections

I love it when the kids come back and give advice and updates and let us know what it's like on the other side. One of our active Redditors from last year emailed me with this update at the beginning of the fall semester: **"I went to orientation last week and remembered just how nervous I was at the beginning of this process, then realized that despite not being exactly where I dreamed of being, I had in fact gotten everything I wanted. Thank you. :)"** To me, this pretty much says it all.

u/TheNextFaker

Hey again! So, I didn't get into any of my 8 reaches, and I'll be going to my 9th choice school

but I just wanted to say thanks a lot for everything. For all the advice, help editing my essays, and comforting words when I needed it most. I've previously never been big on Reddit and used it primarily to burn time, but I'd never imagined I'd use it for help on my college applications.

Again, thanks a lot of everything. I've only become more motivated to work harder, accomplish more things, build a more competitive profile, and achieve all my dreams.

> [−] admissionsmom
>
> Congrats to you! You were going for some pretty extreme reaches. I'm sorry that didn't work out for you, but it seems like you have learned a lot about yourself in the process. Good luck and keep in touch!

u/GammaHuman

Hello AdmissionsMom!

I just thought I'd give you a little update on my going to A&M, partially because I think you might be proud and partially because I'm telling everyone who will listen. I got accepted off of the waitlist for their Honors Program! I'm super-duper excited about the opportunities it should bring. Thought I would let you know. I hope you, your children, and your advisees are all doing well. Best wishes, Gamma

> [−] admissionsmom
>
> Hi Gamma! Wowee and Mazel Tov! That is so cool and well-deserved! Yes. Definitely thanks for updating me. Can't wait to hear about more of your successes next year.

u/admissionscousin

Accepted to Columbia

You may remember me from "So you wanna work for Google," which I posted during the holidays. I noted at the bottom that, despite being a dropout with a good career, I was looking to transfer somewhere to finish school. At the time I wasn't sure where, but with the help of my username-aunt /u/admissionsmom, I was able to get into Columbia University's School of General Studies. I'm absolutely thrilled to have the opportunity to study at a competitive and rigorous university! I'm not like most students on this subreddit in that I was very disinterested in school growing up. I didn't take APs, didn't study for the SAT/ACT, etc. I did have a lot of ECs back then and continued to pile them on since, but that was only out of personal interest. It wasn't until last summer when I found this subreddit that **I learned there was more to college apps than high test scores**. I look forward to connecting with the brilliant students, getting a well-rounded education via the Core, and finally proving to myself that I can stick with it and earn a degree. Thanks a billion /u/admissionsmom!!

> [–] admissionsmom
>
> You're very welcome! It was all my pleasure, and I'm so excited for you. You'll definitely have to keep me updated!

u/zztempo314

Personal Reflections on this College Season

Now that my last decisions from colleges have come out, I'm going to reflect on my experiences this season, as well as give some of my final thoughts. WARNING: THIS POST IS VERY LONG.

When I was in elementary school, my parents decided to homeschool me.

I made it to the AIME (~top 1% of all competition math takers) in 7th grade and went to ARML in 6th grade. I placed in top 10 in SoCal MATHCOUNTS twice (those of you who know SoCal also know how ridiculously competitive the math competitions are there), and I even represented the USA in several math competitions in China (no, not the IMO lol, I wasn't that good. It was the WMTC).

However, since I was an Asian male, my parents soon realized that I didn't stand out. How would I get into a good college if I am simply one of the other 9999999 Asian males that are good at math? So, I decided to tone down the competitive math study-ing a bit and pursued piano and Boy Scouts. I ended up receiving national awards from both fields (I was invited to play in Carnegie Hall, and I became Eagle Scout).

Just as college application season came around, my parents were confident. After all, I had a 1530 SAT, a decently strong GPA especially for a homeschooler (3.9uw/4.4w), and I was great at math, piano, and community service. I spent weeks on all of my apps, and in fact, during January of this year, my dad said, "You'll definitely get in all of the colleges you applied to." Yes, really, they were that confident.

Fast forward to today. 7 applications, 7 Ls. Not a single W, not even to a safety. I was devastated. $515 down the drain, along with hours and hours of painstaking essay refining. One of my first thoughts was "HOLISTIC REVIEW MY ASS," cuz I mean CLEARLY I stood out, and I was even homeschooled, so I didn't get to just take 50 AP classes at a super good high school. I had really good ECs (for the sake of space I only listed the ones where I received national awards), and I had volunteered A TON for community service.

Despondency started to kick in. I was known among many friends as "that smart guy; that nerd." How would they feel or make me feel when they ask, "Where are you going to college?" and I respond, "Uh, I'm going to community college?" And worst of all, whenever I compared myself to other people, that's when the bad attitude gets worse — it turns into jealousy. How the hell did those people with much lower test scores/GPA and barely any ECs get in, whereas I didn't? How it is fair, that they get to slack their asses off in school and watch TV/play video games for 6 hours each day while I am busy studying all that time, skipping all the parties?

However, after calming down at last, I am able to think posi-tively. Going to community college isn't a bad thing at all. Sure, I miss "the true college experience." Sure, that means I have to drive every day, potentially into rush hour traffic. But, it saves a LOT of money, and I can potentially transfer after 1 year, thus sav-ing even more money by finishing college a year early.

This college process has humbled me but invigorated me as well. I can continue to work my ass off in CCs and give all the colleges that rejected me the middle finger, cuz they'll regret it big time that they didn't take me.

Generic TL;DR: **Where you go to college does not define you as a person.** Many successful people didn't go to a top school. Try to look at things from the positive side, no matter what.

Become a storyteller.

I got an email with some advice for you all from u/BigManFromAFRICA88. Although his words weren't posted on our subreddit, he wanted to share what he learned, and I felt you should hear what he has to say:

> I never expected to get into all the schools I applied to. I fully expected to take a bunch of losses (read: rejections) because, you know, I didn't have a company, cure cancer, etc., on top of applying to so many scholarship programs, BS/MD programs, and such that I worried that I spread myself thin. So, was I still special? Yes! I prided myself on being an awesome student with dedicated extracurriculars (like you, the reader, are as well!). But to be honest, unless you're Malia Obama, there are tons of people like you and me and now at a bunch of top schools, including mine, acceptance rates are in the single digits. But how did I differentiate myself? I became a storyteller.

> This is my main piece of advice: **MAKE SURE YOUR APPLICATION TELLS A POWERFUL STORY ABOUT YOURSELF — meaning TAKE YOUR ESSAYS SERIOUSLY.** These essays are literally the only story of your life you are giving, so treat them as such! But

be creative. If you are a music aficionado and maestro, chase that edge but also subtly mention how you struggled with math and it made you a much more analytical person. For me, I combined lifelong dreams of medicine and engineering with an "insatiably curious" (the flagship phrase of my application profile) mind and raw, down-to-earth humor. Hard to communicate, right? Sure, but as long as you are authentic about yourself and write your essays like you were sitting with the admissions officers themselves and chatting with them, you can effectively have your personality shine through your words on paper. Talk about your favorite poem. Drop your 3rd-grade rap name. **Be ostentatiously you, and you have a much better chance of getting in.**

Make sure you are confident during interviews. If you need, fake it till you make it. Make eye contact, sit up straight, and keep your legs wide to impose confidence. Know yourself and your strong points — a place I could have personally improved on.

Combine this aspect with your academic achievements and you're set. If you're passionate about medicine, go shadow a doctor or watch some surgeries. If you're passionate about research, go and find opportunities that might even pay you. If you're passionate about entrepreneurship, try to start a business. If you're passionate about all three, chase all three; even though it is sometimes tiring, you can always sacrifice for the things and people you love and still stay happy.

GOOD LUCK CHIEF.

— u/BigManFromAFRICA88

"Be ostentatiously you." Honestly, my little golden dumplings, I don't think anyone could say this any better. Buy it. Inhale it. Believe it.

tl;dr

- Your essays should reflect who you are and act as channels for your thought processes.
- Do what you love and pursue it hard.
- Be authentic — they want to see that you're a person. A real, live person with genuine interests, not someone that's just doing things so that they can get into college.
- Actively try to make your life better, happier.
- There's more to college admissions than high test scores.
- Where you go to college doesn't define you as a person.
- Tell a powerful story about yourself. These essays are literally the only story of your life you are giving, so treat them as such!
- Write your essays like you were sitting with the admissions officers themselves and chatting with them, you can effectively have your personality shine through your words on paper.
- Know that you are loved by those around you and by whatever community that you become a part of next year.
- Be ostentatiously you.

Gen Z Glossary

AF – acronym of "as f*ck;" ex. "That first trigonometry problem on the SAT Math Level 2 test was hard AF."

AFAIK – as far as I know.

Basic – someone who is interested in mainstream or popular things not because of any genuine interest, but because those things are mainstream and popular; ex. "I swear I'm not basic—I really do love pumpkin spice lattes, and I won't apologize for it."

Bi – short for "bisexual"; ex. "Is it okay to write my essay about coming out as bi?"

Boi – literally means "boy" but is used in situations where one is ridiculing another; ex. "You thought you could get away with tooling around on Reddit all night before the ACT and still do well? Boi, what were you thinking?"

Bread – slang for the object of your desire, as in pursuing something you want; ex. "I'm scared of how hard I'm going to have to study to get this bread – any advice?"

Buzzkill – a person or thing that spoils what would otherwise be a fun/enjoyable experience for others, usually by bringing down everyone else's good mood; ex. "Damn, Alec was being such a buzzkill today by refusing to talk about anything else but college applications."

Dat – slang for "that"; ex. "I'm trying hard to get dat thick acceptance envelope from Emory."

Deadname – The birth name of a person who has changed their name; often used in the trans community to refer to the name a person was given before their transition; ex. "Please don't use "Jacob" to address Christie—that's her deadname, and it's rude to do that."

Def – short for "definitely"; ex. "As a freshman, you should def not be worrying about personal essays right now."

Esketit – slang for "let's get it"; popularized by rapper Lil' Pump; ex. "'Bout to register for my last semester of high school! Esketit!"

Extra – dramatic, excessive to the point of ridicule; ex. "My parents are being soooo extra about not being allowed to read my personal statement."

Fam – inspired by the word, "Family," but intended to refer to a group you closely identify with and belong to; ex. "I don't know what I would do without my environmental club fam to back me up."

Fecking – a less profane and more acceptable way of saying "fucking"; can also be used as feck, fecker, or feckhead; ex. "The UCLA website crashed just as I logged in to see if I'd been accepted or not! I'm so fecking mad!" Also, see frick and fricking.

Feels – emotions or feelings, generally used to describe something profound or poignant; ex. "Your personal essay about reconnecting with your grandfather hit me right in the feels."

F – in order to pay their respects, online commenters will use the letter "F" to pay their respects; ex. "User 1: My mom had to go to the hospital this morning — and I have my SAT too! User 2: F."

FFS – acronym of "for f*ck's sake," a term of frustration and exasperation; ex. "ffs, I've been trying to meet with my college counselor for weeks, but she keeps cancelling!"

Finna – short for "fixing to" or "going to"; ex. "I'm finna to lock myself in my room all weekend to knock out these essays."

Fire – blazing hot, wickedly cool, incredible, awesome; ex. "I worked so hard on my portfolio for my RISD application, and it's straight fire."

FML – acronym of "fuck my life"; used to express exasperation, disappointment, or frustration at a recent development. "I just found out I didn't get as much financial aid as I needed for my early action school. FML!"

FOMO – acronym of "fear of missing ou"; for example, you might feel FOMO when having to choose one college over another.

FR – acronym of "for real"; ex. "What the hell? Harvard's transfer acceptance rate is 1%? Can that be fr?

Fuccboi – a boy/man who mistakes his blasé attitude for suaveness and assumes this will land him girls. He often will say or do anything to convince an unsuspecting girl to commit to a relationship and then treat her very poorly by running around on her; can also be used to refer to a young man with poor judgment and/or taste who tries way too hard to be perceived as manly or cool; ex. "My ex would not stop texting me last night to help him with his resume, so I finally just told him to put down that he was a fuccboi for all junior year."

GOAT – acronym for "Greatest of All Time": ex. "Is it too obvious to write my essay about how much Lebron James inspires me? He's the GOAT."

HAM – acronym of "Hard as a motherfucker"; used to communicate the power with which a person performs an action; ex. "I'm about to go HAM on the SAT."

Hella – used in place of "very" or "really"; ex. "What did you do to make your resume look hella streamlined?"

Hype - to become very excited: ex. "I get hype whenever I get acceptances from my safety schools."

IDK – acronym of "I don't know"; ex. "IDK if I want to consider schools in the Midwest."

IMO – acronym for "in my opinion"; ex. "It's not a good idea to take easy A classes instead of challenging yourself, IMO."

"L" – stands for "loss"; ex. "Now sister, they told you not to slack off your last semester of senior year, but you did anyway. You're the only one to blame for being rescinded—take the L."

Legit – short for "legitimate"; can also mean "dope," "cool," or "awesome"; ex. "Not going to lie, but *Colleges That Change Lives* is legit. Trust me."

Let's get this bread – expression used as a rallying cry to encourage oneself or others to work hard towards a goal; ex. "Speaker 1: 'Instead of shopping, let's study for APs this weekend.' Speaker 2: 'Let's get this bread!'"

Lowkey – to feel casually toward something; ex. "I lowkey wanna apply to some Ivies, but I know I won't get in.

LMAO – acronym for "Laughing my ass off"; ex. "Did you get the memes I sent you about applying for college? LMAO!"

Lurk – to read the posts on a message board or internet forum but not comment or otherwise actively interact with other users; ex. "I spend a lot of time lurking on Reddit but rarely post."

osu! – an open-source, free rhythm game; ex. "I spent way too much time last night playing osu! when I should have been studying for my AP Chem test."

Real Talk – slang for the truth, and for being candid and direct; ex. "Real talk, Mom, you have to accept that Stanford is a reach for everyone."

RIP – acronym for "rest in peace"; could be used to pay respects to a deceased person; can also be used to express a general sense of suckiness or disbelief; ex. "Nooooo I forgot to save the work I did last night filling out the Common App online, and now it's all gone! RIP!"

Salty – to be angry, upset, bitter, or agitated, often over things that are seen by others as small or unimportant; ex. "Gillian is still salty about not getting a likely letter from Barnard, and she needs to get over it."

SMH – acronym for "shaking my head," used to express frustration, disbelief, world-weariness, or disappointment; ex. "No matter how much I explain to my mom that no one is guaranteed a full ride to Yale no matter how good their stats, she insists I can get one if I 'apply myself.' SMH."

Stan – slang for an over-the-top, obsessive fan; can also mean to idolize someone; ex. "As a future English major, I stan Tracy K. Smith."

TMI – acronym for "too much information"; used to express that a person has overshared or volunteered more than anyone else needed to know about a situation; ex. "I'm worried that my personal statement about how my sucky deployment to Iraq is TMI—what do you think?"

Trynna – short for "trying to"; ex. " I'm trynna figure out how to fill out this Common App, but it's hella confusing."

YMMV – your mileage may vary

YOLO – acronym for "you only live once"; ex. "You've been studying so hard. You can def take a night off to go to a concert. YOLO."

"W" – stands for "win"; ex. "Getting all my apps done was a struggle, but I came out with the hard W because I got accepted to 7 of 9 schools."

Wholesome – something that makes you feel good, positive, or hopeful; ex. "Speaker 1: 'I was so freakin' angry about my Calc grade for the semester, but then I remembered to meditate. Now I think my bad grade was a good thing because it made me consider how I need to practice self-care more.' Speaker 2: 'Wow, that's so wholesome.'"

WTF – acronym for "What the f*ck?"; ex. "My teacher is taking forever to turn in his recommendation letter for my applications! WTF am I going to do?"

Yee/Yeet – an exclamation of excited agreement; ex. "Yeeeeeee, I do want you to proofread my essay for me! Thanks!"

Resources

I'm not going to lie to you. As much as I like to play up the positives of learning more about yourself than you ever have and using the admissions journey as an opportunity to really get in tune with who you are and what you want out of life, the truth is that the college admissions journey can be long and arduous. But during my time helping kids like you get into college, I've come across lots of great resources that will guide you along the way and make everything easier. I'm all about relieving stress during the admissions process and doing that *while* dotting every 'i' and crossing every 't' requires outside help. Below are my favorite resources for everything in college admissions, from essay writing, test prep, and application websites to visiting colleges, affording college, making a list of schools, mental health and wellness, and mindfulness.

TESTING

College Board

The College Board administers the SAT, SAT II, PSAT, *and* AP tests. It's a lot, I know. As providers of these tests, the College Board provides extensive free tests, test-taking tips, and contains exam policies on their website. The best way to study is by taking as many practice tests as possible. Questions on these sorts of tests are generally predictable, and the highest scoring kids are generally the ones who are most familiar with the test. Additionally, you should read any important test day information from the College Board so that you have all the right test-taking materials on test day and so that you are not surprised when you show up at the test location.

ACT

The ACT website provides free test questions in addition to paid test preparation resources. The ACT is notorious for leaving students with very little time to answer many questions. It's important to take practice tests so that you are familiar with the test's time constraints. While the ACT website does not offer as many free tests as the College Board, a simple google search can you lead you to free ACT practice exams.

Princeton Review

Princeton Review offers tutoring services and administers free practice tests. Princeton Review tutors are very good but also very expensive. However, the Princeton Review's practice tests are completely free of charge. They offer free practice ACT and SAT tests at sites across the United States and likely offer one near you. Taking a practice test with the Princeton Review is a really good idea for a number of reasons. Taking a test at a mock site ensures you will be unbothered from distractions, simulates the real test experience, and provides immediate score feedback. The Princeton Review also sells good books for test preparation. Inside their books are practice tests, answer keys, and helpful lessons. Taking practice tests and completing the lessons from a Princeton book is often a sufficient way to study.

Khan Academy

Khan Academy has been one of my favorite YouTube channels for a while now. Khan Academy offers helpful videos to prepare for the SAT, in addition to practice tests. If you are having trouble on a particular section or just want to improve your scores generally,

Khan Academy is a valuable resource. I would advise watching their videos and then applying their lessons after you take your first practice test.

Applerouth Testing (applerouth.com) is another great resource for test prep. In addition to offering tutors and free practice tests, Applerouth offers free online seminars to help with test prep, financial aid applications, and admissions timelines.

COLLEGE LISTS AND COLLEGE SEARCH

The Fiske Guide

This is my #1 go-to college guide. Fiske covers over 400 colleges and is the perfect book to read or skim to start your search. The book offers a college self-quiz to help you start making a list of colleges.

Colleges that Change Lives

CTCL is a website and book about 40 unique colleges that often fly under the radar but focus on their students' development. CTCL colleges have small student bodies, professors that are mentors more than just teachers, and are liberal arts schools. If you are having trouble searching for the right school for you and don't mind a small campus, I recommend at least venturing to CTCL's website or picking up a copy of their book.

The College Finder

Most college guidebooks are thick books that offer "snapshots" of hundreds of colleges. Instead, *The College Finder,* by Dr. Steven Antonoff is composed of hundreds of lists that cover areas such as Great College Cities, The Most Underrated Colleges, Colleges That Go the Extra Mile to Make It Financially Possible to Attend, Colleges Where Sports Rule, and more. Antonoff's book will point you toward colleges that are a good fit for you and lead you toward hidden college gems.

Princeton Review's Best 384

The Princeton Review's annual book on the "Best" 384 colleges is a good place to start if you are having trouble making a college list. The book boasts an expansive, but still in-depth look at close to 400 colleges. The book organizes colleges by best academics, administration, campus life, financial aid, college character, and social scene to help you better compare colleges.

College Admissions Websites

Honestly, this should be your first stop. Check here for any admissions information about deadlines, required or recommended courses and testing, and testing deadlines. Additionally, if you read carefully, most college admissions websites pretty much describe the student they are looking for. Do you see yourself in that description? Also, some of them have some pretty amazing admissions help in general, along with fantastic blogs about admissions and essay writing. Some of my faves are MIT Admissions, Tufts Admissions, Tulane Admissions, UVA Admissions, and Georgia Tech Admissions.

College Publications

Many of the best insights into a college come from colleges themselves. Student newspapers, admissions pages, and college social media accounts provide info on college campus culture, happenings, and student life. Follow all the colleges on your list on social media and browse their websites. Colleges often give away student magazines or newspapers at college fairs. If you cannot access one at a college fair, look online for any student publications. Just reading one student newspaper can give you a much better idea of what life is like on campus.

Department Course Offerings

Each academic department (ex. Sociology, Biology, English, etc.) at a college or university posts public course offerings, essentially a list of all the classes offered each semester. It is a good idea to glance at the course offerings of the schools you are interested in. See if there are courses you'd be interested in taking. Additionally, each department will list a brief bio for every professor on staff. If you are interested in comparing departments across colleges, professors who are doing leading research, have tenure, and have taught at the school a long time are good signs of a healthy academic department.

Common Data Set

According to their website, "the Common Data Set (CDS) initiative is a collaborative effort among data providers in the higher education community and publishers as represented by the College Board, Peterson's, and U.S. News & World Report." To find out all sorts of information about a college like average financial aid, admissions rates, or what they emphasize in their admissions offices, you can google the name of the college and "common data set."

College Match Self Survey is similar to a personality test for choosing a college. If you have a free half-hour, you should take the test and see what is important to consider as you search for a college. Remember to take the test results in consideration, but also keep in mind that they can be interpreted in a variety of ways.

Corsava Cards (corsava.com) are a unique approach to building a college list and a useful tool for students who do not have access to a reliable college counselor. Corsava asks students to sort 125 college characteristics into the categories, important, neutral, and not important. Corsava then uses your geographic location preferences and produces a list of six colleges and asks your impression of them. If you are stumped or need help starting a list, Corsava is a great tool.

Niche.com is essentially the Yelp of colleges. The site has many college reviews from students and alumni. Additionally, Niche has tools to help you calculate your chances of applying to college and an informative section that details where most graduates of a college end up after graduating. Take each college review with a grain of salt, though even the most cynical reviews can contain helpful information.

Diversity Fly-Ins

Increasingly, colleges offer free fly-in programs, travel scholarships, or overnight-stay programs for students who are accepted to their schools. Some colleges even offer these programs to students who are simply thinking of applying. College Greenlight has compiled a list of colleges that offer financial assistance for students to visit and Get Me to College also has a list of diversity fly-ins (and much more!). Even if a school on your list is not listed there, do not get discouraged. Email an admissions officer and ask if their college has a program that can be of help. Admissions officers are always willing to assist students who are interested in their college.

Get Me to College (getmetocollege.com) is a premier resource for first-generation and low-income students who have dreams of going to college. This is one of my favorite websites and offers free advice on getting ready for college, college application timelines, visiting campus for little or no cost at all, and paying for college. Get Me to College is great at getting students to campus using free diversity fly-in programs. Additionally, the site has academic and standardized test readiness tips, even scholarship resources for students and undocumented students.

FINANCIAL AID

Net Price Calculator

Every college is required to have a Net Price Calculator on their website, but sometimes it can be hidden or hard to find. Before you apply to a school, google "name of college" and "net price calculator" and then sit down with your parents and fill out the info. Never assume that you will get more money than the net price calculator says you will. That's a dangerous game and can either leave you with loads of student loan debt or a school you've been accepted to but unable to attend.

FAFSA

FAFSA is the first stop you make after the net price calculators to receive financial aid. You will need to gather all the materials they say and sit down with your parents to fill these forms out. They will open on October 1, and each college will have differing dates for deadlines, so be sure to check out your college's admissions and financial aid web pages.

CSS PROFILE

Many private colleges require the CSS Profile in addition to the FAFSA. Be sure to check your college's admissions and financial aid websites to see whether they require it or not, and what the deadlines are.

APPLICATION PLATFORMS

The Common App

The Common App is the most popular college application site and contains applications to over 700 different colleges of all shapes and sizes. To start your app, you will need to fill out some basic biographical information and eventually be ready to select a group of colleges to apply to. For every application, you will need a copy of your high school transcript, list of extracurricular activities, official test scores, and information about your parents or legal guardian. The Common App goes live August 1st and, depending on where you want to apply, most application deadlines are in the fall or early January. The Common App has a mobile app to help you manage your deadlines. It is a good idea to start thinking about your Common App essays as soon as you can.

The Coalition App

The Coalition App is a useful tool to help students and families get through college with little to no debt. The goal of the Coalition App is to help make college affordable to guide first-generation students through the college application process. While fewer schools are on the Coalition App than the Common App, the Coalition App offers free online college prep, and you may be able to submit your application without paying a single dollar. Colleges on both the Common App and Coalition App do not prefer one site to the other, and the Coalition App offers more flexible essay options.

QuestBridge (questbridge.org) is a non-profit organization that connects high-achieving, low-income students to selective colleges. The goal of QuestBridge is to make sure smart low-income students can still afford to attend the best colleges. QuestBridge is connected with over 40 of the top schools in America and has helped thousands of students gain admission with full scholarships or generous financial aid to top colleges. If college is something your family struggles to afford on its own, you should definitely apply to one of QuestBridge's several programs, regardless of your citizenship status. Additionally, even if you aren't admitted as a Quest Scholar, QuestBridge has great resources to help you prepare for college.

ApplyTexas (applytexas.org) is the application site for all public and many private Texas colleges. This includes four-year universities, as well as public liberal arts colleges and community colleges. ApplyTexas is particularly useful if you want to go to school in Texas because it is easy to copy your application and apply to multiple Texas schools without filling out additional essays or applications. That being said, most Texas universities have rolling admission, so the sooner you apply, the better your chances.

UC App

The UC App is essentially ApplyTexas but for California schools. The California higher education system is the largest of any state. The UC App also allows you to submit applications to different schools with one application.

SPECIAL RESOURCES FOR LOW INCOME, FIRST GEN, OR POC

QuestBridge (questbridge.org)
see info above

Jack Cooke Kent Foundation (jckf.org)
Offering freshman and transfer scholarships, Jack Cooke Kent Foundation offers up to "$40,000 per year, college planning support, ongoing advising, and the opportunity to network with the larger Cooke Scholar community" for high achieving students.

Gates Millennial Scholarship (gmsp.org)
"The goal of the GMS program is to promote academic excellence and to provide an opportunity for outstanding minority students with significant financial need to reach their highest potential."

The Posse Foundation (possefoundation.org)
"The Posse Foundation identifies, recruits and trains individuals with extraordinary leadership potential. Posse Scholars receive full-tuition leadership scholarships from Posse's partner colleges and universities."

ESSAYS

The Most Dangerous Writing App (themostdangerouswritingapp.com)

The most difficult part of writing is often just getting started. The Most Dangerous Writing App deletes all your progress if you stop writing for too long. This gimmick doesn't make it a serious writing app, but it can be a really useful tool to complete the first draft. If you are having trouble starting a college essay, TMDWA is an excellent place to start.

College Essay Guy (collegeessayguy.com)

Ethan Sawyer, a.k.a. College Essay Guy, is one of the leading experts on college essays and applications. College Essay Guy has free video resources, webinars, blog posts, and guides to help you write the best essay possible. Additionally, he offers several online courses and e-books. If you are willing to shell out for a college essay course, his videos and sample essay are hard to beat. Sawyer is the real deal and an incredibly nice guy.

ThisIBelieve.org

The best writers are also the best readers. Similarly, reading good personal essays will help you write your own quality personal essays. ThisIBelieve.org is filled with quality essays that are fun, moving, and easy to read. Before you start writing, I recommend reading their essays and picking up on the rhetorical techniques that strong writers use. There are also tons of them that you can listen to if you prefer.

AdmissionsMom's Book Club!

Confession: I've been a lifelong reader and have a kind of, sort of book addiction. I started reading books about parenting when my oldest was in utero and started reading books about college admissions when he was a freshman in high school way back in 2005. I'm pretty sure I've read nearly every college admissions guide there is to read. This is a long list of books, but it really just touches the surface of the books I've read. These were my favorites...my greatest hits. I've held on to these and bought and shared multiple copies over the years. The mindfulness books came about more recently, but they have burrowed their way deep into my heart — and my advice. Some of them have truly been life changing for me, and I hope you can find your way to read a few and discover what might resonate with you, too.

Mindfulness/Self-Reflection/Personal Development (These books are not only fantastic for personal development and learning about mindfulness, but they also are amazing examples of personal writing and being able to write with your voice.)

10% Happier by Dan Harris
The Antidote: Happiness for People Who Can't Stand Positive Thinking by Oliver Burkeman
Big Magic: Creative Living Beyond Fear by Elizabeth Gilbert
Brave Enough by Cheryl Strayed
Daring Greatly by Brene Brown
Full Catastrophe Living by Jon Kabat-Zinn, PhD
The Happiness Equation by Neil Pasricha
Meditation for Fidgety Skeptics by Dan Harris and Jeff Warren
The Mindful Teen by Dzung Vo, MD
The Mindful Twenty Something: Life Skills to Handle Stress and Everything Else by Holly Rogers, MD
The No F*cks Given Guides by Sarah Knight
Smiling Mind: Mindfulness Made Easy by Jane Martino and James Tutton
The Subtle Art of Not Giving a F*ck by Mark Manson
Tiny Beautiful Things: Advice on Love and Life from Dear Sugar by Cheryl Strayed
Wild by Cheryl Strayed

Year of Yes: How to Dance It Out, Stand in the Sun, and Be Your Own Person by Shonda Rhimes
You are a Badass by Jenn Sincero

College Admissions (I really narrowed this list down to my favorites, and it's still really really long :)!

Admission: A Novel by Jean Hanff Korelitz
College Essay Essentials by Ethan Sawyer, College Essay Guy
The College Finder: Choose the School That's Right for You by Steven Antonoff, PhD
College Match: A Blueprint for Choosing the Best School for You by Steven Antonoff, PhD
Colleges that Change Lives by Loren Pope, revised by Hillary Masell Oswald
Crazy U: One Dad's Crash Course in Getting His Kid Into College by Andrew Ferguson
The Fiske Guide by Edward Fiske
Generation Z Goes To College by Corey Seemiller and Meghan Grace
Guide to College Visits by Princeton Review
The Hidden Ivies by Howard Greene, M.Ed, and Matthew Greene, PhD
I'm First! Guide to College: by ImFirst.org and striveforcollege.org
I'm Going to College — Not You! by Jennifer Delahunty
The Insider's Guide to Colleges by Yale Daily News
Looking Beyond the Ivy League: Finding the College That's Right for You by Loren Pope
The Neurotic Parent's Guide to College Admissions by J.D. Rothman
What Colleges Don't Tell You by Elizabeth Wissner-Gross
What High Schools Don't Tell You by Elizabeth Wissner-Gross

Where You Go is Not Who You'll Be by Frank Bruni

Parenting (I've got parenting books going back over 30 years, but this list has some of my faves that I felt would be most relevant here.)

The Blessing of a Skinned Knee by Wendy Mogel, PhD
The Blessings of a B Minus by Wendy Mogel, PhD
The Gift of Failure: How the Best Parents Learn to Let Go So Their Children Can Succeed by Jessica Lahey
The Gift of an Ordinary Day by Katrina Kenison
How to Raise An Adult by Julie Lythcott-Haims
The Price of Privilege by Madeline Levine

Education
The Naked Roommate and 107 Other Issues You Might Run into in College by Harlan Cohen
A Practical Education: Why Liberal Arts Majors Make Great Employees by Randall Stross
The Smartest Kids in the World by Amanda Ripley
You Can Do Anything: The Surprising Power of a "Useless" Liberal Arts Education by George Anders

Writing and Grammar
Between You and I: A Little Book of Bad English by James Cochrane
Bird by Bird by Anne Lamott
Eats, Shoots & Leaves: The Zero Tolerance Approach to Punctuation by Lynne Truss
The Grammar Devotional: Daily Tips for Successful Writing From Grammar Girl by Mignon Fogarty
Grammar Girl's Quick and Dirty Tips for Better Writing by Mignon Fogarty
On Writing: A Memoir of the Craft by Stephen King

Woe is I: The Grammarphobe's Guide to Better English in Plain English by Patricia T. O'Conner

Good Fiction to Read to Develop Writing Skills (Just read!)
Me and Earl and the Dying Girl by Jesse Andrews

The Catcher in the Rye by JD Salinger

Anything written by Haruki Marukami, John Steinbeck, Anne Lamott, Ernest Hemingway, Jane Austen, a Bronte sister, or Kurt Vonnegut.

Shout Outs

Obviously, I didn't write this book myself, just as I wasn't the only one giving advice and offering support on r/ApplyingToCollege. So, let me thank all the kids, advisors, parents, and other kind souls who spent hours and hours contributing to the positive atmosphere of our growing community. Specifically, I want to thank the following individuals who were happy to and agreed to share their anxieties, advice, and words with you all:

4m_33s	University of Illinois, UC
Admissionscousin (CJ Johnson)	Columbia University
AdmissionsSon	Harvard College
Adrian Velonis	Haverford College
Aerophage1771 (Germaine W.)	Princeton University
Alexander Kuptel	
Andrew Chambers	University of Virginia — WAHOOWA!!
Anonymous	Carleton College
Ashley Chen	
BioticAsariBabe (Nicolas Suter)	
BlueLightSpcl (Kevin, Founder, Tex Admissions LLC UT Austin, 2011)	
Bhushan Patel	Harvard College
Carmen Alvaro	University of Southern California
Crowbarmlgjenkins	University of Chicago '22
D6410 (Katherine Phillips)	George Washington University
Dimitri Z.	
Doubutsuai	Columbia University
Elkakey (Ella Keymer)	Sarah Lawrence College

F.R.	Yale '22 -- BOOLA BOOLA!
Franklin	Yale
GammaHuman	Texas A&M '21
Halima Abshir	Columbus State CC
Heymylittlefishies (Hassan Rashid)	Trinity College, CT
Ian Benedict	University of Washington, Seattle
Iphsyko (Raini Huynh)	Trinity University, TX
Jonathan Qi	
Josh	Stanford
Juju	Michigan State University
Kaisersand (Daniel Edrisian)	UC Berkeley
Kamille Suayan	UC Irvine
Kevin Fillhouer	
Kian B.	University of Michigan/ ENG.
Konrad Cheng	University of Southern California
Laura Goon	Rice University
Madeleine24	University of Florida
Maggie Pierce	University of Central Florida
Memeoneco	Columbia University
Mmmya	
Ninotchka123	Wellesley
Paolo Adajar	MIT
Patricia Fernandez	Temple University
PeperoniTrain	Wash U St Louis
PeteyMIT (Chris Peterson)	
PhAnToM444	Loyola Marymount University
PM_ME_UR_GAMECOCKS (Andrei Robu)	University of South Carolina
Robertobaz (Rob Bazaral)	University of Edinburgh
RouJoo (Ralph Uy)	University of British Columbia
Saada100 (Saad Ahmad)	
Samantha Good	University of Indianapolis
Secretgeek69	UC Berkeley
Senatorswank (Joshua Swank)	UC Irvine
Sherrie Wang	Yale
Shoham Sengupta	College of William and Mary
Shoulderofgiantx (Joseph Zhang)	
Simon	

Skrapman2 (Nick Riveira)	UT Austin, Hook 'Em!
Sonja Marcus	Western Washington University
Spherical_Melon	UC Davis
Szi8890 (Ivan Zhao)	Brown
Thebigdog420	Vanderbilt
TheDuke127 (Michael Duquesnel/)	Moody Bible Institute
TheRealClyde1 (Cameron Chin)	University of Southern California
TwinPurpleEagle (Maybel Oo)	California Lutheran University
USS-Enterprise	WPI
VA_Network_Nerd	
Voltroom	Johns Hopkins University
Wilandhugs	SUNY Buffalo
Zac Walsdorf	
zztempo314	San Diego CC DIstrict

Thank you, thank you, thank you to all of you and to all of the other amazing contributors to our subreddit whose words continue to inspire and educate (and make us laugh…. and cringe sometimes, too!).

Acknowledgements

Of course, huge thanks to the entire A2C community, especially to the mod team who keep it in order the best they can and all the kids who share their hearts and souls, laughter, jokes, anxieties, worries, fears, and excitement on a daily basis. Big thanks to my amazing real-life fam, husband Billy and my three mostly grown and flown kids, Henry, Sara Rose, and Joseph for supporting and encouraging me. Extra special big thanks to Joseph for pushing me to check out Reddit and look for a college admissions community. Extra extra special big thanks to Sara Rose and Joseph for their editing expertise and insight into Gen Z, even though they are millennials themselves. Also, thank you, Sharon and Gisela for your amazing edits! Chloe, Raini, and John, my fabulous summer interns, this book wouldn't be happening without you. Susannah and Cindy, you were awesome; thanks for making the magic stuff happen. Many thanks to everyone else who has been with me on this journey — you know who you are. And to my mom, my example in life – thank you.

A-Mom's Mom Club

Carolyn and her mom, junior year at The University of Texas at Austin.

I was lucky enough to have an amazing role model and mom. A college dropout who didn't return to college until her forties, Mom was a hard-working, kind, caring, intelligent person, who never failed to stop to bring food to the homeless or push education for the undereducated. After receiving her master's degree in Early Childhood Education in her late forties, she created and instituted the Early Childhood Program at her local college and was a huge supporter of engaging students in college life who otherwise wouldn't have been engaged.

When she died a few years ago after a long illness, I was devastated. A wise friend encouraged me to find a way to live my life in ways that would honor her. This advice led me to my adventures on the subreddit, r/ApplyingToCollege, where I found a place that I could follow her example of engaging students in the college process who might not otherwise be engaged. It was also a place where I could help others find their way through the intricacies of the journey with perhaps just a little bit less stress. Of course, I'm putting my spin on it with mindfulness and my own naturally more open-minded philosophies of life, but my time on Reddit definitely has her roots.

In fall of 2016, during my first few months on the subreddit, I was frustrated by how many of our A2C kids couldn't afford to pay for application fees or send their test scores, among various other application expenses. I have to give the College Board, ACT, and many of the colleges themselves a lot of credit for making great efforts to mitigate these issues of costs with fee waivers and self-reporting over the last year, but the fact remains that many high school seniors looking to go to college are still limited by the cost of applications.

So, in my mom's memory—and also in honor of countless fellow Redditors who've inspired me in so many ways—I've created the A-Mom's Mom Club, collecting from the sales of the book to help our very own r/ApplyingToCollege applicants with the financial burdens and fees of the process, like submitting test scores and application fees. So, by buying this book, you're helping applicants, from literally every corner of the world, to reach their goals and discover their future lives.

About Carolyn

Carolyn Allison Caplan is a lifelong reader (think flashlight-under-the-covers-as-a-child reader), and an admitted all-things education and college admissions junkie. She has a BA in English from the University of Texas at Austin, and a Masters in Liberal Arts (MLA) with a concentration in English from the University of St. Thomas in Houston. In the last few years, while dealing with empty nesting and other life stuff, she has discovered mindfulness, meditation, and yoga, and is in the process of becoming both a certified Yoga teacher and a Koru Mindful Meditation teacher. Additionally, Carolyn has recently completed the UCLA College Counseling certificate, and is a member of HECA, IECA, NACG, and TACAC. She estimates that in the last three years she has read over 2000 Reddit kid essays, and chatted with over 25,000 kids from A2C. You can find out more about Carolyn at www.admissionsmom.college.

CPSIA information can be obtained
at www.ICGtesting.com
Printed in the USA
LVHW050022240919
631983LV00004B/831/P